Generously
Reformed

Generously Reformed

Theology Rooted Deep and Reaching Wide

J. Todd Billings, Suzanne McDonald,
and Alberto La Rosa Rojas

Baker Academic
a division of Baker Publishing Group
Grand Rapids, Michigan

© 2026 by J. Todd Billings, Suzanne McDonald, and Alberto La Rosa Rojas

Published by Baker Academic
a division of Baker Publishing Group
Grand Rapids, Michigan
BakerAcademic.com

Printed in the United States of America

Library of Congress Cataloging-in-Publication Data
Names: Billings, J. Todd author | McDonald, Suzanne, 1973– author | Rojas, Alberto La Rosa author
Title: Generously reformed : theology rooted deep and reaching wide / J. Todd Billings, Suzanne McDonald, and Alberto La Rosa Rojas.
Description: Grand Rapids, Michigan : Baker Academic, a division of Baker Publishing Group, [2026] | Includes bibliographical references and indexes.
Identifiers: LCCN 2025029618 | ISBN 9781540963321 paperback | ISBN 9781540969934 casebound | ISBN 9781493453016 ebook | ISBN 9781493453023 pdf
Subjects: LCSH: Reformed Church—Doctrines
Classification: LCC BX9422.3 .B543 2026
LC record available at https://lccn.loc.gov/2025029618

26 27 28 29 30 31 32   7 6 5 4 3 2 1

To the graduates of
Western Theological Seminary,
serving around the globe

Contents

7. Eschatology: In the End, What?   139

Key Question: What Does Reformed Theology Teach About the End Times?

Acknowledgments

We have written this book as those welcomed into the Reformed theological tradition, finding it a spacious place where we can put down deep roots and reach wide as members of God's household. While we are responsible for this book, with all its shortcomings, we are grateful to belong to a tradition much larger than ourselves, sharing in gifts we did not originate or create.

We give special thanks to Western Theological Seminary in Holland, Michigan, for their support and encouragement as both a community and institution, as well as for the sabbatical time to focus on this project. We are also grateful to the donors of the Gordon H. Girod Research Chair in Reformed Theology for funding research assistants and for their commitment to cultivating pastor-theologians within the Reformed tradition.

We are deeply appreciative of the students who contributed to this project through their research assistance, feedback on chapter drafts, and other invaluable support. Their dedication and insights enriched this work in countless ways, for which we are truly grateful. The work of Nathan Longfield was especially instrumental in launching this project, as Nathan conducted essential research and interviews on pressing questions within the Reformed theological tradition. We are also thankful for the great help provided by Anna Anderson, Jake Chipka, Drew Craddock, AJ Funk, Nasario Guzman-Peña, Tom Oord, Nicholas Rogalski, James Schetelich, Breno Nunes de Oliveira Seabra, Emili Shepperson, Rebekah Taylor, and Madelyn Vonk.

Thank you to Bob Hosack at Baker Academic. Your belief in this project from the outset and your input at every stage have been invaluable—even as you exercised the virtue of patience awaiting its final completion. Alex DeMarco and his team at Baker Academic have also done exceptional work!

Special thanks to Katlyn DeVries for sharing her remarkable organizational and editing skills. We are deeply grateful for your assistance and for the privilege of working alongside you as a colleague at the seminary.

This book is dedicated to the graduates of Western Theological Seminary who serve in a variety of ministries around the globe. Your curiosity, thought-provoking questions, and joyful discoveries within the Reformed tradition have fueled and guided this project.

Soli Deo Gloria

Introduction

"Wait, is that what Reformed theology says?"

We have often witnessed this surprised reaction from students, pastors, church members, and other Christian friends. Sometimes it's sparked by something they've read or heard that claimed to be Reformed. Other times it comes after we've taught, preached, or discussed a point of Reformed theology that completely defied their expectations.

We love the Reformed theological tradition, but in this cultural moment, misunderstandings of Reformed theology are legion. Whether a person was raised in this tradition, is inquiring about it as an onlooker, or is genuinely discerning whether they would want to inhabit a Reformed vision of faith, the conflicted messages of what *Reformed* is can leave them perplexed and, perhaps, a bit skeptical. Does a celebrity pastor who is labeled Reformed decide what teaching belongs to Reformed theology? How many "points" does Reformed theology encompass—four, five, seven, or dozens? If someone has started to discover beauty and depth in the Reformed theological tradition, what exactly are they finding there?

This book offers a substantial, yet accessible, introduction to Reformed theology as a frequently misunderstood, yet expansive and generative, tradition. The idea arose from a survey of pastors within the Reformed tradition. We asked, "What are the common questions you hear from people who are new to the Reformed tradition? What misunderstandings do you see?" This book names those common questions and addresses them in a way that not only clarifies misunderstandings but also puts a more fulsome account of Reformed theology on the table. Because the starting place is common questions, this book does not offer a full systematic theology, which would cover all main points of Christian doctrine. Some areas of Reformed theology are not addressed or are addressed only briefly. In being a substantial, yet accessible, book introducing Reformed theology and correcting common misunderstandings, this book follows a path made by two much older books written by earlier generations of professors at our seminary: Eugene Osterhaven's *The Spirit of the Reformed Tradition* and I. John Hesselink's *On Being Reformed: Distinctive Characteristics and Common Misunderstandings*. Both of these valuable books address misunderstandings and questions of earlier generations, seeking to give a substantial vision in the place of caricatures.

In contrast to all three of us coauthors of this book, Osterhaven and Hesselink both grew up in the Reformed tradition. They were raised Reformed within Dutch immigrant communities in Michigan and Iowa. But interestingly, it was through academic and ministry experience around the world that they became capable and enthusiastic purveyors of the Reformed tradition. Over the course of two decades, Hesselink served as a missionary in Japan, along with his wife, Etta; then he wrote a doctoral dissertation on John Calvin's theology under the supervision of famed theologian Karl Barth in Basel, Switzerland, before returning to Western Theological Seminary as president in 1973. Osterhaven and Hesselink both learned the weaknesses of the Reformed tradition in their international encounters, but they grew in their depth of appreciation as well. Hesselink writes, "All of these experiences—academic, spiritual, ecumenical, and international—over a twenty-year span meant an increasing understanding and appreciation of what was distinctive and beautiful about the Reformed tradition."[1]

We three coauthors also have a comparative perspective on the Reformed tradition. Todd was raised Baptist in the Midwest and had formative experiences with interdenominational evangelical mission groups and schools until he started to embrace the Reformed tradition shortly before graduating from Wheaton College in 1995. Alberto was born in Peru to a pious Roman Catholic mother and Methodist father. After immigrating to the United States, he embraced his faith as a teenager in a nondenominational Christian and Missionary Alliance youth group. He encountered the Reformed tradition as a student at Trinity Christian College, a Dutch Reformed Christian school in the south suburbs of Chicago. Suzanne was not brought up as a Christian and came to faith in her late teens. Her first denominational homes were the Anglican Church of Australia and then the Church of England, before she discovered that she belonged more clearly in a Reformed theological and church context.

Each of us has scholarly training that shapes our descriptive work about what the Reformed tradition is and is not, but we also write as believers who

1. Hesselink, *On Being Reformed*, x.

have discovered the Reformed tradition to be a spacious, compelling, and worshipful place for living as Christians in our complex world today. While we recognize it as imperfect and tainted by sin, the Reformed tradition is a deeply generative way to inhabit the historic tradition of the Christian church, with resources for renewing its life and witness through deepening its nourishment in God's Word through the Spirit.

The primary focus of this work is the theological dimension of Reformed confession and theology; it is not a work in cultural anthropology, sociology, or church history. The Reformed theological tradition is not disembodied; it is an approach to growth in Christ by the Spirit that comes from and finds expression in many cultural and historical locations. This is not an aberration of Reformed theology; it is encoded in Reformed DNA, to be rediscovered and inhabited.

In the Global South, membership in Reformed congregations is significant and growing.[2] In the United States, Canada, and the United Kingdom, official membership in Reformed denominations is on the decline, but many nondenominational congregations, or congregations within Pentecostal/charismatic and Baptist denominations, have been finding their home within the Reformed theological tradition.[3] Indeed, in the United States around 30 percent of pastors would describe their congregations as Calvinist or Reformed.[4] While the meaning of their self-understanding as Calvinist or Reformed may vary dramatically, it does display a strong ongoing interest in the Reformed theological tradition, whether or not a congregation is a member of a historically Reformed denomination.

Why is there widespread interest in Reformed theology among a variety of Christian traditions in the West and significant growth of Reformed

2. Benedetto and McKim, *Historical Dictionary*, 2.

3. Millions of Christians today belong to the Reformed theological tradition while also embracing charismatic beliefs and practices, both in the Global North and in the Global South. This may surprise some readers, as certain Reformed groups hold a cessationist view—the belief that certain spiritual gifts (e.g., tongues or prophecy) ceased after apostolic times. Though the Reformed confessions affirm Scripture's sufficiency, they do not explicitly address the issues surrounding these spiritual gifts. For a brief overview of the global Reformed charismatic movement, see McCracken, "Rise of Reformed Charismatics." For accessible-yet-contrasting perspectives on the relationship between Reformed theology and the charismatic movement, see Smith, "Teaching a Calvinist to Dance"; and Schreiner, "Why I Am a Cessationist." Regarding those who self-identify as Reformed from within Pentecostal denominations, see note 4 below.

4. See Barna Group, "'Reformed' Movement"; and Rankin, "SBC Pastors Polled." The Barna study highlights the multidenominational nature of interest in Reformed theology, noting that "31% of pastors in traditionally charismatic or Pentecostal denominations were described as Reformed, while 27% identified as Wesleyan/Arminian. This is somewhat surprising given that these denominations—including Assembly of God, Vineyard, Foursquare, and Church of God-Cleveland—are generally viewed as stemming from Wesleyan or Holiness traditions."

denominations in the Global South? There are many reasons, to be sure. But from our experience as professors introducing students from a variety of backgrounds to the Reformed tradition, we have seen how they find it a hospitable way to uncover deep truths that enrich their understanding of God's Word in Scripture. They often find that it broadens their connections with the household of God through the ages and across cultural divides. This tradition sets them on a pilgrim's path of faith seeking understanding as children of God who are joyfully nourished in Christ by the Spirit. It gives guidance to their lives and witness in a confusing world, with many "lords" that vie for their attention. It centers us in the grand story of the triune God—the loving Father who sent his beloved Son to restore a good creation corrupted by sin and who adopted us into God's household by the Spirit and united us to that same Christ. Through the Reformed tradition, we live as pilgrims in our short mortal days, rejoicing in God's promises and aching for his kingdom to come in fullness.

Rooted Deep in God's Word, Reaching Wide in God's World

What does it mean for diverse groups to inhabit the Reformed theological tradition in a generous and generative way? This question is not first and foremost a question about denominations, or a question about how churches organize together in terms of polity (governing structures), denominational offices, or to make names like *Presbyterian* or *Reformed* seem trendy in the late modern West, which is sometimes described as a religious marketplace. It's not about capitalizing on cultural trends to find something new or something traditional; neither is it about settling our most pressing questions about God so we can feel that we have "arrived," that we are not the pilgrims we actually are, those "on the way."

We write to explore how the Reformed theological tradition can be passionately and generously inhabited as a way for the contemporary church to rediscover its life as a creature of the Word, an imperfect human fellowship that finds its life in clinging to the Word of God in Christ for nourishment. At the center of the Reformed tradition is a delight in and longing for the Word and work of the triune God. Thus, the tradition reaches down with deep roots for life outside of itself (in God) and branches out widely to the life of the world in which we live.

This analogy of a tree, deeply rooted and reaching wide, is taken up in Psalm 1. The psalmist speaks of those who "delight" in the "law of the LORD," who "meditate" on it "day and night," for "they are like trees planted by streams of water, which yield their fruit in its season, and their leaves do not wither. In all that they do, they prosper" (Ps. 1:2–3). This love of the Word of the Lord sends our roots deep into the soil of Scripture, where we draw life from God's Word within a Spirit-enlivened tradition. Yet the journey is not only downward but outward, as we grow toward maturity in Christ and bear fruit for the world through abiding in Christ by the Spirit. We do not do this as solitary individuals but as adopted members of the Father's household in Christ by the Spirit, which spans many cultures, ages, and locations. We are rooted deep. And this rootedness lets us reach wide.

Reflecting on the biblical image of a tree as a vision of the church's vocation in a fractured age, theologian Kristen Johnson describes what flourishing looks like: "Trees offer these life-giving gifts to all around them, not only to their own kind. They are rooted in one location and make that particular place better by their very presence. And with deep roots, trees can develop wide branches that enable them to find places of overlap with other branches, even branches that come from different kinds of trees with their own deep roots."[5] The work of a tree does not provide a quick fix to its environment and ecosystem. A tree goes deep for nourishment and nutrients; in doing this, its slow growth and wide expansiveness provide shade, rest, and joy to the neighborhood and the world in its midst. This is how we seek to embody the Reformed tradition: not with celebrity heroes or special techniques to renew Christ's church and its theological vision but, rather, as generously positioned within a long, multigenerational, and global theological tradition that is *located* rather than vague and *expansive* rather than defensive. Together with members of the body of Christ past and present, we seek life and nourishment in God's Word, accessed by the Spirit, as adopted children of the Father. As members of God's household that extends through the ages, we reach out in a spacious way that cultivates deep discipleship, rest, joyful play, and witness to a world in need.

The Reformed Tradition as "Catholic"

We seek to inhabit a tradition substantially, not avoiding the truth claims and real differences among Christians. But we believe that the Reformed tradition can be inhabited in a way that has generosity as well as depth, such that, as in Johnson's framing of the tree, it provides "fruit, shade, and sustenance to the people and institutions around us, generously finding places of overlap rather

5. Johnson, "The Way of Jesus in a Divided Nation."

than demarcating lines of division. By their fruit you shall know them."[6] As we describe in our "wager" below, we believe that inhabiting the Reformed tradition, deeply and generously, can lead to a discipleship that is deeper than that which comes from assuming that we can stand above historic Christian traditions by identifying simply as "biblical" or "Christian." In this, our goal is that in being Reformed we can inhabit the broader catholic (i.e., "the whole" or "universal") church with a particular goal in mind: "building up the body of Christ, until all of us come to the unity of the faith and of the knowledge of the Son of God, to maturity, to the measure of the full stature of Christ" (Eph. 4:12–13).

Some readers may find it strange that we speak of ourselves as "catholic." In this book, the lowercase term *catholic* does not refer to the Roman Catholic Church. In a basic sense, the term *catholic* points to a confession of God's work reflected in early Christian baptismal creeds, like the Apostles' Creed. In saying that we are catholic, we are acknowledging that we are children of the Father who belong to the Son through the Holy Spirit, that we "belong to the holy, catholic church." We are not a movement. We are not part of a voluntary organization. We are not self-made, autonomous followers of Jesus. We are not members of a church that was started fifty or four hundred years ago. Fundamentally, we have been incorporated, by the Holy Spirit, as adopted children, into God's household—a household that extends back to the early church described in Acts. Indeed, this household extends back further still, in various forms, even to "the beginning of the world."[7]

In some contexts, Christians will say they are catholic, belonging to the universal church through time, but this is a passing comment on the way to naming a deeper identity, such as Baptist or Presbyterian or Wesleyan or Reformed. Internal ecclesial discussions then center around whether someone is "authentically Baptist," or "Presbyterian enough," or "truly Reformed."

We believe that the ordering should be reversed, and that this reversal has far-reaching consequences. We see the Reformed tradition (which can include many denominational and nondenominational expressions of the church) as a pathway to inhabit the larger and even more expansive catholic Christian faith. Traditions are not dispensable or arbitrary; there is no generic way to open oneself to the doctrine, patterns, and wisdom of the historic catholic faith. The Reformed tradition gives one possible way to inhabit the wide and rich land of God's household, which extends around our globe and through the ages.

---

6. Johnson, "The Way of Jesus in a Divided Nation."
7. Belgic Confession, 27 (*Our Faith*, 53).

Through the Spirit, we've been adopted into God's household as children of the Father in Christ. In reaching deep into the nourishment of God's Word by the Spirit, we dwell in, feed on, and delight in God's Word as acts of communion with the Lord, a communion that moves us to embrace our identity in Christ and reach out in compassionate witness. Thus, the Reformed tradition is not just a set of propositions to affirm, but rather a set of theological convictions and dispositions that find expression in our ache for and delight in God's Word. We believe that we receive God's Word communally, in preaching and in the sacraments, in the midst of a newly adopted and reconciled identity as the people of God. We don't master Scripture and then leave it alone. We go again and again to commune with God in Christ by means of Scripture.

Unlike congregations that claim to have "no creed but Christ," or to be simply "reviving the New Testament church," churches within the Reformed tradition dig deeply into the history of the Christian tradition. They expect to find both truth, as a result of the Spirit's work, and distortion and sin, as the Christian church is fallible in its history and present. While open to the questions and critiques of the church's shortcomings, the Reformed tradition nevertheless seeks to inhabit the historic Christian tradition in a way that is catholic, not seeking to reinvent Christianity in each generation.

And yet, the catholic path of the Reformed tradition is self-effacing in relation to Scripture. As we introduce a generous Reformed tradition in this book, we will draw on Reformed confessions—doctrinal statements and catechisms from Reformed Christians around the world, testifying to their faith.[8] But ultimately, we care about the confessions because we care even more deeply about Scripture. Rather than saying that we have "no creed but Christ," we have discovered, like many others over the centuries, that confessions actually deepen our roots in Scripture, enlivening our nourishment in God's Word. If we draw on the wisdom of just one person (our pastor or our favorite theologian) or one short era of history (e.g., the past thirty years) in our reception of Scripture, our engagement with the vast depth of God's wisdom in Scripture is bound to be superficial. Confessions point us to a community that goes beyond

---

8. The Reformed confessions present themselves as faithful yet fallible testimonies to the teaching of Scripture. In most Reformed denominations, ordained leaders pledge to uphold the confessions in what is called *subscription*, a term that means "to sign," or formally affirm, the confessions in their role within the church. Because Scripture is the supreme authority, there is some flexibility in how subscription is applied. Some denominations require strict adherence but allow candidates to register specific "scruples," or conscientious reservations—points of disagreement rooted in their interpretations of Scripture. Others take a more flexible stance, simply asking candidates to be guided by the confessions. Though practices differ, all aim to honor the confessions as valuable testimonies to God's Word while recognizing that they are fallible, not final, authorities.

ourselves and our own age—and even beyond the Reformation era—as a chief task for the Reformed confessions is to testify to ancient Christian theologies about God and Christ. Confessions point beyond themselves, assisting in the interpretation of Scripture and providing an aid in our God-given journey of growing in communion with God through God's Word in Christ.

Misunderstandings about the Reformed tradition are widespread, both outside of and within Reformed circles. Thus, in each of the topical chapters below, we begin with a critical question about the Reformed tradition (e.g., Does Reformed theology teach us to see God as a controlling tyrant or as a loving provider? Or, Is the Reformed tradition just for white Westerners?). Each chapter will address the concerns underlying its key question and will correct common caricatures. Then each chapter will develop a positive vision of how that aspect of Reformed teaching can move congregations deeper into fellowship with God in Christ as they feed on Scripture. Correcting misunderstandings is necessary, but the heartbeat of this book is how the Reformed tradition can be a compelling way to inhabit the historic, catholic Christian tradition, one that leads us toward growth in joyful witness to the "manifold wisdom" of God displayed in Jesus Christ (Eph. 3:10 NIV) and displays the constructive contributions that Reformed theology can make to the communal life of discipleship.

A Wager

Why would someone want to inhabit a particular theological tradition like the Reformed tradition? For many, the list of reasons "why not" is likely to be longer than the list of reasons "why." Distrust of institutions—from the government to church denominational structures—has been increasing in Western contexts. Sadly, all too often this distrust of the institutional church is for good reason: abuse of power, confusion of cultural status with a Christ-following way, wearisome debates that seem to indicate to the world that Christians are ones who bicker together rather than ones who love one another.

This book is not an apology or defense for belonging to a Reformed denomination or network or inhabiting a particular polity. Denominations and structures matter, of course. But for too long they have been confused with something quite distinct: inhabiting a historic theological tradition. It is possible to be part of a Reformed or Lutheran or Methodist or Baptist denomination and to inhabit those traditions in reductionistic ways. In some contexts, theological points can quickly become weapons in warfare, meant to secure the fortress against the onslaught of "the liberals" or "the fundamentalists."

In other contexts, due to exhaustion from years of denominational bitterness, a congregation tries to hide their heritage under the rug. As long as it is a fairly homogeneous group, it can seem plausible for a congregation to be "generically Christian." But when the first controversy related to baptism or church leadership or generational change or accountability emerges, a church split naturally follows.

We understand that while many readers may desire to connect with the Christian faith of the past, the obstacles to committing oneself to a historic Christian tradition are considerable. Is the historic Reformed tradition really worthy of trust? Has it been an ideal church through history? Was it complicit in the horrors of slavery and the history of racism? Did this tradition avoid the cultural Christianity that left behind the Bible when Scripture became unfashionable? Has it resisted the allure of power and chosen the way of the cross?

Let us say this at the outset: The Reformed tradition, as expressed in its confessions, in its theologians, and in the lived reality of history, avoided none of these horrors and errors. It is not an untainted church in its past or its testimony. It has, as we will describe in chapter 2, a "non-innocent history."

Yet, here is our wager: If we are followers of Jesus, we *must* decide how we will relate to the larger, historic Christian tradition—with its beauties and profound shortcomings. On the one hand, we can pretend that we belong to a church that is only a few decades old and avoid these larger questions; but that is a decision. That decision assumes a church exists that somehow floats above flesh-and-blood mortals who have followed Jesus for centuries. On the other hand, we can decide to make our home in a much older tradition, whether Reformed or Lutheran or Roman Catholic or Orthodox. There are no perfect options, no innocent possibilities, no churches whose history and life represent unerring purity and faithfulness. Whether we like or dislike church or history, our life decisions display a sense of what it means to belong to the household of God, the church catholic, present through history and in various cultural contexts.

We authors of this book believe that even with its flaws and shortcomings, the Reformed tradition can be a fruitful pathway for growing deeper into maturity in Christ, for hearing from the testimony of the whole counsel of Scripture, and for strengthening our witness—in word and deed—to the good news of Jesus Christ in a hurting and often cynical world. Indeed, the Reformed tradition gives an account of the church as a creature of God's own Word. The church is fallen and fallible. Yet, through God's mercy alone, God created a people where there were no people. In union with Christ through the Spirit, we are adopted into God's household and given new life, an identity to grow into. In this process, we do not need to sugarcoat the church's sins, yet we also need not despair. God alone is the hope for the church, and his life-giving Word continues to call his household to repentance, growth, and witness.

What is at stake in calling this a wager? We use the word to evoke the reflections of the seventeenth-century French mathematician, physicist, and philosopher Blaise Pascal. He offered a careful argument that often shows up in philosophy classes about the existence of God. He does not provide *evidence* for God's existence but, rather, gives practical arguments for why it is wise to commit oneself in trust to God, even if plagued with doubts. In essence, his wager is that, given the potential eternal rewards and consequences, it's wiser to believe in God than not, even without certainty of God's existence. Uncertainty should not be an obstacle to commitment.

We believe that an adapted version of the wager has implications for Christians considering whether to commit themselves to a particular theological tradition. All traditions are imperfect, and there will always be uncertainties about what such a commitment entails. As Pascal reflected on his life slipping away, he noted that questions of religion and theology can be debated interminably, so one will be paralyzed if one requires certainty before acting. "If we must not act save on a certainty, we ought not to act on religion, for it is not certain. But how many things we do on an uncertainty, sea voyages, battles! I say then we must do nothing at all, for nothing is certain, and there is more certainty in religion than there is as to whether we may see to-morrow."[9] This is true in the question of whether or how to occupy a particular theological tradition. Learning about that tradition and others is important. Logical reasoning has a place as well. But if we always stay outside all historic Christian traditions, then the tradition we *functionally* embrace will put the self, our own preferences, at the center: We decide what to eat at the smorgasbord of Christianity.

We may think that we are keeping our options open by staying in this smorgasbord mode of relating to the Christian tradition; but in matters of faith, there is no way to opt out. In the words of Pascal, "You must of necessity choose. This is one point settled."[10] He notes that we are likely to spend much of our lives avoiding such commitments through distraction. "All of humanity's problems stem from man's inability to sit quietly in a room alone," he writes.[11] We do need to sit alone and consider the questions of faith because to avoid acting in this instance is, in fact, an action.

9. Pascal, *Pensées*, 70.
10. Pascal, *Pensées*, 67.
11. Pascal, *Pensées*, 39.

Indeed, choosing how and whether to commit to a particular Christian tradition can be like standing before the Grand Canyon or trying to take in the scope of Mount Everest on a flight around it. Before something so grand, we realize our limits anew. We take in much, but much of what we observe is how little we can fully process. For Pascal, and for other mortals like us, this is the setting within which we commit on questions of faith: "The eternal silence of these infinite spaces frightens me. How many kingdoms know us not! Why is my knowledge limited? Why my stature? Why my life to one hundred years rather than to a thousand?"[12] We are small, our lives are short, and we cannot wait on the sidelines when it comes to matters of faith.

We encourage readers to bring their hearts and minds to this book, but we use the concept of a wager to describe the decision of whether and how to inhabit a theological tradition because we know that, on this point, it can be tempting to simply defer—as if we could opt out, stand on the sidelines. If we decide to take a smorgasbord approach, viewing theological traditions as consumers (and ourselves as those who should be in charge), then we should be honest about that decision. But we authors of this book are willing to wager that diving into a particular pathway to inhabit the broad, catholic tradition will be a richer, more fruitful path. And we think that the Reformed tradition, despite all its defects and shortcomings, can provide a deeply biblical, refreshingly God-centered, and profoundly generative pathway into the catholic Christian faith.

12. Pascal, *Pensées*, 61.

1

A Reformed Theology Primer: Misconceptions and Realities

Key Question: What Is Reformed Theology, Anyway?

Because the Reformed tradition is such a broad and misunderstood topic, we need to give some orientation, a primer, before we get to the key questions that will form the focus of this book. Although I was not raised in the Reformed tradition, I (Todd) have had "Reformed theology" in my job title for two decades, and I was deeply interested in the subject more than a decade before that. The phrase *Reformed theology* has a quite different meaning, and quite divergent associations, in various contexts. Even in my own experiences, from Pasadena to Addis Ababa, Ethiopia, from Harvard to a small nondenominational church in Kansas, the range of assumptions, hopes, and suspicions about the Reformed tradition are almost too many to number.

Perhaps a tiny snapshot from these contexts might give a sense of the kaleidoscope. In Pasadena, *Reformed* was used to speak about an approach to culture in which Christians did not simply separate from or imitate culture and the arts but became creators of culture for Christ's kingdom. I recall lively conversations in Addis Ababa in which the Reformed were praised for rightly confessing God's kingship over creation but also suspected of having deficient doctrines of baptism and the Lord's Supper. While I was doing doctoral work at Harvard, some colleagues assumed that Karl Barth, the Swiss theologian who resisted Nazism, was my primary interest. Although many theologians span the Reformed tradition, Barth's significant influence in twentieth-century academic discussions meant his name was the first to come to mind when they heard I was Reformed. I recall a conversation in Kansas in which *Reformed* was understood to designate a group of people who "thought that they alone were elect because they were better than everyone else."

More puzzling (and fascinating) are the cases in which suspicions or celebrations of the Reformed tradition contain contradictions. "The Reformed have too high a doctrine of Scripture," I have been told. Because the Reformed prioritize the hearing of God's Word in Scripture over general categories like experience, these critics think the Reformed place mind over body, rationality over emotion. Others think the Reformed have too low a doctrine of Scripture because they are not quite rational enough. Why else would the Reformed have confessions and catechisms? If the Reformed rightly applied reason in response to Scripture, they would realize that Christians need nothing beyond a careful, literal-grammatical interpretation of the Bible, they say. Ideas such as that Christian tradition could be helpful in receiving Scripture, and that practices in worship and prayer that engage our affections may be key aspects of cultivating a receptive posture to Scripture, are seen as absurd ways of rationalizing sub-biblical practices. In the end, the critics are right and wrong. They are wrong in some of their misconceived assumptions about Reformed theology, but they are right in that all attempts to talk about God are fallen and finite.

Indeed, the mess and irony involved when small mortals like us talk about God is something we can and should openly embrace. The subject of theology is the joy of all joys, the living God and his gospel! We affirm Thomas Oden's instinct that "the disciplined study of God is best experienced from within a light-hearted, caring community that laughs at its own soberest undertakings."[1] But there is a danger that, in the heady dynamics of human discourse about God, we lose a sense of proportion. As mortal creatures with aches and blind spots and the tendency to deceive ourselves, we should note the absurdity involved if we try to elude our stubborn limits. Oden writes, "We students of God, look at us: God's own image, scratching our eczema; irritated by hemorrhoids, yet capable of refracting divine goodness; biped animals who dream of eternity; playing God yet being bums, clowns, and louts—yet bums who can say from the heart, 'God bless.'"[2] Reflection on

1. Oden, *Classic Christianity*, 858.
2. Oden, *Living God*, 405.

Scripture and the study of God in theology are acts of praise, songs of thanks. But if we attempt to study God like we would study an object of wood, or if we discuss theology like we are competitors in a boxing match, the entire quest will be clownishly inadequate.

As we unpack some myths and set the stage for a generous Reformed theology, we seek to do so from a posture of humility and hope. From a Reformed perspective, theology is not primarily a human effort to make claims about God; rather, it is an attentive act of receiving, of hearing, and of testifying to the Lord of creation, covenant, and redemption. It is a humble rejoicing in revelation that we could not have invented ourselves. Even as we testify to the goodness, power, and mercy of the Lord, we can join the psalmist in admitting that our knowledge of the Lord is not like his knowledge of us: "Such knowledge is too wonderful for me; it is so high that I cannot attain it" (Ps. 139:6).

Making It Complex: A Variety of Confessions from Refugee Theologians

What is Reformed theology? It seems like a simple question. As we've just noted, all human discourse about God is messy, an incomplete testimony from mere mortals. We are absurdly limited in comparison to God's eternal way of knowing and being. Both our knowledge and our will are tainted, and we are inclined to hide from a God who does not appear according to our wishes. These factors alone suggest that Reformed theology, like Lutheran theology or Catholic theology, will be messy and complicated, at least at particular points.

Dear readers, fasten your seat belts. Additional factors, distinctive to the Reformed tradition, make discussions of Reformed theology complex and multilayered. To begin with, particular confessions and catechisms are the central, shared authorities—under Scripture—that identify Christian communities as Reformed. But there is no uniformity in the sources or the content among these Reformed standards. Stated differently, the central identifying sources for the content of Reformed theology vary in different regions and different parts of the Reformed tradition. While the Reformed tradition values the discipline of theology, no single theologian defines what it means to be Reformed. That is established by assemblies in particular regions, with unique histories and cultures. In most regions, as the Reformed faith spread, the church adopted two types of theological documents that its pastors embraced as shared authorities, under the prime authority of Scripture: catechisms (teaching tools) and confessions (supplemental statements of faith including expositions of key scriptural sources for the doctrines).

The Reformed Church in Hungary, founded in 1567, is still active today with around 3.5 million members in the church worldwide.[3] In addition to its catechism, its single confession is the Second Helvetic Confession (1536), written in Switzerland by Heinrich Bullinger in the second generation of the Reformation. A generation later, Guido De Bres, a pastor in a persecuted underground church in what would become the Netherlands, wrote the Belgic Confession (1561), which became the main statement of faith for the Dutch Reformed Church. In the same generation, John Knox and five other Scottish reformers wrote the Scots Confession (1560). There is significant theological shared ground among the confessions written by Bullinger, De Bres, and Knox and his colleagues. But there are differences as well, and these are quite intentional. Each wrote with the specific challenges and needs of their context in mind.

What were the underlying factors leading to these different Reformed confessional traditions? Sociologically, Reformed theology was often birthed in the pain of exile, among religious refugees. As one historian notes, "The Reformation stands out as the first period in European and possibly global history when religious refugees became a mass phenomenon."[4] This reality was central for the development and growth of the Reformed movement. Although Reformed Christians sought to cooperate with governing authorities who would give them clemency, leading Reformed theologians such as John Calvin, John Knox, Peter Martyr Vermigli, and Theodore Beza all lived away from their home regions and cultures for decades. A common destination for these refugees was Geneva, Switzerland. Geneva became the destination for thousands of displaced people with physical and spiritual needs that stretched the capacity of the city. Among the displaced were pastors. This led to a reorganization of the diaconate to provide for physical needs and the founding of the Genevan Academy in 1559 by Calvin. For generations, the Genevan Academy was a launching pad for training pastors and other reformers who were then sent to do ministry elsewhere. Whether in Switzerland, Germany, Scotland, or even Brazil, the Genevan Academy became a theological and missional catalyst for the Reformation.

In addition to the sociological reason for this multiformity was a theological one: The Reformed held to a theology of the Spirit and the church that did not insist on uniformity to have unity. It was enough for these sister

---

3. Global Ministries, "Reformed Church in Hungary."
4. Terpstra, *Religious Refugees*, 4.

churches to have *similar* confessions, for there was a range of differences in culture and custom that could be fitting in different places. These differences could reflect the Spirit's work in distinct contexts and ultimately fit within the Reformed sense that they belong to the church catholic, the universal church, in all times and all places. Later chapters in this book will examine this point further—that Reformed Christians embraced the Reformed faith as a way to be catholic Christians, even though their movement had been rejected by the Roman Catholic Church.

For the Roman Catholic Church, especially in the early modern era, this "universality" of the Christian faith was displayed through the church's magisterium, or teaching office. This involves a hierarchy of offices as well as sources, with the office of the pope and the decisions of church councils playing central roles in holding together the unity of the Roman Catholic faith. The Reformed tradition locates itself as belonging to the catholic faith, but with a different way of inhabiting this shared faith. It not only sought to reject the "innovations" of the church of Rome but also developed a variety of regional confessions of faith and catechisms that expressed this unity in a variety of forms. Dutch theologian Herman Bavinck (1854–1921) put it this way: "That church is most catholic that most clearly expresses in its confession and applies in its practice this international and cosmopolitan character of the Christian religion. The Reformed had an eye for it when in various countries and churches they confessed the truth in an indigenous, free, and independent manner."[5]

Although he wrote over a century ago, Bavinck's phrasing here is significant for Reformed Christian communities around the world today: The Reformed goal is to confess the faith "in an indigenous, free, and independent manner." By *indigenous*, Bavinck means something more like *local* or *contextual* than *Native American* or *Aboriginal*, as we sometimes understand the term today. Indigenization is how the diverse-yet-unified catholicity and universality of the church is expressed, rather than in a top-down approach or a uniform collection of Protestant confessional statements.

While the Reformed indigenizing principle will be explored further in later chapters, it should be clear already that having a variety of differing Reformed confessions and catechisms gives a certain messiness to the definition of *Reformed theology*. It can be messy and also profoundly generative. Reformed churches around the world—from South Africa to Cuba—have continued to generate confessional documents that clarify the gospel's witness in their own times and places.

5. Bavinck, *Reformed Dogmatics*, 4:323.

Contextual Flexibility: Order of Worship and Church Government

The complexity of what is meant by *Reformed theology* goes even further as we move to two areas in particular: worship and polity (church government). In these two major areas, a Reformed approach operates on a principle of deep contextual flexibility, refusing to require a particular approach in order to belong to the Reformed theological tradition.

Orders of worship and church government are both vital areas of church life. They are deeply important for the Reformed tradition. However, from early in the Reformation it was clear that one order of worship or polity would not dictate the singular way to be Reformed.

The Scots Confession gives one example of this principle. The confession notes that "good policy and order should be constituted and observed in the Kirk [church] where, as in the house of God, it becomes all things to be done decently and in order." Yet, rather than stating what these policies should be, it clarifies that no polity or order of worship "can be appointed for all ages, times, and places; for as ceremonies which men have devised are but temporal, so they may, and ought to be, changed, when they foster superstition rather than edify the Kirk."[6] In God's household, the church, there is a place for order and structure, echoing the apostle Paul's imperative that "all things should be done decently and in order" (1 Cor. 14:40). But there is not a singular biblical or Reformed way to enter into this structure; it is a temporal matter of discernment amid various possibilities. The contextual, temporal character of the order of worship means that it not only *can* but "*ought to*" be reassessed and changed, so that it cultivates true worship of God rather than distracting idolatries and "superstition."

This approach to Christian worship keeps a God-centered focus. Worship encompasses daily life in family and vocation, and congregational worship is a divinely given means for communion with God and one another by Word and sacrament. But when it comes to the particulars of worship, the Reformed tradition strives to be attentive to how different regions and cultures have different histories. Sometimes it has failed to do this, leading to "worship wars" of various kinds, but because flexibility about matters of worship is an underlying assumption within the Reformed tradition, at its best it has incorporated and celebrated quite diverse cultures and histories.[7] By the second generation of the Reformation, it was clear that there was not just one Reformed way of worship in terms of a shared liturgy, a dependence on fixed prayers in a prayer

6. Scots Confession, 20 (Dennison, *Reformed Confessions*, 2:201).
7. For an excellent historical and global overview of approaches to worship in the Reformed tradition, see Vischer, *Christian Worship in Reformed Churches*.

book, or spontaneous prayer. Different approaches to music and singing were used in different places. Even assemblies that produced a range of significant confessions and catechisms refused to prescribe particular liturgies or set orders of worship, as can be seen in the *Directory for Public Worship* issued by the Westminster Assembly (1643–49). The *Directory* was intended to be a helpful-yet-flexible handbook for ministers to cultivate orderly and reverent approaches to prayer, worship, and the sacraments.

In a similar mode, rather than promoting a singular model for church governance, Calvin reflects the early Reformed tendency to take a contextual and pragmatic approach to church polity: "We know that church organization admits, nay requires, according to the varying condition of the times, various changes."[8] Calvin's preference was for church authority to be exercised by assemblies, rather than by individuals like bishops and archbishops, who were given broad regional authority. But in response to queries from England and Poland, he accepted the episcopal system (governance through bishops and archbishops) as a possible form of the church's life, particularly when that structure was part of the region's history and culture. In the words of one prominent translator and scholar of Calvin's work, "Calvin accepted the episcopal system where it existed so long as it was purged of the trappings of imperial status and tyranny and so long as bishops were active in preaching, teaching, and pastoral care."[9]

As an example of this contextual flexibility, it is helpful to note that the Hungarian Reformed Church has had bishops since the late sixteenth century. For this Reformed denomination, the episcopal system is adapted by incorporating the role of assemblies more prominently than most episcopal-based polities do. But it is still an authentic expression of Reformed polity. On the other end of the polity spectrum, a wide range of Reformed denominations and churches have been congregationalist in their church government since the beginning of the seventeenth century. They cooperate with other Christians but function autonomously on a congregational level, even as they hold to Reformed doctrine.

Reformed Indigenization: A Coherent Multiformity

For the Reformed, contextual flexibility in confessional traditions, worship, and polity is not a crass pragmatism. The valuing of particular peoples and regions with their history and culture emerges from a set of theological

8. Calvin, *Institutes* 4.7.15.
9. Leith, *Reformed Tradition*, 159.

convictions about creation, the Spirit, and the church. The Spirit, who moves in the whole of creation, works differently among those with different histories and cultures, even as they share the main substance of their Reformed and catholic faith. The Reformed enthusiastically affirm that worship is central to the Christian life and the church. The gathered congregation is framed as imperative in the Reformed confessions, to worship the triune God, pray, sing, preach, and celebrate the sacraments. In the words of the Belgic Confession, believers are "obliged to join [the church] and unite with it, keeping the unity of the church by submitting to its instruction and discipline, by bending their necks under the yoke of Jesus Christ, and by serving to build up one another, according to the gifts God has given them as members of each other in the same body."[10] Participation in the life, worship, and structures of the church (which guide discipleship and discipline) is seen as vitally important.

Thus, when it comes to worship and polity, Reformed Christians seek to value the distinctive gifts within different contexts by narrowing the qualifications of what is required to be a sister church in the Reformed tradition. This narrowing is not meant to set limits on who is in or out of the communion; narrowing requirements is actually a widening that recognizes the vast range of variety in worship styles and practices, organizational structures, and polity. None of these ways of functioning determine whether or not a church or a fellowship of churches is considered Reformed, for *Reformed* is a designation based on the theological confession of the church. The Reformed confessions, as we refer to them in this book, usually consist of a general doctrinal statement (such as the Scots, Belgic, French, Second Helvetic, or Westminster confessions) and a catechism (such as the Heidelberg, Genevan, Anglican, or Westminster Shorter and Longer catechisms). These are the "standards" that are shared among church leaders. While the exact content of these doctrinal and pedagogical statements varies according to the region, history, and context, they share a great deal of commonality in their Reformed theology.

Admittedly, the terms *flexible* and *contextual* may not be the first that come to mind for some readers when they hear the phrase *Reformed theology*. In the late twentieth and early twenty-first centuries, many people in the West developed their impressions of the Reformed tradition from celebrity preachers. Search engines, friends, and neighbors are likely to name one or more well-known preachers as representative of Reformed theology. Sadly, this hides the deeper wisdom of the transgenerational Reformed tradition, with its contextual flexibility on the points we have been describing.

---

10. Belgic Confession, 28 (*Our Faith*, 54).

I recall conversations where questions were raised about the Reformed approach to women in ordained ministry or a complementarian account of family, which holds a particular view of gender roles and male "headship" in the family. Answers seemed to be ready at hand. A celebrity preacher who was outspoken on these topics would be brought up, and the conversation partners would deduce, "He is Reformed, he has this view on gender roles, thus his view is the Reformed view." This may seem logical, according to current ways of thinking. Many churches and interdenominational ministries describe their position on these topics. So what is the Reformed view?

The question itself (and the impulse to find the answer through a representative pastor) is deeply problematic. With a Reformed way of inhabiting tradition, no individual, whether theologian or celebrity preacher, can decide what Reformed theology teaches. Sources of authority (beneath Scripture) are shared communally in confessions and catechisms. A search through historic Reformed confessions and catechisms shows that *there is no Reformed confessional position on these topics*. These documents seek to portray and communicate historic Christian theology in a Reformed way. They do not focus on presenting a singular model for church governance, or a shared understanding of gender in relation to the family. Churches and denominations in the Reformed tradition are welcome to develop policies that relate to gender in church governance. However, differences along that line cannot, by definition, define whether one is Reformed theologically, but only whether one conforms to one particular polity or another.

We think that, overall, this flexibility is an *asset* of the Reformed theological tradition, though at times this ambiguity has led to fierce infighting among Reformed communities about modes of worship and polity. In addition, in an age of digital media and communication, this flexibility can often lead to misunderstanding and confusion, even from well-known preachers and teachers who are known for giving expositions of Reformed theology.

The Beauty and Messiness of Being Reformed

The flexibility of the Reformed tradition can be beautiful but also confusing. A range of other traditions—including Roman Catholicism, Eastern Orthodoxy, and some Protestant traditions—have more symmetrical layers to their life together. The doctrine, liturgy and worship, and church governance all belong to that tradition in a way that clearly fits together. But while the Reformed tradition *values* worship and polity, it does not consider those layers to be *constitutive* of being Reformed in the same way. In other words, Reformed congregations can have quite radical differences in order of worship and liturgy and still all be Reformed.

A specific comparison with Lutheranism may be helpful here. There are a variety of Lutheran denominations, and Lutheran theology has a rich and lively tradition in academic, denominational, and congregational contexts. But there's a sense in which the main sources for Lutheran theology are relatively clear: the confessions and catechisms in the Book of Concord, as collected in 1580.

Lutheran theology shares some aspects with the Reformed tradition, and these can be confessed within a variety of denominations. But on the whole, the different layers of Lutheran identity tend to be symmetrical. The confessions and catechisms are shared internationally; churches share a liturgical tradition and polity, which includes bishops and synods.

With the Reformed tradition, in contrast, these layers are often quite asymmetrical. In terms of polity, not only those who embrace a presbytery system are Reformed. There is a vast variety in church governance among churches with a Reformed confession or a Reformed theological heritage, including Anglican, Congregationalist, and nondenominational churches. What about worship? There is a rich history and tradition of Reformed worship. But as I (Todd) have expounded elsewhere, it is far from homogeneous. There are long, multicentury Reformed traditions that cultivate a reverent piety with the use of fixed liturgical forms, and there are also traditions of Reformed worship that are much more charismatic in expression. A highly emotional and affective mode of worship also has a multicentury heritage in the Reformed tradition.[11] These varied expressions of worship have deep roots in the historic church and in the multifaceted Reformed expression of the catholic Christian faith.

Reformed over Calvinist

As a way of recognizing the coherence yet multiformity of the Reformed theological tradition, we prefer to speak of this tradition as *Reformed*, rather than as *Calvinist*.[12] Whether consciously or not, speaking about the Reformed tradition as Calvinist is a way of reducing church history to a great-thinker

---

11. See Billings, *Remembrance, Communion, and Hope*, 1–3.

12. For readers who would appreciate further clarification about what the term *Reformed* means, including a response to some common misunderstandings of the term and a widely used maxim often framed as "Reformed and always reforming," we recommend reading appendixes A and B in this book.

model: viewing church history as a sequence of great thinkers who define and exemplify whole traditions.[13] Although at points in the nineteenth and early twentieth centuries the terms *Calvinist* and *Reformed* were basically synonymous with Reformed theology, we advocate using the term *Reformed* because it is misleading to see the theological tradition as derivative from Calvin alone, or even from Calvin primarily. In addition, as we will see below, some self-designated Calvinists today use that term because they teach the so-called five points of Calvinism but not the rest of Reformed doctrine. Thus, *Reformed* remains the broader, more expansive term.

For centuries, in its self-understanding, there was no single "founding father" for the Reformed tradition. Calvin was a prolific biblical commentator, and as a second-generation reformer he was an effective codifier of key aspects of Reformed theology. In contrast to Martin Luther, Calvin is not the author of any widely used confession of faith or catechism. Calvin did not seek to be unique in his teaching, separated from other reformers whom he considered to be peers, such as Guillaume Farel, Peter Martyr Vermigli, or Wolfgang Musculus. Calvin is an important Reformed theologian, but he was not considered the originator of the Reformed tradition in his own day or in generations that followed.

In sum, while the multiform character of Reformed confessionalism can be overstated (the confessions of the same era share a significant amount of common ground), the differences are still significant. The confessional witness of a Presbyterian with the Westminster Standards has commonality with, but also differences from, someone whose standards are the "three forms of unity" (the Belgic Confession, Canons of Dort, and Heidelberg Catechism) or someone from a Swiss Reformed heritage (such as the Hungarian Reformed Church, with the Second Helvetic Confession and the Heidelberg Catechism). Some doctrinal points within Westminster are not included in these other confessions. Because of its multiform character, it would be a mistake to use such points as the criteria for what belongs to Reformed theology overall.

Heuristics for Reformed Theology, Keywords, and Group Identity

At this point, it should be clear that the answer to the question "What is Reformed theology?" is complex and layered. And yet, as human beings, we naturally want—even need—to simplify. We put complex realities into neat categories, both as a help for our understanding and so that we can connect

---

13. For a description and critique of the great-thinker model in viewing church history, see Bradley and Muller, *Church History*, 30–31.

with one another. As we consider different heuristics (mental shortcuts), key-words and phrases that are used to sum up Reformed theology, a question arises: How does this process of simplification work, and what does it mean for how we talk about Reformed theology?

This question struck me after I had an interview with a journalist who was investigating the "young, restless, and Reformed" movement in 2009—not long after a *Time Magazine* article had named "New Calvinism" as one of "10 Ideas Changing the World Right Now."[14] The journalist, eager for a quick summary of Reformed theology, zeroed in on the TULIP acronym. When I pointed out that TULIP wasn't a comprehensive take on Reformed theology and that the acronym itself had problems, she grew impatient. "Then what's a better acronym?" she asked. Wanting something that offered more possibili-ties, I suggested, "How about chrysanthemum?" She paused—then quickly shifted the conversation.

While the journalist seemed impatient at the time, I've come to realize that her question was more probing than I initially thought. Essentially, she was asking for an accessible shorthand both for her and for her readers. As Nobel Prize–winning social scientist Daniel Kahneman explains in *Thinking, Fast and Slow*, our brains rely on heuristics and biases to ease the cognitive load of constant deliberation. If we consciously analyzed every action throughout the day, we'd be paralyzed, unable to function or survive in our world. Instead, our brains use "fast" thinking—"automatic and often unconscious processes that underlie intuitive judgment." Moment by moment, this system "con-structs a coherent interpretation of what is going on in our world,"[15] relying on various biases, heuristics, and emotionally charged shortcuts. As mortals seeking to find food and shelter and connection and meaning, we operate in "fast thinking" most frequently, on a day-to-day level.

But sometimes our intuitive judgment doesn't serve us well. Our biases push us into misunderstanding rather than into deeper understanding, getting us into trouble. At that point, Kahneman says, we must transition to a differ-ent system of mental processing: "slow thinking." Enormously fruitful and generative, slow thinking can lead to a joyful state that some call "flow." But it also requires an enormous amount of mental and physical energy. It takes concentration to learn a new language or skill, analyze a text, or weigh the pros and cons of a major decision. "The often-used phrase 'pay attention' is apt," Kahneman says, because "you dispose of a limited budget of attention that you can allocate to activities, and if you try to go beyond your budget,

14. Van Biema, "New Calvinism."
15. Kahneman, *Thinking, Fast and Slow*, 13.

you will fail."[16] When our minds get tired, they enter triage mode, sliding back into the shortcuts of fast thinking.

When it comes to Reformed theology, many keywords and phrases are frequently used to help with fast thinking, to simplify the complex. Each one not only relates to the content of theology but also provides a yardstick for who belongs and, consequently, who does not. "Are you a five-point Calvinist, or a four-point Calvinist?" "Do you embrace covenant theology? Because Reformed theology *is* covenant theology." "We agree with the *solas* of the Reformed tradition, unlike that church down the street." If Reformed theology is a journey of faith seeking understanding, new terms and key phrases can help us navigate our way; but, on their own, the keywords can easily become "rites of entry" to certain conversations or in-groups. In our view, healthy Reformed theological reflection resists the notion that we should seek to separate ourselves into an enlightened in-group. Rather, instead of belonging to an exclusive club, we are on a shared journey of faith seeking understanding.

For example, I've had numerous conversations with Roman Catholic, Eastern Orthodox, and Wesleyan Christians, and I've repeatedly noticed a now-familiar response in them when they learn that I teach Reformed theology. Their body language changes—their gaze moving away, their shoulders tightening—and they shyly imply that I must think they are part of the "out-group." Ironically, the more deeply I have embraced Reformed theology in my own theological journey, the more commonalities I have found with Christians of these traditions. Many of my closest and longest friendships are with Christians who very much disagree with the Reformed tradition. Yet, as I have moved from generically Protestant to distinctively Reformed, my curiosity and appreciation for these other traditions, and those within them, has deepened, not become shallower. Various theological traditions form a kind of "ecumenical water table." Digging small holes here and there can get you only so far. But dig *deeply* into one tradition, in a healthy way, and you'll hit the water of *catholicity*. There, we do not all agree. But appreciation, curiosity, and friendship can be a wellspring.

This requires entering into a tradition with generosity toward others, even while celebrating the unique gifts of our own traditions discovered in the process of digging. It requires slow thinking. It also requires seeing the goal as inhabiting the catholic Christian tradition, rather than as being more "truly Reformed" than one's neighbor.

Because we see the Reformed tradition as one way to enter the ecumenical water table, we don't advocate a short acronym or phrase to sum up the

16. Kahneman, *Thinking, Fast and Slow*, 23.

Reformed tradition. Instead, this chapter closes with two sets of reflections that express some basics of a Reformed approach to Scripture, creation, and its own task. We name certain key themes, such as a *Spirit-enabled pilgrimage in Christ*, which is *theocentric*, *trinitarian*, *Christocentric*, and *personal*. These are characteristics of the Reformed tradition. In naming them, we intend to chart a slow-thinking entry point to Reformed theology. These characteristics don't work as code words that separate the Reformed from the non-Reformed, and they can't really be used to win theological arguments. But that's OK. We believe that in theology, as in the rest of life, we are called to love our neighbors and not bear false witness against them or twist their words. As C. S. Lewis points out, discussion as warfare tends to devolve into a maxim: "Assume that your opponent is wrong, and then explain his error."[17] While it may provide a spectacle for onlookers, it usually generates more heat than light.

The Place for Theological Shorthand

We do need a place for theological shorthand, for fast thinking and healthy pre-understandings in theological discussion. All specialized forms of inquiry develop their own shorthands and technical apparatuses. As we use technical terms in this book, we will seek to define them as we go. There are also some helpful and accessible dictionaries of the Reformed theological tradition that give definitions and details about theologians, doctrines, and events that are much more reliable than an internet search.[18] Like a guest in a new country, a newcomer is sure to encounter surprises, both puzzles and insights. While theological dictionaries do not offer an overview of Reformed theology, they can function like travel guides for terms and ideas that are new and puzzling.

What about the *solas*, covenant theology, or the five points (with the handy acronym TULIP) as a guide to Reformed theology? Each of these may have some fast-thinking value in particular contexts. But as ways of summarizing Reformed theology as a whole, they underdeliver. They cannot bear the weight.

The Solas

For some, the *solas* can be helpful as memory hooks. Michael Horton gives a brief exposition: "Scripture alone (*sola scriptura*) is the source and norm

---

17. C. S. Lewis, "'Bulverism' or The Foundation of Twentieth Century Thought," quoted in Jacobs, *How to Think*, 78. We are indebted to the insights of Jacobs in this section, especially in his *How to Think*, 96–102.

18. See Kapic and Vander Lugt, *Pocket Dictionary*; McKim, *Reformed Theology from A to Z*.

of Christian faith and practice, and this Word proclaims a salvation that is by God's grace alone (*sola gratia*), in Christ alone (*solo Christo*), through faith alone (*sola fide*). Consequently, all of the glory goes to God alone (*soli Deo gloria*)."[19]

At their best, the *solas* can help us remember some of the pressing theological issues at stake in the Reformation. On the doctrine of salvation, they point to the theocentric and Christ-centered vision underlying Lutheran, Reformed, and other Protestant movements in the sixteenth and seventeenth centuries. Yet as a set of keywords to summarize Reformed doctrine, they fall short. There is much that they do not include related to the Spirit, the church, eschatology, and so on. And the emphasis on *alone* is often misleading to hearers; for example, "Scripture alone" implies that Scripture is the *only* authority in theology, which has never been the historic Reformed position.[20]

Reformed Theology as Covenant Theology

The saying "Reformed theology is covenant theology" highlights an important aspect of Reformed thought but is insufficient as a complete summary. A widely used introduction to Reformed theology by R. C. Sproul notes that this phrase served as a "nickname" to distinguish Reformed theology from dispensationalism, particularly after the Scofield Reference Bible popularized dispensationalism in the early twentieth century.[21] The maxim is meaningful in that specific context, as the two traditions offer distinct models for understanding God's covenantal work throughout the biblical canon.

Sproul frames Reformed theology in terms of three covenants—redemption, works, and grace—grounding this framework biblically and referencing the Westminster Standards. He fails to mention that this approach, known as *federal theology* in technical terms, is just one among several traditions of covenant theology in the Reformed tradition. While it appears in the Westminster Standards, it is absent from most non-Presbyterian Reformed standards. Observing this maxim's use over the years, it often serves as a litmus test for in-group versus out-group status, implicitly suggesting that non-Presbyterians are excluded from the Reformed tradition.

To be clear, Reformed theology as a whole offers a rich doctrine of the covenant, further explored in this book through the theology of infant baptism. For both new and seasoned readers of the Bible, understanding the

19. Horton, *For Calvinism*, 28.
20. For more on this, see chap. 3.
21. Sproul, *What Is Reformed Theology?*, 117. For more on dispensationalism, see chap. 7 of this book.

covenantal aspects of God's relationship with creation and his people can be enormously illuminating, particularly in appreciating the crucial role of the Old Testament in Christian theology. Moreover, federal theology is a venerable tradition within Reformed thought; it has provided valuable insights for pastors, biblical scholars, and theologians alike. Recent books have explored its historical development and ecumenical potential with substantial depth.[22]

However, using federal theology as a summary of Reformed theology is misguided, as it is absent from the sixteenth-century confessions. Many Reformed Christians belong to undeniably Reformed traditions whose confessions, catechisms, or standards do not explicitly teach the threefold covenant of federal theology. Thus, federal theology cannot serve as a comprehensive summary or definition of Reformed theology as a whole.

The Five Points of Calvinism

The most widespread shorthand for summarizing Reformed theology is the five points of Calvinism. This refers to the five points of doctrine in the Canons of Dort, often summarized via the widely used but quite misleading acronym TULIP. We will explore these issues more fully in chapter 4. For the moment, though, it's important to acknowledge that debates about the five points are especially heated, with each point commonly being used as a fist in theological boxing matches. A Reformed Christian would be wise to reframe the parameters, but this is a difficult task.

For example, consider the decisions that Reformed theologian Michael Horton had to make when he was invited to what promised to be a profitable theological brawl. A publisher wanted him to write a companion book to Roger Olson's *Against Calvinism* and to call it *Against Arminianism*. Knowing that audiences always enjoy a good fight, they wanted Horton to make a case against Arminian theology's rejection of the five points of Calvinism.

Horton wisely declined this offer. Eventually, he agreed to write the book if he could "write a positive case" for what he believed, rather than attacking what he opposed. The book was published as *For Calvinism*.[23] Within it, Horton speaks about the danger of turning theology into a battlefield, sharing that when he first discovered the Reformed tradition in high school, he

22. For an accessible-yet-substantial overview of covenant theology, see H. Perkins, *Reformed Covenant Theology*. John Fesko has several monographs providing historical insight on covenant theology, and a four-volume series of books by Michael Horton, beginning with *Covenant and Eschatology*, displays the considerable constructive and ecumenical promise of Reformed covenant theology.

23. Hayes, "Interview with Michael Horton."

became "imprisoned" by "pride" by entering into acrimonious debates with brothers and sisters in Christ.[24] In the opening chapter, Horton removes the scaffolding for a "Calvinist against Arminian" theological boxing match on the five points. He declares that "the nickname 'Calvinism' is unfortunate," a misleading term applied to Reformed theology.[25] While he addresses the five points, as the publisher asked, they are just a few among many points of Reformed doctrine, which sees itself as broadly catholic,[26] evangelical,[27] and Reformed. The five points are valuable as expressions of components within a Reformed doctrine of grace, but they were never intended to stand on their own or to provide a summary of Reformed doctrine.[28]

As Richard Muller explains, the five points were always intended to be understood within the broader context of the church's confession. The idea of a "five-point Calvinist" or a "five-point Reformed Christian" overlooks the fact that Reformed theology encompasses far more than these doctrines. These points "are not an arbitrary list of more or less biblical ideas—they are carefully embodied patterns of teaching, drawn from Scripture and brought to bear on the life of the church." Without "less-famous points of Reformed theology" such as infant baptism, justification by faith, the sacraments as means of grace, and a Reformed understanding of union with Christ and sanctification, "the remaining famous five [points] make very little sense."[29]

To be clear, the five points in the Canons of Dort, later incorporated into confessions like the Westminster Standards, offer valuable Reformed teaching on a cluster of theological topics; they provide not only doctrinal exposition but also significant pastoral insight on issues like the relationship between salvation and works, evangelism, and the Christian life. However, asking these five points to represent the entirety of Reformed theology exceeds their purpose and capacity.

In sum, there can be some value to shorthand ways of seeking to name or categorize aspects of Reformed theology, but it is a fraught endeavor that inevitably underdelivers when we ask a fast-thinking tool to introduce us to

24. Horton, *For Calvinism*, 303.

25. Horton, *For Calvinism*, 19–21; see also 23–25, 28–31.

26. Horton notes that Reformed theology embraces the "one holy, catholic, and apostolic church" through time, in contrast to Protestants who call themselves "restorationists." "That is, [Reformed theologians] do not believe that the Reformation was a break from Catholic Christianity, or that the church had ceased to exist until the Reformers came along." Horton, *For Calvinism*, 27.

27. Horton helpfully clarifies that "to be Reformed is to be *evangelical*, not in the sense of a party label or social movement, but as those who believe, confess, and spread the good news of God's saving work in Jesus Christ." Horton, *For Calvinism*, 27.

28. Horton, *For Calvinism*, 15–16, 19–21.

29. Muller, "How Many Points?," 427–28.

the overall Reformed theological tradition. Let us move now to slow thinking to put into words some key elements of a Reformed approach to theology.

Slow Thinking on the Basics: Faith Seeking Understanding in a Reformed Key

Christian theology in a Reformed key is a worshipful pursuit of knowledge of God and all things in relation to God. God is the object of our pursuit. With Psalm 27, the theologian longs to "behold the beauty of the LORD" and prays, "your face, LORD, do I seek" (vv. 4, 8). This is an aspect of discipleship in Christ, a pathway of longing and delight in God that reflects the foundational shape of our calling within God's household. In response to the question, "Which commandment is the first of all?" Jesus replies, "'Hear, O Israel: the Lord our God, the Lord is one; you shall love the Lord your God with all your heart, and with all your soul, and with all your mind, and with all your strength.' The second is this, 'You shall love your neighbor as yourself.' There is no other commandment greater than these" (Mark 12:28b–31).

This pursuit is unlike any other. We pursue knowledge of God as an aspect of offering our whole selves in love to God and others, of seeking to behold the Lord who has claimed us as his own, in Christ. Along the way, we discover the joy of meditating on God's mighty acts, for "great are the works of the LORD, studied by all who delight in them" (Ps. 111:2).

What does it mean to meditate on God's mighty works? We can get a glimpse by drawing on Calvin, who writes that God's creation is a good gift, a "theater" of God's glory; thus, "there is no spot in the universe wherein you cannot discern at least some sparks of his glory."[30] For, as the psalmist testifies, "The heavens are telling the glory of God; and the firmament proclaims his handiwork" (Ps. 19:1). The theologian ought to be attentive to the order and wonder of the creation as "a mirror in which we can contemplate God, who is otherwise invisible."[31] This knowledge through careful attention to God's handiwork of creation is valuable for many purposes and vocations in creaturely life: for science and medicine, for music and the arts, for cultivating the fruit of the land in farming, for building shared communal life in families and neighborhoods, for stewarding the shared resources and challenges in political life.

But when it comes to our knowledge of God, even though humans are aware of a "seed of religion" giving us a fragmentary knowledge of God, this

---

30. Calvin, *Institutes* 1.5.1.
31. Calvin, *Institutes* 1.5.1.

seed is insufficient.[32] In the words of the apostle Paul, "For though they knew God, they did not honor him as God or give thanks to him, but they became futile in their thinking, and their senseless minds were darkened" (Rom. 1:21). Because of our human feebleness and our inclination to follow false gods, creation is insufficient as a guide for distinguishing the God of Jesus Christ from "the throng of false gods."[33] Thus, we need the "spectacles" (eyeglasses) of Scripture to see the things of God more clearly and distinctly. For "no one can get even the slightest taste of right and sound doctrine [Christian teaching] unless he becomes a pupil of scripture."[34] In all of this, the process of pursuing God is not one of mere obligation to obey Christ's commandments. It is a process of joining in God's delight in the wonder of creation and rejoicing in the light of God's Word in Scripture, so that we can pray with the psalmist, "How sweet are your words to my taste, sweeter than honey to my mouth!" (Ps. 119:103).

Unlike many other human journeys toward understanding, the knowledge of God is not a knowledge of control. We will never master the subject matter of theology—the mysteries of God, Christ, the Holy Spirit, and so on. God is not an object in the world to be examined. God is the alpha and the omega, the source and end of all creation, the one in whom "we live and move and have our being" (Acts 17:28). Theological knowledge is infused with mystery; positive knowledge is intertwined with the declaration that God is incomprehensible to creatures. As finite creatures in our brief, earthly pilgrimage, we cannot know God in fullness. Even as the Lord declares his love, he discloses a deep asymmetry between his own knowledge and ways and those of his creaturely covenant partners:

> For my thoughts are not your thoughts,
>   nor are your ways my ways, says the LORD.
> For as the heavens are higher than the earth,
>   so are my ways higher than your ways
>   and my thoughts than your thoughts. (Isa. 55:8–9)

Mindful of the exalted glory of the Lord and our own meager capacities, Reformed theology seeks knowledge of God, and the world in relation to God, but with reverence and modesty. Christians are not ones who have "arrived" at all the answers about God and our world. We do not own the truth. We do not perfectly embody the right way. Indeed, as this book will

32. Calvin, *Institutes* 1.3–4.
33. Calvin, *Institutes* 1.6.2.
34. Calvin, *Institutes* 1.6.1.

explore at various points, the Reformed tradition is far from innocent in its history. All too often it has claimed to possess the truth and the way, all the while wandering from the great Shepherd. Yet in its theological confession, the Reformed tradition calls sinners to turn from this death-directed path, recognizing that the heart of the Christian claim to uniqueness in a world with many paths is not that we have everything figured out. Rather, we claim to be owned by the One who *is* "the way, and the truth, and the life" (John 14:6), the great *I Am*, Jesus Christ. Like John the Baptizer, we do not point to ourselves; rather, we testify, "Here is the Lamb of God who takes away the sin of the world!" (John 1:29). We have not mastered the things of God. We are disciples, pilgrims on a journey. Thus, in Bavinck's words, "Mystery is the lifeblood of Christian theology."[35]

Reformed theology teaches that we cannot know God fully (i.e., in the same way that God knows himself). And yet, we are not abandoned, not left in the dark. In his astonishing love, God comes to us—God condescends, and he accommodates to our limited capacity. To use an analogy from Calvin, through Scripture God "lisps" (or, literally, "babbles") to us "as nurses commonly do with infants." Calvin highly values Scripture as God's Word to us. But its expressions "do not so much express clearly what God is like as accommodate the knowledge of him to our slight capacity."[36] The Lord of the universe stoops over, condescends, and speaks baby talk to us in Scripture. His Word is fully sufficient for its purpose—to speak, through the Spirit, to small, finite creatures like us, bringing us into covenantal fellowship with him and with one another. This is deeply relational knowledge, not just data.

Likewise, theology in a Reformed key is not the mere systematizing of data or organization of information. It is knowledge inseparable from worshipful fellowship with God and his household. Knowledge of God cannot be reduced to true information that can be digitally encoded on the internet or processed through an AI text generator. As the apostle James writes, "You believe that God is one; you do well. Even the demons believe—and shudder" (James 2:19). Believing truths about God is good. But the point of God's condescension to us is to restore fellowship with us in covenantal faithfulness, as children adopted into his household in Christ by the Spirit, and flowing from that, to restore communion with others, bearing witness to his love to all creation.

---

35. Bavinck, *Reformed Dogmatics: Abridged*, 147.
36. Calvin, *Institutes* 1.13.1.

Slow Thinking in the Center and the End: The Triune God's Glory and Creation's Restoration

Reformed theology is theocentric, focused first and foremost on God. This is a deeply countercultural emphasis. Sociological studies in the United States have shown how the "self" is central for many, with the vast majority of Americans claiming that "enjoying yourself is the highest goal of life."[37] Sadly, this is true also among many Christians, who tend to see God as a butler who serves our own interests—namely, to pursue "the central goal of life [which] is to be happy and to feel good about oneself."[38]

In contrast, Reformed theology finds its central delight in the beauty, majesty, and glory of God as displayed to us in Jesus Christ. For many, this is a refreshing emphasis, leading to prayer and worship and lives of gratitude and thankfulness. In contrast to the endless quest to "discover oneself," the Reformed confessions clearly testify to God as the source of our hope and life. This theocentric focus is displayed elegantly and simply in the opening of the Westminster Shorter Catechism, which declares that the human purpose is "to glorify God, and enjoy him forever."[39] Human beings were not created for the purpose of being happy in themselves. God created humans to delight and enjoy, to find their purpose in bringing glory to God, living in testimony to his beauty, honor, and love.

This theocentric emphasis certainly invites us to transcend an obsession with ourselves, but it is also deeply existential and even personal in its implications. The opening section of the Heidelberg Catechism displays how this theocentric focus has deeply experiential implications in how we view ourselves:

Q. What is your only comfort in life and in death?
A. That I am not my own, but belong—body and soul,
in life and in death—to my faithful Savior, Jesus Christ.[40]

Echoing the apostle Paul in 1 Corinthians 6:6–20, the catechism begins with the basic reality that we do not belong even to ourselves. In each day of life and as we face death, our hope is not in our success or accomplishments; it is not even based on the goodness of our acts of love toward God and others.

37. Eighty-four percent of Americans believe that "enjoying yourself is the highest goal of life," while 66 percent of church-going Americans share this view. Kinnaman and Lyons, *Good Faith*, 58.
38. See Smith and Denton, *Soul Searching*, 162–63.
39. Westminster Shorter Catechism, Q and A 1 (Dennison, *Reformed Confessions*, 4:353).
40. Heidelberg Catechism, Q and A 1 (*Our Faith*, 69).

Our only true and final hope and consolation is extrinsic, coming from outside of ourselves. It is the new identity we receive through the Spirit: We belong— "body and soul, in life and in death"—to Jesus Christ, our faithful Savior.

As the Heidelberg Catechism continues in its answer to this first question, the trinitarian framing for Christian identity is accented. One's comfort in life and in death is found in belonging to Christ, who has delivered believers from the penalty of sin and the "tyranny" of the devil. Because we belong to Christ, the Father of Jesus is now our Father, active in providential care. And as we are in union with Christ, the Spirit "assures [us] of eternal life," generating signs of the new creation now and making us "wholeheartedly willing and ready from now on to live for him."[41]

Thus, although Reformed theology is theocentric, accenting God's sovereign transcendence, it is deeply Christ-centered and profoundly personal in its implications, with the Spirit mediating both forgiveness and new life through Christ. Crucially, this new life also reflects a high theology of creation because salvation itself is approached not as a deliverance from the created world but as a restoration of creation's goodness through the work of the triune God. Stated differently, God's grace does not destroy creation's nature; it restores it. The enemy that is conquered in Christ is not creation or human culture; it is sin.

In its focus, Reformed theology is theocentric and Christocentric, yet it is also deeply personal in its doctrine of the Spirit and the Christian life. Bavinck frames the restoration of God's good creation through grace as foundational to his theological approach and to discerning the Spirit's ongoing work: "The reality [is] that the creation of the Father, ruined by sin, is restored in the death of the Son of God and re-created by the grace of the Holy Spirit into a kingdom of God."[42] The problem is not with creation, but its corruption. Christians of all occupations and vocations are called to bear witness to Christ's kingdom, his reign, which has implications for all spheres and areas of life. Thus, in the words of Bavinck, Reformed theology "shows us how God, who is all-sufficient in himself, nevertheless glorifies himself in his creation, which, even when it is torn apart by sin, is gathered up again in Christ."[43] By the Spirit, those who have been adopted into the household of the Father are called and enlivened to gather up that which sin has torn, and continues to tear, apart.

Theology in a Reformed key is not only theocentric, trinitarian, Christocentric, and personal; it is also a *Spirit-enabled pilgrimage in Christ*. We

41. Heidelberg Catechism, Q and A 1 (*Our Faith*, 70).

42. Bavinck, *Reformed Dogmatics*, 1:112.

43. Bavinck, *Reformed Dogmatics*, 1:112.

rejoice that the Spirit enables us to receive and abide in the Word, bringing us into the household of God not simply as servants but as adopted sons and daughters. For "when we cry, 'Abba! Father!' it is that very Spirit bearing witness with our spirit that we are children of God" (Rom. 8:15b–16). The joy of this adoption and the new household that we have been adopted into (the church) are gifts we do not achieve. We were graciously incorporated into this people and this inheritance by the Spirit. It is a present reality, but it is also bent forward, in trust, in ache, and in hope. We "groan inwardly while we wait for adoption, the redemption of our bodies. For in hope we were saved. Now hope that is seen is not hope. For who hopes for what is seen? But if we hope for what we do not see, we wait for it with patience" (Rom. 8:23–25).

We have been adopted, yet we groan as we await adoption. We are on a journey. Through the Spirit, we have been incorporated into Christ, the Word of the Father. Yet, we look forward to the hope we have not yet seen, when Christ, who is our life, comes again in his second advent. "When Christ who is your life is revealed, then you also will be revealed with him in glory" (Col. 3:4). We know that there is much we don't understand; there is much that we cannot see now, "For now we see in a mirror, dimly, but then we will see face to face. Now I know only in part; then I will know fully, even as I have been fully known" (1 Cor. 13:12). But we are not looking for an end beyond encountering God's glory face-to-face with Jesus Christ. "For it is the God who said, 'Let light shine out of darkness,' who has shone in our hearts to give the light of the knowledge of the glory of God in the face of Jesus Christ" (2 Cor. 4:6).

How do we think theologically about the fact that our own knowledge is incomplete, in process, on a journey? Reformed theologian Franciscus Junius (1545–1602) can help us here. He developed a theocentric, Christ-centered, Spirit-enabled way to speak about the reality that we have genuine knowledge of God on this journey, even as it is indirect and partial. He makes two levels of distinctions to help clarify our situation. First, he distinguishes between *archetypal knowledge* of God (God's knowledge of himself) and *ectypal knowledge* (a mediated, accommodated, human knowledge of God).[44] God truly makes himself known to us through Scripture, but he does not thereby convey archetypal knowledge of himself. Instead, through Scripture, God graciously gives us ectypal knowledge—knowledge born of a relational way of knowing God that is appropriate for small, mortal creatures like us.

Within this indirect, accommodated knowledge of God, Junius introduces three further distinctions to help give us proper perspective about our current pilgrim knowledge of God in Christ. The highest creaturely form of the

---

44. See Junius, *Treatise on True Theology*, 105–6.

knowledge of God is present within a mystery at the center of the universe—
the Word made flesh, the union of God and humanity in Jesus Christ, the covenant Lord and Servant in one person. This is a *theology of union*, for "it exists
in Christ according to his humanity."[45] As John 1:18 testifies, "No one has
ever seen God. It is God the only Son, who is close to the Father's heart, who
has made him known." Thus, according to Junius, all creaturely knowledge
of God stems from this theology of union, for Christ, as the "prototype and
essential wisdom of God," is the source of every other level of knowing God.[46]

The second-highest knowledge of God is a *theology of vision*.[47] It is a
knowledge of God afforded to the redeemed at the *beatific vision*, the final
face-to-face vision of our Lord when Christ "will come again in glory to
judge the living and the dead, and his kingdom will have no end."[48] We look
forward in hope to this vision because we don't yet see face-to-face. But on
that day, we will "acquire in the heavens the glorious vision of God and by
which we ourselves will, in the same ways, see God."[49]

Finally, we come to the most modest form of theology, the *theology of
pilgrims*. It is a humble type of theology, for this theological vision is "indis-
criminate, vague, and incomplete"; it is imperfect compared to a theology of
vision. Even our best theological reflection now falls short, for it is "mixed
with our weakness and imperfection."[50] But Junius insists that it has dig-
nity as well. Through divine revelation, our pilgrim theology is sufficient for
its purpose on our sojourn. Moreover, along with vision theology, pilgrim
theology is a gift established in Christ himself: "Christ sanctified both these
types of theology in His own person, since He both experienced the humble
theology in the humiliation of the flesh, and now enjoys the exalted type in
that very exaltation by which He now has been exalted above every name,
evidently so that He might show that the common principle of each theology
resides in Himself."[51]

In this way, a Reformed vision of our theological journey and end is both
modest and audacious. In modesty, we can openly admit that our knowledge
of God is incomplete and indirect, for "we see in a mirror, dimly" (1 Cor.
13:12), giving testimony to our hope as we cry out, "Come, Lord Jesus!" (Rev.
22:20). Audaciously, we can do theology as children of God in Christ who have

---

45. Junius, *Treatise on True Theology*, 119–20.
46. Junius, *Treatise on True Theology*, 129.
47. Junius, *Treatise on True Theology*, 119.
48. Nicene Creed (*Our Faith*, 14).
49. Junius, *Treatise on True Theology*, 120.
50. Junius, *Treatise on True Theology*, 136.
51. Junius, *Treatise on True Theology*, 129–30.

been graciously adopted into God's covenant household and inheritance. As ones united to Christ and his body, we are gifted a genuine, relational knowledge of God, as the Spirit cries "Abba! Father!" in our hearts. We belong to God, in life and in death. We are not masters of "the way, the truth, and the life." Rather, we belong to the one who is himself "the way, the truth, and the life." And by the Spirit, we seek to grow into maturity in him.

2

The Church in a Reformed Key: Ethnocentric Compliance or Multivalent Catholicity?

Key Question: Is the Reformed Tradition Just for White Westerners?

A stumbling block for many considering the Reformed tradition is that it can appear to be a largely white, Eurocentric tradition—one in which Eurocentric values provide the furniture and set the table for the conversation. Is the Reformed tradition defined by the values and culture of "old white men" who want others to join, as long as others inhabit their clique with compliance and conformity?

Both sociological studies and personal narratives in the United States, particularly in majority-white contexts, show that Christians from ethnic minorities often experience a dissonance in Christian spaces where the value of cultural diversity is lauded but, in practice, minorities are treated as outsiders. One significant study concluded that in spite of many white evangelicals being "well-intentioned," their "values and their institutions actually recreate racial divisions and inequalities they ostensibly oppose."[1] Both the history

---

1. Emerson and Smith, *Divided by Faith*, 1.

of exclusion and the ongoing reality of church membership based on market principles mean that Christian leaders are shaped to orient their ministries to the self-interests of racially homogeneous in-groups, even if they would desire to move a different direction.[2] Kathleen Garces-Foley notes a common theme: "Those in the minority group face the problem of being treated like perpetual visitors." Rather than feeling like church members, they can feel they are treated like guests, outsiders in their own congregations.[3] For an ethnic minority in a predominantly white context, the phrase *the Reformed tradition* might seem risky, if not outright daunting.

On the one hand, traditions can suggest conformity, uniformity, or compliance. Traditions can be exclusive and ethnocentric. For Christians, traditions can function as excuses for not stepping out in faith in new ways. On the other hand, many today, particularly in the younger generations, long to be part of something bigger and more transcendent than the endless trendy programs found among some churches. "Seeker-sensitive," "attractional," "emergent," "new monasticism"—the list of trendy programs goes on and on. But these Christians long to inhabit a rich history of ideas and practice; they long to be rooted in a Christian tradition.

Both sides of this tension are very real. In our daily lives as Christians, we face the reality that the historic church, and its institutional structures, have not only generated beauty and goodness but have also caused real harm. Rather than loving God and neighbor, at times Christians have enslaved fellow image-bearers, seeking to justify that horror by the witness of Scripture. At times, Christians have offered their lives to the gods of nation or race or wealth or power. And, like the rest of the history of Christianity, the history of Reformed Christianity has a profoundly mixed record. Sometimes Reformed theology has been used as a catalyst to rise up in protest and compassion in response to idolatry, abuse, and injustice. At other times, rather than acting as ambassadors of the one true king and Lord, Jesus Christ, Reformed Christians have distorted elements within Scripture and the Reformed tradition to serve the "rulers" and "authorities" in "this present darkness" (Eph. 6:12).

This chapter responds to the concern that the Reformed tradition may be an ethnocentric tradition, one requiring compliance and conformity in its view of the church and the power dynamics within its structure. At times, unfortunately, this concern arises justifiably from our experience. Though the Heidelberg Catechism confesses, "I am not my own, but belong—body and

2. See Emerson and Smith, *Divided by Faith*, 1–2, 160–68.
3. Garces-Foley, *Crossing the Ethnic Divide*, 124.

soul, in life and in death—to my faithful Savior, Jesus Christ,"[4] Reformed Christians sometimes insist in practice, "I *am* my own; I belong to my own people, my social group."

Yet, the Reformed tradition also has real assets to discern the work of God within the church, to celebrate gospel work wherever it occurs, and to seek unity and catholicity within the church in a way that is confessionally multiform yet pursues maturity in Christ. Historically, this has resulted in a tradition that celebrates the act of listening to other believers across the bounds of time and culture to discern the Word of God in Scripture. It has resulted in a tradition that has a wide, global presence and exists predominantly in the Global South today. It has resulted in a tradition that is attentive to how the Word of God intersects with both the gifts and the idols of a cultural moment, calling the church to celebrate the diverse, created goodness of different cultural expressions, but also to stand against attempts to serve a lord other than the one Lord Jesus Christ.

Reformed theology provides a theological architecture for being realistic about the fact that the church is always broken and sinful and yet, as a creature of the Word, the church finds her life and identity in entering into the Spirit's work of dying and rising with Christ. Even when church leaders and hierarchies betray their Lord and their flocks, the Reformed tradition frames a way to call the church back to Christ, the unique Lord. Jesus Christ is the way, the truth, and the life. His people do not own the way, the truth, and the life; they are owned by *him*. The Reformed tradition inhabits a vision of the church's multiform unity in Christ that compels the church to hear God's Word anew by the Spirit in a variety of cultural contexts, while being firmly located within the historic Christian church.

Catholicity: Reformed Retrieval of an Ancient Theology and Practice

As noted in the introduction and first chapter of this book, the Reformed theological tradition sees itself as *catholic*. Early Reformed leaders and confessions did not attempt to start a new church but to inhabit the household of God through the centuries, united by the Spirit in Christ. The church is *catholic*, sharing one faith and one baptism. This oneness is a gift of God, not a product of human effort. Yet catholicity is also an *ongoing calling* of the church and requires a posture of learning from those in the household of God of diverse cultures and ages as the adopted people of God grow up into Christ, the Head. Testifying to this catholicity is an article of faith from the

---

4. Heidelberg Catechism, A 1 (*Our Faith*, 69).

Apostles' Creed (to believe in "the holy catholic church"), reflecting baptismal creeds from the earliest centuries of the Christian church. Inhabiting the church as catholic is the opposite of inhabiting the church as an ethnocentric sect or faction.

The word *catholic* originates from the Greek words *kath* and *holou*, which together mean "on the whole," in contrast to something narrow or restricted. Although the word doesn't appear in Scripture, by the second century, Ignatius of Antioch referred to the "catholic church," understood as the whole church of Jesus Christ, transcending regional and linguistic boundaries. This designation specified a community that baptized members in the name of the Father, Son, and Holy Spirit, in obedience to Christ's commission (Matt. 28:19–20).

The teaching of the catechism and early creeds was part of a holistic ancient Christian strategy to help Christians, especially ones from pagan backgrounds, to grow in their understandings of Scripture and the church's teaching and to be incorporated into a new network of relationships in the church. As one historian notes, "The catechumenate functioned much like a total immersion program in language study."[5] Catechumens were immersed in a new language of relationships (including mentoring and the examination of life) and in the new language of the Bible and Christian teaching.

Why was this deep, formational immersion necessary? Because in developing the catechumenate, the church catholic was rejecting both the ideal of accommodation to the dominant culture and the ideal of isolation from the surrounding culture.[6] The catechumenate was relationally intense, deeply connected to community, worship, and Christian practice. Its content was deeply biblical: overview of the biblical story, studies of the Ten Commandments and the Lord's Prayer, and teachings on baptism and the Lord's Supper.

On this path, this catholic church was not only claiming to be the true (nonheretical) church; it was also pursuing a calling. To confess the church as catholic was not a shrug that indicated "Everyone baptized must be fine," or "All who say they believe are good." It was a confession of a gift: the Spirit's work in creating one, new humanity. It was also a calling to patiently yet fervently grow into maturity in Christ through the Scriptures, through baptism and the Lord's Supper, through obedience (the Ten Commandments), and through fellowship with God (the Lord's Prayer).

The Reformed and Lutheran branches of the Protestant Reformation retained a commitment to the catholicity of the church. In 1530, not even a

5. Sittser, *Resilient Faith*, 157.
6. In the words of Sittser, "Rejecting both accommodation and isolation, early Christians immersed themselves in the culture as followers of Jesus and servants of the kingdom of God." Sittser, *Resilient Faith*, 17; see also 175–76.

decade after Martin Luther's excommunication in 1521, Philipp Melanchthon (in the Augsburg Confession) and Huldrych Zwingli (in *Fidei Ratio*) both fully embraced Nicene trinitarian proclamation and the Chalcedonian christological formulation. In the Second Helvetic Confession of 1566, Heinrich Bullinger states it directly: "We retain the Christian, sound, and catholic faith, whole and inviolable."[7] Since there is "one mediator" between God and human beings, "one shepherd of the whole flock, one head of this body," there is "one church: which we, therefore, call catholic because it is universal," spread "abroad" through the world, and it "reaches unto all times."[8] In the words of John Calvin, "The church is called 'catholic,' or 'universal,' because there could not be two or three churches unless Christ be torn asunder—which cannot happen!"[9]

By claiming to be an extension of catholic theology in core confessions, the Reformed tradition was intentionally linking its heritage to a set of theological creeds, exegetical practices, and catechetical traditions that played key roles in the church's life in ancient Christianity.

Is It Eurocentric to Retrieve Ancient Catholicity?

At this point, some readers may object: Does it really matter if the Reformed and Lutheran traditions sought to ground themselves in this ancient catholic theology and practice? Doesn't early Christianity itself arise from and reflect Eurocentric cultures? Christianity has rapidly grown as a global, multiethnic, and multinational faith as a result of modern missionary outreach since the nineteenth century. Doesn't this make a Reformed and Lutheran retrieval of ancient Christian theology simply a doubling-down on Western, Eurocentric heritage?

This question can arise from a genuine concern about multiethnic inclusion. For example, in the early twentieth century, the Black Muslim movement in the United States emerged in response to the horrors of slavery, lynching, and the ongoing reality of oppression by white Christians. Christianity was framed as a "white man's religion," and Islam as a more empowering alternative. In recent decades, the ongoing experience of racial injustice in the United States has given many the impression that the Christian faith is fundamentally a European and white reality to be opposed for the sake of liberation. While the concern is well-intended, it contains two misunderstandings: It gives white

---

7. Second Helvetic Confession, 11 (Dennison, *Reformed Confessions*, 2:831).
8. Second Helvetic Confession, 17 (Dennison, *Reformed Confessions*, 2:845).
9. Calvin, *Institutes* 4.1.2.

and European strands of Christianity too much credit, and it fails to recognize the enormous contributions of African, Middle Eastern, and Asian Christians to the development of Christianity.

The earliest centuries of the Christian faith were not monocultural, as if they took place in a time before encounters with cultural and linguistic differences. To the contrary, ancient Christianity was fundamentally multinational, multilinguistic, and multiethnic. The Christian faith was not predominantly European. Alexandria (in northern Africa) and Antioch (in Asia Minor) were important centers for early Christian communities, in addition to Rome. By the fourth century, there was an active Christian community in ancient Ethiopia. Beginning in the second century, Syriac-speaking Christian missionaries planted churches along the Mediterranean, then followed the Silk Road trade route to plant churches in central Asia and modern India, making their way to China by the early seventh century.[10] Even as we consider the spread of Christianity in regions we now call Europe, it would be a mistake to call this European in a modern sense. Indeed, some scholars argue that speaking about Europe in a unified way before the seventeenth century is usually a dangerous anachronism.[11]

Of course, early Christians had cultural biases, blind spots, and other shortcomings. Like Christians today, they were an imperfect people, wrestling with sin and tempted to bend their knees to lords other than Christ. But it was also the site of the Spirit's activity—the one Spirit who brought diverse peoples into one faith and one baptism, adopted by "one God and Father of all" (Eph. 4:4–6).

Is Reformed Catholicity a Biblical Identity and Calling?

So far, we have noted how ancient Christianity and early Reformed and Lutheran Protestants saw themselves as catholic and that this catholic heritage

10. Syriac churches were "strongly evangelistic and carried the gospel beyond the Mediterranean world in an expansion unparalleled in either antiquity or the Middle Ages. This effort is all the more remarkable as these churches were not supported by a state that could sponsor or sustain their mission. Syriac missionaries did not arrive as part of an army or invading power, but rather in merchant caravans and among refugees." Chatonnet and Debie, *Syriac World*, 113. For more on the missionary efforts of Syriac churches into Asia, see Chatonnet and Debie, *Syriac World*, chap. 5.

11. In light of the work of Edward Said in *Orientalism*, many scholars see the notion of a unified European identity as a development of the seventeenth and eighteenth centuries, coinciding with the Enlightenment and the rise of colonialism. The colonial ethos postulated a unified "European heritage" among divergent and competing European nations, framing non-European societies as exotic and backward in contrast to the "progress" of European societies.

was culturally, geographically, and nationally diverse. This is important for countering a misleading narrative that seeks to credit Europe, or "the West," with the formation of core Christian doctrines and practices. But is this vision of the church as catholic also *biblical*?

This was a significant Reformation-era question for Protestants, who approached Scripture as the final authority in doctrine and practice, and it is equally significant today. Early Reformed and Lutheran theologians looked to a variety of texts in the Old and New Testaments to answer this question, but a brief exposition from the book of Ephesians can illustrate some of the most salient features of their claim.

Ephesians describes the church as those chosen, adopted, and graced in Christ, forming "one new humanity" (Eph. 2:15) with "one Lord, one faith, one baptism, one God and Father of all" (Eph. 4:5–6). This oneness is a gift from God, and it's also a calling; it's something we continually strive for. In Ephesians, the calling to live into God's gift of oneness has a purpose: for believers to be equipped for service "until all of us come to the unity of the faith and of the knowledge of the Son of God, to maturity, to the measure of the full stature [*plērōma*] of Christ" (Eph. 4:13). *Plērōma* is a rich word. It portrays a multifaceted wholeness. Paul connects it to the process of "grow[ing] up in every way into him who is the head, into Christ" (Eph. 4:15). This *plērōma* is ultimately possessed by Christ alone (Eph. 1:23), yet believers are called to live into this fullness and wholeness by the Spirit.

Thus, on our Christian pilgrimage, maturity and *plērōma* in Christ is an ongoing goal and destination. As Reformed theologian Michael Allen observes, Ephesians 4 suggests that growing into the *plērōma* of Christ is a permanent calling for the church. At least until Christ's return, no church can say, "I have arrived at full maturity; I fully display the *plērōma* of Christ." For just as God is "unbounded and unending," growth into the fullness of maturity in Christ, by the Spirit, is unending as well.[12]

From the opening generations of the Protestant Reformation, the Reformed understanding of catholicity, rooted in Scripture and the early creeds, affirms the church's universal and unified nature. In biblical terms, catholicity is both a gift and a calling. The gift includes the oneness and unity that the people of God could not generate on their own, apart from the Spirit. The calling is to share in the Spirit's work of continual growth into the fullness of maturity in Christ. This growth and its purpose toward full maturity are about growth in Christ, not cultural uniformity or ethnocentric intimidation. The calling toward multifaceted fullness is a calling to share in Christ himself, the risen

---

12. Allen, *Ephesians*, 102.

and exalted Lord, for he is "far above all rule and authority and power and dominion" (Eph. 1:21), and his *plērōma* as Head of the church "fills all in all" (Eph. 1:23).

Fruit from Desolate, Divided Ground: The Church as Creature of the Word

The scriptural witness to the identity and calling of the church can sound lofty, even idealistic. It may seem plausible in some moments and places that the church is a diverse people united in Christ, in a reconciled communion. But when the church is divided, antagonistic, alienated—championing one group's history and culture against another—it can seem like a delusion.

By the late twelfth century, four major groups claimed to be the true church: the Roman Catholic, Eastern Orthodox, Assyrian Church of the East, and Oriental Orthodox.[13] Divisions stemmed from the Council of Chalcedon (451) and then the Great Schism (1054). While theological rifts formally led these churches to separate, the theological disagreements were deeply intertwined with the linguistic, cultural, and ethnic differences that deepened through the course of history.

Thus, when Protestant calls for reform took place in the Roman Catholic Church, the world's Christians were already quite divided: Each claimed to be the one, catholic, universal church of Jesus Christ, to the exclusion of the others. These exclusions largely corresponded to the different geographical locations that centered each communion. The Assyrian Church was in parts of North Africa and the Middle East, but it had also spread Christianity to China by the ninth century. The Oriental Orthodox had a vibrant presence in the regions known today as Egypt and northern Ethiopia. The Eastern Orthodox were in various other regions of the Middle East and Greece, along with Eastern Europe and parts of modern Russia. The Roman Catholic Church had its center of power in Rome but extended to other regions of Europe and England, as well as to regions within the Americas (South, Central, and North) and some regions of Asia and Africa. Christianity was still a global religion, but each of these four communions understood itself alone as the true church. This often led to pronouncements that members of the other churches were heretics and schismatics, without salvation in Christ. Indeed,

---

13. See Ortlund, *What It Means to Be Protestant*, 21. For a detailed discussion of "institutional exclusivism," which Ortlund defines as the view that "the real church of Christ is restricted to one visible, institutional church with its own unique hierarchical structure," see *What It Means to Be Protestant*, chap. 2.

even into the twentieth century the starting point for official Roman Catholic and Eastern Orthodox theological approaches was to begin with the declaration that theirs was the only one, true, visible church of Jesus Christ. As Pope Pius XI wrote in his 1928 encyclical, "The union of Christians can only be promoted by promoting the return to the one true Church of Christ of those who are separated from it," which requires that one "accept, recognize and obey the authority and supremacy of Peter and his legitimate successors."[14] Particularly within Roman Catholicism, the reforms of Vatican II have significantly softened the posture toward non-Catholic Christians, with openness to recognizing "separated brethren" in Christ who are Christians outside of the visible membership of the Roman Catholic Church.[15]

Yet the overall point here is worth lingering on, in light of this chapter's focus: After the Great Schism in the eleventh century, this ecclesiological exclusivism—identifying the one true church with just one of the groups claiming that title—inevitably narrowed the church into different cultural, linguistic, and regional enclaves. In relation to one another, different cultural expressions of the Christian faith were often evaluated on either/or terms: "Either you belong to the true church, or you are heretics. Either you belong to God's people, or you are headed for damnation." Although the Christian faith was still multinational and multiethnic, the geographically and culturally distant Christian was often approached with suspicion rather than as part of the multifaceted fullness of the catholicity of the church.

Although the original goal of early Protestant Reformers, such as Luther in Germany and Zwingli in Switzerland, was to bring reform within the Roman Catholic Church, the path they traveled led to a different way of *discerning* the church, one that refused to identify "the true church" with the hierarchy and culture of just one dominant group. This openness to cultural and ethnic differences came from a theological understanding that the church is a creature of God's Word. The Word and action of the triune God define the church, enabling a more flexible and self-effacing criteria for where the "true church" might be found.

While it might seem a bright, forward-thinking idea, like a mission statement we might write for a church today, for Luther and Zwingli, as Roman Catholic priests, this way of discerning the church was born of a sense of desolation. In Luther's region of Germany, the pope put a man named John

14. See Pope Pius XI, "Mortalium Animos." With the phrase "supremacy of Peter and his legitimate successors," the encyclical is speaking of the *office* of the pope. It is important for Protestants to note that in the Roman Catholic view of papal authority, encyclicals like this one are not considered infallible but are part of the ordinary teaching office of the church.

15. See Pope Paul VI, "Unitatis Redintegratio."

Tetzel in charge of selling indulgences.[16] Tetzel was corrupt, convincing people to buy indulgences to build St. Peter's Cathedral in Rome on the grounds that the purchase would make sinners "cleaner than Adam before the Fall." Like a sales representative, he assured those wanting to buy indulgences for a deceased loved one suffering in purgatory, "As soon as the coin in the coffer rings, the soul from purgatory springs."[17]

As priests, Luther and Zwingli became increasingly troubled by abuses such as these, so they preached and wrote to advocate for a return to the primacy of Scripture and against growing papal power, including abuses related to indulgences, purgatory, and clergy corruption. Yet, calls for reform from Catholic priests could easily lead to a death sentence. This had been the case in earlier reform efforts, but the execution of Jan Hus and the crusades against the Hussites were especially poignant reminders for these Reformers.[18]

Thus, Luther's friends were wise to fear for his life when he refused to recant his teachings and submit to the pope's authority in 1520. Pope Leo X indicated that such a refusal would mean excommunication, including exclusion from salvation in Christ, as a "wild boar [who] has invaded" the Lord's "vineyard." His supporters were prohibited from reading or publishing his work, and his published writings were ordered to be burned.[19] Still, Luther refused to recant.

And yet, just three years after being excommunicated as a heretic by the pope and being declared an outlaw by the state, Luther wrote movingly about the one hope of the church. It was not hope in the church community, its inherent goodness, or its collective possibilities. It was not in its visible spectacle or displays of power. The church's hope was in its identity as a "creature of the Word" of God: "For since the Church owes its birth to the Word, is nourished,

16. Indulgences were "the remission of the time to be spent in purgatory in purification and punishment for sins." González, *Story of Christianity*, 1:418.

17. González, *Story of Christianity*, 2:27. The Council of Trent rejected the profit-driven sale of indulgences and exaggerated promises that undermined the sufficiency of Christ's cross, differentiating Tetzel's views from Roman Catholic doctrine. However, some Protestant-Catholic differences endure, as indulgences continue to be part of Catholic practice. E.g., Pope Francis authorized plenary indulgences during the Extraordinary Jubilee of Mercy in 2015–16. The Catechism of the Catholic Church defines an indulgence as "a remission before God of the temporal punishment due to sins whose guilt has already been forgiven," which may be "applied to the living or the dead." Holy See, "Catechism of the Catholic Church," sec. 1471.

18. About a century earlier, Bohemian priest Jan Hus had advocated for many similar reforms. After being promised safe passage, Hus attended the Council of Constance, where he was quickly imprisoned, tried, and then later burned at the stake as a heretic in 1415. In 1420, Pope Martin V initiated the first of five Crusades in Bohemia to exterminate Hussites as heretics. Reforms of this sort were supremely dangerous to attempt.

19. Pope Leo X, "Exsurge Domine."

aided and strengthened by it, it is obvious that it cannot be without the Word. If it is without the Word, it ceases to be a Church."[20]

That same year (1523), Zwingli wrote "Sixty-Seven Articles" to call the church to reform its approach to merit, indulgences, and worldly power by the standard of Scripture. The first of Ten Theses of Berne (1528) states the Swiss Reformed vision of the church vividly: "The holy, Christian Church, whose only Head is Christ, is born of the Word of God, and abides in the same, and listens not to the voice of a stranger."[21]

When hope for the church could seem foolish, it was the Word of God, accessed by the Spirit, that was the defining hope of the church. In other words, something *external* to the community of the church, the active speech of the triune God, was the ground and ongoing life of the church. The church is not an affinity group, a volunteer organization, or an instrument of charity; the church is a result of God's redemptive Word, which is the source of its ongoing life.

Because God's Word and work define and animate the church's life, the Lutherans and the Reformed both came to affirm two "marks" of the church: God's Word received in preaching and God's Word received in the sacraments. The marks of preaching and the sacraments were *not* intended as a full catalog of the church's calling. The church has many callings in many different contexts. Rather, as marks, they affirm that the Spirit of God is free to generate the church as a creature of God's Word wherever God's Word is spread and received—in whatever culture or history, and within a variety of ecclesial structures. Luther rejoices in the simplicity of this basic claim, that "a seven-year-old child knows what the Church is, namely, the holy believers and lambs who hear the voice of their Shepherd."[22]

This dynamic of the Word, received by faith through both preaching and the sacraments, became the central Lutheran and Reformed framework for discerning the visible church, even amid the desolation of the church's corruption: "From this the face of the church comes forth and becomes visible to our eyes. Wherever we see the Word of God purely preached and heard, and the sacraments administered according to Christ's institution, there, it is not to be doubted, a church of God exists."[23]

These marks were expressed widely among Reformed confessions. In 1553, Thomas Cranmer wrote this simple and elegant account of the marks in a foundational document of the English Reformation, being incorporated into

20. Luther, "Concerning the Ministry," 37.
21. Cochrane, *Reformed Confessions*, 49.
22. Luther, Smalcald Articles, 3.12.2–3.
23. Calvin, *Institutes* 4.1.9.

what the Anglican tradition calls the 39 Articles of Religion: "The visible Church of Christ is a congregation of faithful men, in which the pure Word of God is preached, and the Sacraments be duly ministered according to Christ's ordinance in all those things that of necessity are requisite to the same."[24] At times, Reformed confessions added a third mark as well. In addition to Word and sacrament, the Scots Confession lists "ecclesiastical discipline uprightly ministered, as God's Word prescribes, whereby vice is repressed and virtue nourished."[25] Yet, even this mark is best understood as pointing the discernment of the church back to God, back to discerning how the Spirit is active in the hearing and receiving of the Word, in preached and sacramental forms.

Are these marks of the church self-congratulatory, such that Reformed (and Lutheran) churches would always be considered "pure" and others would not? That was not their intent. Using these criteria, Lutheran and Reformed Christians came to discern the Spirit's work among many whom their contemporaries had written off. When leading Roman Catholic theologian Johann Eck forcefully claimed that churches in the East had lost the true Christian faith and would be damned, Luther vigorously objected. Likewise, while Calvin called for reform and repentance from abuses of the Roman Catholic Church, he also said, "We categorically deny to the papists the title of *the* church, . . . [yet] we do not for this reason impugn the existence of churches among them."[26] As the Westminster Confession would articulate in the seventeenth century, "The purest Churches under heaven are subject both to mixture and error."[27]

Discerning the presence of the *invisible* church through these marks in the *visible* church allows the Reformed tradition to be spacious and open to the variety of cultures and expressions that the Christian faith takes on.[28] At the same time, since purity in preaching and sacraments is a qualitative category, it is properly a category of self-scrutiny for churches in the Reformed tradition as well.[29] Congregations and communions in the Reformed tradition are invited to ask: Are we placing the Word of the gospel at the center of our life and trust, as expressed through Word and sacrament, and through discipline and discipleship in obedience to that Word? For being a creature of God's Word is both a God-given identity and an ongoing calling.

24. Dennison, *Reformed Confessions*, 2:760–61. While written as part of Article 20 in the Forty-Two Articles of the Church of England (1553), this sentence remained within Article 19 of the final 1571 version of the 39 Articles of Religion.

25. Scots Confession, 18 (Dennison, *Reformed Confessions*, 2:199).

26. Calvin, *Institutes* 4.3.12 (emphasis added).

27. Westminster Confession, 25.5 (Dennison, *Reformed Confessions*, 4:264).

28. This is explicitly noted in Calvin, *Institutes* 4.1.9.

29. Small, *Flawed Church, Faithful God*, 73.

Multiform Catholicity in the Global Reformed Tradition Today

So far, we have explored some key historical and theological dimensions of whether the Reformed tradition is an ethnocentric enclave of white Western Christians. A Reformed vision of a culturally diverse catholicity, as we've described—which extends through time across numerous different forms of church government, worship styles, and histories—is key to addressing the question. But to what extent, and in what ways, is this multiform catholicity on display in the global Reformed tradition today?

This is a difficult question to briefly address. Describing the "now" is challenging because we live within the flow of change, and we cannot see where the developments will lead. And because of the complexity of the many ways to be Reformed, we work with imperfect measures. But we can highlight certain key realities:

First, lest we lose sight of the forest for the trees, it is clear that *the Reformed tradition today is multinational and multiethnic in its global expression*. Far from being a largely Western phenomenon, the vast majority of the members of Reformed denominations and fellowships are now in the Global South. These are also the sites of large and expansive growth.

There is no perfect way to measure this, but the reality is clear: The majority of Reformed Christians today live in the Global South, not in North America, Europe, or the United Kingdom. The largest Reformed ecumenical group is the World Communion of Reformed Churches, with 230 denominations in 108 countries and 80 million members.[30] In South Korea alone there are over 10 million Presbyterians, compared to around 1.5 million Presbyterians in the United States, if one combines the totals of the two largest Presbyterian denominations.[31] Well over 30 million Reformed Christians live today in various regions of Africa,[32] and millions live across Latin America, especially Mexico and Brazil. And in addition to those in South Korea, millions more members live in various other parts of Asia, including 3 million in Indonesia.[33] All these estimates from the Global South are very modest, significantly underestimating the actual reality, for millions more Reformed Christians belong to other Reformed ecumenical groups or do not participate in global fellowships. In addition, internationally, there are congregations that belong to the Anglican Communion, or are congregationalist in polity (whether Baptist or nondenominational), who seek to inhabit the Reformed theological tradition.

30. Benedetto and McKim, *Historical Dictionary*, 2.
31. Benedetto and McKim, *Historical Dictionary*, 495.
32. World Council of Churches, "Member Churches."
33. Benedetto and McKim, *Historical Dictionary*, 642.

Second, *speaking of the culturally multiform character of this Reformed tradition, numerous new Reformed confessions and testimonies of faith have been written by Reformed communions in the Global South, attentive to express the catholic Christian faith in a Reformed key for their contexts.* As noted in chapter 1, a decisive difference between Lutheran and Reformed is that the Reformed have not sought to find one set of doctrinal standards for the whole tradition. The Reformed tradition has valued regional and local differences in polity, worship, and even in theological confession. In the words of Heinrich Bullinger in 1536, in signing the First Helvetic Confession, "We wish in no way to prescribe for all churches through these articles a single rule of faith," for "we grant to everyone the freedom to use his own expressions which are suitable for his church and will make use of this freedom ourselves, at the same time defending the true sense of this Confession against distortion."[34]

While Reformed confessions continued to be written into the eighteenth century, the number of new confessions generated decreased in the nineteenth century and at the beginning of the twentieth century. Then an event took place in Germany that led to the writing of a new confession, the Barmen Declaration (1934). It is worth taking a moment to consider this confession in light of the challenges of ethnocentrism, for in the decades that followed, dozens and dozens of confessions were written by Reformed communions around the world.

After the devastation of losing World War I, with burdensome reparations imposed by the Treaty of Versailles (1919), Germany underwent economic crisis, political instability, and deep social unrest. Amid this, the fires of German racial and ethnic nationalism grew through the 1920s and early 1930s. Even before Adolf Hitler's 1933 appointment as chancellor, a group called the German Christians promoted a form of racial nationalism, claiming that "the existence of different races and people was God's design and that each group was to be kept distinct."[35] This ideology supported Nazi policies like the 1935 ban on intermarriage between Aryans and Jews, and with the Nazi rise, they framed it "in spiritual terms and took [it] to be the direct work of God's providence in history for the salvation of the German nation."[36] The German Christians aimed to reshape the church's theology and practice to align with Nazi ideology, demanding loyalty to the state over faith.

In response, Protestants in Germany refusing to submit to Nazi ideology had to discern whether this was a moment to confess the faith anew, meeting

34. Bullinger, quoted in Small, "Reformed," 157.
35. Bender, "5 Lessons."
36. Bender, "5 Lessons."

the high bar of *status confessionis* (a state or situation of confession). This principle frames the possibility of drafting a new confession in a situation where *failing* to confess would injure the gospel and its witness. (The purpose of a new confession is to clarify and supplement existing confessions rather than supplant earlier ones.)

Thus, in 1934 a group of Protestants called the Confessing Church, who rejected the so-called German Christian movement, adopted the Barmen Declaration to confess its refusal to submit to Nazi ideology. Drafted primarily by Karl Barth, it proclaimed that "Jesus Christ, as he is attested for us in Holy Scripture, is the one Word of God which we have to hear and which we have to trust and obey in life and in death." It affirmed Christ's "mighty claim upon our whole life," rejecting "the false doctrine, as though there were areas of our life in which we would not belong to Jesus Christ, but to other lords."[37] This confession was also tied to life in community in resistance to these "other lords." Members of the Confessing Church, like Dietrich Bonhoeffer, lived in communal service to Christ and others, rejecting allegiance to the Nazi state and often facing grave risks.

Since then, churches worldwide—both within and beyond the Reformed tradition—have used Barmen as a model for resisting racist and nationalist pressures and asserting loyalty to Christ above all. Barmen has inspired similar confessions in Japan and Taiwan.[38] It has also had an impact among Christians who are not Reformed, such as in a 2022 Orthodox declaration condemning the Russian Orthodox Patriarch's support of Russian President Vladimir Putin, decisively rejecting "any teaching that attributes divine establishment or authority, special sacredness or purity to any single local, national, or ethnic identity."[39]

While some confessions were written in moments of crisis, others were written to supplement older Reformed confessions in a way that expressed the particular issues and challenges of receiving the gospel in particular global contexts. This is a characteristic Reformed approach, with contextual judgments made at a regional level, yet confessed as part of the historic, catholic Christian faith. The Indonesian Toraja Church confesses "together with the saints of all ages and places," and the United Church of Zambia confesses that it "holds the faith which the Church has ever held in Jesus Christ, the Redeemer of the World."[40] Yet, within the context of this catholic confession, these new confessions seek to articulate the faith anew. Historic Reformed

37. Barmen Declaration, 311.
38. See Vischer, *Reformed Witness Today*, 64–66, 98–105.
39. "A Declaration on the 'Russian World' (Russkii Mir) Teaching."
40. Vischer, *Reformed Witness Today*, 48, 292.

confessions are not infallible, and the world is ever-changing. So the preamble to the New Confession in 1972 from the Presbyterian Church in the Republic of Korea says, "The truth of the Scriptures empowers us in all time through the Holy Spirit," thus it is "our duty to articulate in a *new way* the truth of the gospel and thereby seek *new ways* of obedience to Christ" in an ever-changing world.[41]

This "newness" should be framed not as a departure from the past but as a way of living into God's calling in diverse cultural contexts. As the World Reformed Fellowship, a global group of conservative Reformed denominations, made clear when they adopted a new Statement of Faith in 2015, the intent is not to "*replace* any of the historic confessions."[42] Rather, in bringing together voices from different cultural contexts, in facing different challenges, in confessing the faith, such "new" confessions belong to a very "old" Reformed tradition. As Indonesian theologian N. Gray Sutanto has argued (while drawing on historic Reformed theologian Herman Bavinck), racism and ethnocentrism not only break God's command to love one's neighbor; they fail to celebrate the multiform beauty of God's good creation. In personal and systemic forms, racism and ethnocentrism tarnish the witness of "the global church" as "a corporate people from every tribe and tongue" being renewed under Christ's lordship.[43] The "newness" of these new confessions can offer gifts of beauty and wisdom to the Spirit's work through their Word in their midst.

Another common theme of these newer confessions is that they apply a testimony of God's great acts on our behalf to concrete public actions of the church, in particular contexts. Some earlier confessions, such as the Heidelberg Catechism, detail the shape of the Christian life and calling, as in the exposition of the Ten Commandments. The Scots Confession implores hearers "to save the lives of the innocent, to repress tyranny, to defend the oppressed."[44] But many of these new confessions address these themes with significantly more depth, both adding to earlier confessions and clarifying their testimony.

A good example of this is the Belhar Confession (1984), written in South Africa in response to apartheid and the church's role in racial injustice. It was written both to clarify and to supplement earlier confessions of faith. The Belhar calls for repentance from racially based alienation and irreconciliation in the church, and it testifies to the gift and obligation of pursuing reconciliation

41. Vischer, *Reformed Witness Today*, 89 (emphasis added).
42. "World Reformed Fellowship Statement of Faith" (emphasis original).
43. Sutanto, "Bavinck Warned."
44. Cochrane, *Reformed Confessions*, 173.

and justice in the church and broader society. It is a powerful testimony from the Global South, one that has been embraced by many Reformed denominations around the world as well, including in the United States, Germany, and the Netherlands. Because this confession makes a significant contribution to a Reformed theology of reconciliation and justice, we have decided to include our main treatment of this confession in chapter 6, in its exploration of a Reformed theology of Christian witness and justice.

Third, *although there is a rich multiethnic and multinational Reformed tradition, the global Reformed church (like the church generally) is still weighed down by the corrosive sins of racism and ethnocentrism.* We will explore this more in the following sections. But in terms of our portrait of "now," we need to keep in mind that, while most members of Reformed denominations live in the Global South and there are long and rich traditions of non-white Reformed Christianity in the West, the membership rolls of most Western Reformed denominations are predominantly white. This is not a static reality. In the United States, Hispanic Christians are a rapidly growing demographic, and some congregations are multiethnic. But on the whole, we are sad to say that racial and ethnic minorities within predominantly white Reformed denominations often face obstacles to a belonging that fully celebrates their gifts.

With that said, an increasing number of congregations in the West that do not belong to a Reformed denomination have come to embrace Reformed theology. I (Todd) know many nondenominational churches that are much more intentional about cultivating their Reformed identity than most congregations within a historically Reformed denomination. Moreover, sociologists have been surprised that a large percentage of congregations within denominations not traditionally considered Reformed, such as those in the Pentecostal tradition, identify with Calvinist or Reformed theology.[45] One can infer from the data in the United States that those seeking to inhabit the Reformed tradition from within Baptist, charismatic and Pentecostal, nondenominational, and Anglican contexts is likely a much higher number than the combined membership within historically Reformed denominations. Many congregations within these fellowships enjoy a high level of racial and ethnic diversity and have likely traveled further down the road of opening avenues for multiethnic belonging. In this way, and many others, these Christians have much to teach members of historic Reformed denominations in the West.

---

45. "The study found that 31% of pastors who lead churches within traditionally charismatic or Pentecostal denominations were described as Reformed, while 27% identified as Wesleyan/ Arminian." Barna Group, "'Reformed' Movement."

Heroes, Villains, and Racist Legacies in the Reformed Tradition

This chapter would be easier to write if we could simply stop with particular Reformed conceptions of the church as catholic in its wholeness, united in fellowship in Christ by the Spirit, amid a diversity of cultures, languages, and peoples. But church history is much messier than that.

Even amid the most illuminating parts of the Reformed tradition are pitfalls, caverns, and blind spots. Vince Bacote, an African American theologian in the Reformed tradition, described the way he experienced this in his own theological research: "I experienced this personally when I was considering my dissertation figure, Abraham Kuyper. In a way, I fell in love with this hero because of this theology of culture and politics, and this made me excited. The problem emerged when I learned he was a racist—it was like getting hit by a bus. I did not know what to do because I had great appreciation for part of his work and I also found racism in it. This was a major crisis."[46]

Abraham Kuyper (1837–1920) was a Dutch Reformed scholar, politician, and educator who exercised extraordinary influence in his own day and after. He founded the Free University of Amsterdam in 1880. He later founded a political party, and he served as prime minister of the Netherlands from 1901 to 1905. Known for articulating the notion of "common grace," which recognizes the work of the Spirit in all cultural realms, his work has been particularly generative in recent decades among Christians in the United States seeking to integrate their faith with culture. Contrary to those who would divide the world into "sacred" and "secular" realms, Kuyper's thought has influenced Christians to see the work of artists, caretakers, bakers, government employees, and so on as Christian vocation. Bacote argues that there is much in Kuyper's legacy worthy of celebration and cultivation. He writes, "It is impossible to look at [Kuyper's] career and deny his great intellect, gifts for organization, prolific publishing record, and vision for a Christianity with twin pieties of private and public virtue."[47]

Even so, Kuyper's racism is undeniable and jarring. While he saw himself as a critic of the crude racism he encountered on his trip to the United States,[48] Kuyper's own political and theological writings frequently display a profound ethnocentrism and racism. In his Stone Lectures delivered at Princeton Theological Seminary, published as *Lectures on Calvinism*, he presents a detailed theory of the development of civilization, arguing for the inferiority of African

---

46. Bacote, foreword to *Ownership*, vii.
47. Bacote, "Kuyper and Race," 154.
48. See Eglinton, "Varia Americana and Race," 65–80.

and Asian societies. He draws on the notion of "the curse of Ham" in Genesis 9 as a justification for white racial superiority, even though many biblical scholars and theologians of his day had recognized this as aberrant and baseless.[49] He speaks of the difference between "the Aryan race" and African tribes such as "Hottentot or Kaffir" as a "wide differentiation," with the former being obviously preferable to the latter, just as "if you were a plant you would rather be a rose than mushroom; if insect, butterfly rather than spider; . . . being man, richer than poor, talented rather than dull-minded."[50]

What are we to do? Kuyper's *Lectures on Calvinism* is one of his most influential books, and the racism appears elsewhere also. Although Bacote had found numerous insights in Kuyper's work, when he discovered Kuyper's virulent racism, he found himself at a crossroads: "My experience is not unique. Many who become enamored of a tradition or figure may find themselves in a kind of honeymoon phase where the tradition or figure provides tremendous benefit." What do we do when we discover that this historical figure "said or did things we find shocking or reprehensible?"[51]

The "reflexive response is either to downplay or dismiss the complications or banish figures because of their transgressions."[52] In our late modern culture, Bacote argues, we tend to assume that thinkers can be "neatly divided" into teams, with "heroes" opposing the "villains."[53] When we bring that framework to church history, or a particular tradition (such as the Reformed tradition), we can be tempted to always connect Reformed theologians with the "hero" category, if we have benefitted from the insights of that tradition. But dismissing the effects of sin is not a wise option; if we do so, "we are being set up for at the least disappointment and at the most devastation."[54] Human beings, and their roles in the church's history, are far too complex for a simple either/or between "team hero" and "team villain." As Jemar Tisby notes, "Many individuals throughout American church history exhibited blatant racism, yet they also built orphanages and schools. They deeply loved their families; they showed kindness toward others. . . . Very rarely do historical figures fit neatly into the category of 'villain.'"[55]

For his part, Bacote argues that we should "neither downplay nor totalize the flaws of Kuyper. He is neither mere hero nor mere villain. Rather, he is a

---

49. Bacote, "Kuyper and Race," 156–57.
50. Bacote, "Kuyper and Race," 159.
51. Bacote, foreword to *Ownership*, viii.
52. Bacote, foreword to *Ownership*, ix.
53. Bacote, foreword to *Ownership*, vii.
54. Bacote, foreword to *Ownership*, vii.
55. Tisby, *Color of Compromise*, 22.

man with clay feet who must be critically engaged." Both Kuyper's writing and his legacy include "these problematic, deeply troubling comments on race. What, then, does it look like to take his full legacy seriously, passing on the good gifts that Kuyper offers while lamenting his sin?"[56]

Bacote and other scholars, such as Richard Mouw, Jeff Liou, and David Robinson, have done work on Kuyper that seeks to strike this balance. For decades it has been common for Kuyperians to simply rebut Kuyper's comments about race, seeing him as "a man of his time," and then treating the rest of his theology as untainted by this ethnocentric prejudice and racism. That is not adequate, they say. Kuyper, and those who followed Kuyper (particularly within South Africa), wove his theology of racial supremacy into aspects of his theologies of creation, election, and redemption. Bacote and others point out how this is in great tension with other claims that Kuyper makes about the manifold beauty of creation, restored in redemption (thus, reading "Kuyper against Kuyper"). They also see how the theology of contemporaries such as Bavinck undermine racist facets of Kuyper's theology. In addition, they engage Kuyper together with various other scholarly voices not only to show how Kuyper's theological vision was distorted but also to open new Kuyperian possibilities. As Liou and Robinson note, "Kuyperians throughout history have, for some reason, said the most beautiful things about diversity without being intentionally race-conscious."[57] When one receives Kuyper's theology deeply, and yet critically, along with other voices, new possibilities open up.

> If affirmation of pluriformity includes an approval of racial diversity, then the stories of God's redemption from the pain of racial injustice—even "wounds yet visible above"—should fill a treasure house within the body of Christ. And Christians should energetically seek out and steward such stories of pain and redemption, because such stories would help to ensure that minorities and marginalized lives matter when Kuyperians call governments to enact justice for the citizenry. . . . Such stories would allow them to boldly proclaim that shalom can even break into the all too ordinary racial pain of our national life.[58]

56. Bacote, "Kuyper and Race," 155.
57. Robinson and Liou, "Our Racist Inheritance."
58. Robinson and Liou, "Our Racist Inheritance." Kuyper believed that the vast diversity in God's creation is not a sign of inferiority or disunity but a reflection of God's creative and sovereign design. He called this "pluriformity." As seen in his *Stone Lectures*, Kuyper did not coherently apply this idea to racial diversity; rather, he framed racial differences in terms of superiority and inferiority. Liou and Robinson therefore propose a corrective to Kuyper's view, advocating for an understanding of diversity that fully respects racial differences without implying a need for uniformity.

The response of Bacote and other scholars to Kuyper's racism gives us an instructive example of two components at work when one approaches such authors from within a tradition. This is in contrast to a great-thinker model, which views history in light of individual representatives.[59] Rather than forcing the thinker to be a hero on a pedestal (by minimizing their flaw) or refusing to listen to them because of their transgression, within a tradition, one can listen deeply, reading the thinker's work within their context, but in a way that opens new possibilities. This approach uses two different strategies— identifying internal tensions within their thought that shed new light on the flaw and opening up a wider range of voices (from the author's own age and our own) to probe alternative ways to develop the theology—in the ongoing journey of hearing God speak through Scripture by the Spirit.

Sean McGever models this approach well regarding renowned Reformed theologian Jonathan Edwards (1703–58). In his recent work, McGever recognizes Edwards's extraordinary, generative gifts as a philosopher, theologian, and pastor, with "more than four thousand secondary books [and] dissertations" published on his life and work by 2010, on topics ranging from "conversion, spiritual formation, missions, Reformed theology, politics, pluralism, religious violence, beauty, being, and understanding."[60] Yet McGever also gives an unvarnished account of his complicity with the cruel and racist institution of slavery in eighteenth-century New England: "As soon as Edwards could afford to enslave a Black person, he did, and this pattern continued for the rest of his life. He enslaved Black people as what he understood to be appropriate to his standing as a member of the New England aristocracy and as an extension of his theology of the glory of God reflected in the harmony created by the various roles and social stations in life, including slavery."[61] Edwards eventually came to disapprove of the slave trade (as an act of theft), but he did not criticize the institution and practice of racialized slavery itself.

Yet, within two decades of Edwards's death, theologians who were drawing deeply on his theology came to renounce his approach to slavery, becoming some of the most passionate antislavery preachers in New England: Samuel Hopkins (1721–1803) and Jonathan Edwards Jr. (1745–1801).[62] Moreover, among a number of Black Reformed authors making a case for the abolition of slavery at the time[63] was Lemuel Haynes (1753–1833), the first Black person to

59. See chap. 1, specifically Bradley and Muller's *Church History*.

60. McGever, *Ownership*, 30.

61. McGever, *Ownership*, 107.

62. McGever, *Ownership*, 153–58.

63. Among these eighteenth-century Black Calvinists who were "vigorously antislavery," John Saillant includes "Jupiter Hammon, James Albert Ukasaw Gronniosaw, Phillis Wheatley,

be ordained as a minister in the United States. Haynes delivered over fifty-five hundred sermons along with published theological works. Haynes brought to his ministry a wide-ranging biblical imagination and deep Reformed theological conviction. In key sermons addressing race and slavery, he combined these pastoral-theological gifts with a principled commitment to the ideals of a constitutional republic—an integration that, as historian Mark Noll writes, "fashioned a sophisticated theological weapon against the continuation of slavery in the United States."[64] As he did this, he adapted an idea within the ethics of Jonathan Edwards Sr. to argue that Christians are called to cultivate an interracial society of shared affections and love.

To receive the riches and also confront the deep flaws within the lives and works of Kuyper and Edwards, we need to listen closely to their writings, being attentive not only to insights but also to internal tensions. And we need other voices—from their own contexts and from our own. But in order to do that well, Bacote believes, we need to move beyond the approach of reading within an either/or framework. Note that, within the Reformed tradition, this is not simply a *methodological* move; it also reflects an anthropology and an ecclesiology that takes human sin seriously, in its personal and systemic forms, while being attentive to the Spirit's powerful and at times surprising work through men and women with "clay feet." In our day, with megachurch pastors who build platforms and often found schools or ministries, it can be tempting to downplay pastoral shortcomings. But from a Reformed perspective, that is not being fully honest about who we are as humans who recognize that God alone is the hero of the people of God.

Embracing the Non-Innocent Reality of the People of God

As noted at the outset of this book, many Christians in the West today find themselves disenchanted by the corruption or superficiality of the tradition they occupy. Many enter into a quest to find the "true church," the one untarnished by the earthly, sinful realities that are so obvious in church history. This quest is understandable, borne from disappointment and, often, from deep pain.

But in a catholic-Reformed understanding of the church, this quest may be short-sighted. While the process of inhabiting a tradition involves sorting in light of the biblical witness, the underlying reality of the church community

---

John Marrant, Quobna Ottobah Cugoano, and Olaudah Equiano," as well as Lemuel Haynes. See Saillant, *Black Puritan, Black Republican*, 4.

64. Noll, *Civil War as a Theological Crisis*, 72.

is one in which the final sorting is left to God. A central text for a Reformed vision of the church is Jesus's parable of the wheat and the weeds in Matthew 13:24–30. In the parable, Jesus warns against seeking to "root out" the weeds in the kingdom of God that had been sown by the enemy. Every congregation is like a field with both wheat and weeds, and it is up to God, not humans, to uproot the weeds.

This understanding of the church also fits with the big-picture story of how Scripture was interpreted in the Reformed tradition. Rather than whitewashing the sins of Abraham, David, and other biblical characters, considering these "heroes" of the faith, God alone was framed as the hero. In many instances, Reformed biblical interpreters were the exception, rather than the rule, in interpreting Scripture in this way.[65] Earlier interpreters, and most during the Reformation, tended to read Abraham as a type of hero of the Old Testament. They gave this honorific rendering of Abraham for understandable reasons, as God worked powerfully in making a covenant with Abraham and his descents—a covenant that the apostle Paul says he accessed by faith such that, through grace, Abraham "is the father of all of us" (Rom. 4:16). Clearly, what happens through Abraham is central to God's work in the world. But is he a hero in the sense that his whole life should be an example, or is God the hero who works in and in spite of the weaknesses and sins of Abraham?

This becomes an acute question as we consider Abraham's repeated deceptions, starting with Pharaoh in Genesis 12:1–20, where Abraham, in fear for his own life (v. 12), did not disclose that Sarah was his wife, but said she was his sister. In consequence, Pharaoh took her as a wife and gave Abraham wealth in animals and servants in exchange for her, as a dowry. Abraham not only made Sarah complicit in his act of deception; he also endangered Sarah on various levels, including effectively forcing her into an adulterous relationship out of loyalty to him. God's disapproval of Abraham's action was expressed by a plague that the Lord sent Pharoah, until Pharoah understood that Sarah was already married.

Most early interpreters had a deep desire to justify Abraham, upholding his image as a hero of the faith. Many said that rather than being sinful, Abraham's deceit was an act of prudence under the circumstances—or perhaps was even justified by the divine "mission" that Abraham was sent on. Early Reformed interpreters, such as Calvin and Wolfgang Musculus, would have none of it. Though Abraham was a leader of God's people under the mission of God, they insisted that his action was completely unjustified. "It's

---

65. See, e.g., Thompson, *Reading the Bible with the Dead*, esp. 71–92, which I draw on in Gen. 12:1–20 below.

no work of faith to do what is unjust and dishonorable in order to obtain the promises of God," Musculus asserts.[66] Far from being a model of faith or exercising prudence, Calvin claims that, in this instance, Abraham refused to cast his cares on God.[67] There is nothing at all heroic about this encounter, besides the heroic mercy of the Lord who is faithful to his covenant promise.

Justo González has a compelling way of describing this approach to reading *God alone* as the hero of Scripture: reading with a "non-innocent history."[68] While he does not focus specifically on Reformed biblical interpretation, his description fits with the patterns we see in early Reformed interpreters like Calvin and Musculus. González notes the remarkable fact that the Old Testament does not shy away from disclosing the non-innocence of its central characters. And this shows up also in the genealogy of Jesus. He is framed as heir to incestuous and adulterous unions, the son of a king (David) who murdered a faithful soldier to marry his wife. Jesus, though without sin, entered not into a glorious, untainted history but into a non-innocent one. "The biblical history is a history beyond innocence. Its only real heroes are the God of history and history itself, which somehow continues moving forward even in spite of the failure of its great protagonists."[69]

Because the Bible itself gives a portrait of the people of God through history as sinful, broken, and complicit—with God alone as deliverer—González argues that interpreters who approach the church's history as a non-innocent history have a hermeneutical advantage in interpreting Scripture as the church. We should not be in search of a completely "pure" church, an uncontaminated people of God—that is not the people of God in the Old and New Testaments. Those who interpret Scripture with this understanding are all the more able to see how the church today—like the people of God in the past—looks to God alone as hero, deliverer, and Lord.

Sadly, although this instinct toward a non-innocent history fits well with much in Reformed biblical interpretation and theology of the church, the actual history of the Reformed tradition includes profound failures in honoring God as the true hero and deliverer. Although the Ten Commandments were expounded in Reformed catechisms, the church in the Reformed tradition has (and will continue to be) broken and sinful.

What are we to make of this?

This is an important question, and deeply existential. In some ways, it brings us a step further down the road of the wager. Reformed Christians,

---

66. Thompson, *Reading the Bible with the Dead*, 77.
67. Thompson, *Reading the Bible with the Dead*, 78.
68. González, *Mañana*, 75.
69. González, *Mañana*, 77.

like other flesh and blood people in the history of the church, have beautiful aspects of their history, but they also have broken, complicit, and sinful ones. Sin and abuse and alienation and corruption are ugly. We cannot, and should not, say, "Evil is good." Lament and repentance is a pathway to life; by it, we die to the old self and live into the new creation by the Spirit.

The Living Faith of the Dead and the Living

"Tradition is the living faith of the dead, traditionalism is the dead faith of the living."[70] The Reformed tradition inhabits tradition in a way that testifies to the "living faith of the dead" in a distinctive way. The Reformed tradition does not claim to possess the entirety of the church but, rather, walks the path of witness to Christ the Lord in our fallen world. Yet, this tradition itself is valued as a product of the Spirit's work within the church, as the creature of the Word. Thus, while the Reformed tradition falls short of God's glorious calling for his church, it does enable resources for embracing the reality of our sinfulness—rejecting any triumphalist narrative about the Reformed tradition, or the Christian tradition more generally.

As a result, occupying the Reformed tradition requires discernment. Upholding or maintaining tradition is not the supreme goal. Instead, the process of living within the Reformed tradition is analogous to that of living into God's covenant Word to us in baptism: It is a journey of dying and rising with Christ, living into God's Word as adopted children who die to the old self and live into the new by the Spirit.

As we hear Scripture, the voice of the Shepherd, we seek to listen and obey, attentive to the ways in which we have lost our way. Perhaps we have lost our way through jumping in on a new trend. Perhaps we have lost our way by following a set of practices that we label as tradition but that do not bear fruit. Perhaps we have set the table for people who are "similar to us" in culture, ethnicity, or race, and we expect others to simply *conform* rather than join us in *discerning*. This discernment involves where and how to die through the Spirit's power, to turn from a self-directed, self-focused path to one of deep belonging—belonging first and foremost to Christ, our Life, and to one another as members of God's household.

Thus, while deeply fallible, the Reformed tradition does provide a way to inhabit the historic Christian faith that acknowledges our deep imperfections.

---

70. Pelikan, *Vindication of Tradition*, 65. See Leith's treatment of tradition in these terms, following Pelikan (Leith, *Reformed Tradition*, 31). We join Leith in commending to the Reformed this approach to tradition.

The church is the creature of the Word; we are without hope to truly be the people of God described in Scripture apart from dwelling in God's Word. In finding nourishment by the Spirit in God's Word, we can have hope for the church, even amid the rubble of brokenness and sin. The way forward is not amnesia or forgetfulness, as if we would live without a tradition that extends through time, as if the historic Christian church had not betrayed her Master, her household of faith, and her neighbor. The way forward is not to claim an exceptionalism, that the temptations and idols that have distorted the Christian witness in the past do not apply to us. According to the Reformed, there is a way to inhabit a tradition as creatures of the Word, the new creation in Christ—belonging to Christ and to one another, as we bear witness to the one true Lord of the church.

3

Infant Baptism: Welcomed by Grace into the Covenant Family

Key Question: Why Do Presbyterian and Other Reformed Denominations Baptize Infants?

In this chapter, we make a case for our own position, which is the majority position in the Reformed theological tradition: Believers are invited to baptize their young children as a covenantal sign and seal of God's promise. However, some streams of the Reformed tradition reject this view. In particular, a long tradition of Reformed Baptists affirms most points of Reformed theology but disagrees on the theology and practice of infant baptism.[1]

If you consider yourself a Reformed Baptist, or are part of another Christian communion that does not practice infant baptism, know that we do not view the practice of infant baptism as a lowest common denominator for those who claim to be Reformed. We certainly embrace friends who disagree on this matter as brothers and sisters in Christ. We include this chapter simply because it is one of the most common questions about the confessional Reformed tradition. It is also a very important matter for theology and practice in congregational life.

---

1. A key confession for many Reformed Baptists is an adaptation of the Westminster Standards in the 1689 London Baptist Confession of Faith.

Why is the practice of infant baptism within Presbyterian and Reformed denominations so commonly questioned? One major sticking point is the claim that Scripture is our supreme authority for theology and the life of faith. Some ask how Reformed Christians can affirm this claim and justify baptizing babies when there is no direct evidence of that practice in the New Testament. These friends reject pedobaptism (the technical term for infant baptism) in favor of credobaptism (believer's baptism alongside a profession of faith). They see the latter as much closer to the baptisms described in the New Testament church. Among other questions, they wonder if the Reformed practice of infant baptism devalues the role of faith in salvation or if it devalues baptism itself, since those baptized as infants might never come to profess an individual faith.

Reformed Baptists are not alone in their incredulity. Many of our Roman Catholic friends (and some Lutherans) also ask us why we practice infant baptism, but their questions come from another angle. The historic Reformed tradition does not affirm that the act of baptism conveys any kind of saving or regenerating grace in and of itself. To these friends, it seems as though we don't believe that baptism actually does anything for the infant. In this case, why do we bother?

As we'll see in more detail in a moment, the majority of the Reformed tradition down the centuries does maintain that there is scriptural warrant for baptizing infants.[2] We also maintain a broader scriptural and theological claim: Christ's action on our behalf and in our place applies just as much to infants as to adults. Because this is so, we affirm that, as the sign and seal of what God in Christ has done for us, baptism should be given to infants as well as adults, even though an infant cannot yet declare their response.

While we don't hold to any saving efficacy in the act of baptism, we do think that God is powerfully at work in the sacrament, declaring and doing very important things for those who are baptized, whether infants or adults. Reformed churches generally practice both covenant infant baptism (we baptize the babies of members of a congregation) and baptism alongside profession of faith if someone has not been previously baptized.

2. One very significant exception to this is the twentieth-century giant of Reformed theology Karl Barth (1886–1965), who questioned infant baptism as early as 1948 and gave his fullest account of his rejection of infant baptism in the final (and incomplete) volume of his *Church Dogmatics* (the fragment that is CD IV/4). He did not adopt a conventional Baptist position, however, in that he rejected rebaptism, considering that while infant baptism was "disorderly," it was nevertheless a valid form of Christian baptism. He also insisted that baptism is, above all, the outward sign of what Christ has done, and is only secondarily about profession of faith. For an account and analysis of Barth's rejection of infant baptism, as well as a constructive way forward, see McMaken, *Sign of the Gospel.*

Because we see baptism above all as the sign and seal of God's promises and God's saving work in Christ, baptism reflects a major strand in Reformed theology as a whole. For us, the primary emphasis is always on the loving and gracious action of God toward us; our response is secondary.[3] Moreover, as we will explain more fully in the next chapter, for the Reformed, the gracious action of God toward us not only precedes but also enables our response of faith to God. This means that, whether someone is baptized as an infant or as an adult, baptism is first about the action of God. In believers' baptism, the person responds to the promises and saving actions of God by professing their faith. In infant baptism, the promises and saving work of God anticipate a personal response at a later stage. In both cases, it is the work of Christ, received in faith, that saves, not the act of baptism. The sacrament is not devalued if someone baptized as an infant does not make a personal profession of faith, just as it is not devalued if someone baptized as an adult later renounces their faith. The promises of God and the saving work of God in Christ held forth in baptism remain unshakably true, even if someone rejects them or turns aside from them.

To unpack all of this, we need to dig a little deeper into Scripture, theology, and history. We'll see both why the majority Reformed position upholds infant baptism and why this has always been, and remains, a matter of dispute within Protestantism as a whole and, to a lesser extent, within the Reformed tradition itself.

First, we need to explore some aspects of the objection we mentioned at the outset, that there is no direct evidence in Scripture for pedobaptism. As we'll see, the New Testament does mention the baptism of entire households, and other texts can demonstrate that the scriptural witness does not forbid, and in fact assumes, the practice of infant baptism. Nevertheless, for those who require a clear and specific scriptural mandate for a particular practice in the church, the lack of any mention of infant baptism in the New Testament and the linking of baptism to a personal declaration of faith are seen as more than sufficient grounds to reject the practice of infant baptism.

Some History: Infant Baptism and Differing Views on *Sola Scriptura*

Some Reformation-era church history can help us consider how we draw on Scripture in these debates. Baptism of infants was one of the key issues that split the early Protestant movement. Close to the heart of this dispute was

3. As we will see below, the early Swiss Reformed theologian Huldrych Zwingli took a different view of sacramental action, although he still strongly upheld infant baptism.

how we are to understand the concept of *sola scriptura* (Scripture alone) as it relates to the beliefs and practices of the church.

The Radical Reformation movement largely understood *sola scriptura* to mean that Scripture should be the sole source in matters of belief and practice.[4] When there is a clear and direct mandate from Scripture, a practice is permitted in the church. When there is no mandate, it is not. The Radical Reformers were deeply suspicious of doctrines and practices that had developed in the church since the conversion of Constantine, or even since the death of the apostles. Therefore, there could be no appeal to earlier theology. The hope of *sola scriptura* for the Radical Reformers was to return to what they considered to be the pure doctrine and practice of the very earliest church, without the accretion of the thought and practices of the intervening centuries. This is not the place to critique either the possibility or the actuality of these aims. It is enough for us to realize that, in a broad sketch, this understanding was a significant aspect of what motivated the Radical Reformers and undergirded their rejection of infant baptism. We can see many connections between this kind of approach to *sola scriptura* and the concerns about infant baptism that we find in many Protestant denominations and independent evangelical churches today.

The Magisterial Reformers, such as Martin Luther, Huldrych Zwingli, and John Calvin (the latter two belonging to our Reformed branch of the Reformation), understood *sola scriptura* differently.[5] For the Magisterial Reformers, *sola scriptura* signified that Scripture is the *supremely authoritative* source for belief and practice. Because of this, they drew gladly (though not uncritically) on the theological insights of the past, particularly from the early church, and felt able to adopt and continue a range of practices within the church as long as those were tested by Scripture and found to be consonant with its overall

4. The term *Radical Reformation* has come to be used by historians to refer to an initially very disparate group of Protestants who came to unite under the beliefs set out in the Schleitheim Confession of 1527. In addition to rejecting infant baptism, they came to espouse Christian pacifism. More generally, they rejected, as far as possible, any engagement with the political authorities and civic society, believing that for the church to remain pure in following the way of Christ, it needed to keep itself from contamination by the rest of the world. We should also add that, alongside the account of *sola scriptura* given here, a small number of Radical Reformers contended that personal revelations of the Holy Spirit (e.g., through dreams or visions) could *surpass* Scripture as sources of revelation. This remained a minority position within the Reformation-era movement. Much later, some Quakers, although not George Fox himself, would also advocate for a similar priority to be given to personal revelations from God.

5. The term *Magisterial Reformers* refers to the willingness of these Reformers to involve the political authorities (magistrates) in upholding and promulgating the Protestant movement. This resulted in the close binding of church and state, although there were significant differences when it came to the actual relationship between church and state, between different branches of the Magisterial Protestant movement, and also within the Reformed communion in different states and territories.

witness. Again, we can see the influence of this kind of approach in various branches of Protestantism today.

These differences of opinion about the way that Scripture functions for the church came to a head in the Reformation era over the issue of infant baptism. As we have seen, since there is no direct scriptural example of, or mandate for, infant baptism, the Radical Reformers rejected it and inveighed bitterly against the Magisterial Reformers on this issue, seeing the continuation of the practice as an egregious compromise of *sola scriptura*. Very much a minority group in the overall tapestry of the sixteenth-century Protestant Reformation, they not only refused to practice infant baptism but also insisted on (re)baptizing adults who chose to follow their movement. The name Anabaptists (Rebaptizers) was given to them by their opponents. As far as the Radical Reformers were concerned, they were not rebaptizing anyone; they did not consider infant baptism to be a legitimate Christian baptism in the first place. This was a very dangerous position to hold in the sixteenth century, when the close bond of church and state meant that baptism was not simply a sacrament of the church. The refusal to baptize infants was also a civil offense, implying a rejection of citizenship within a state or territory. Many Anabaptists were exiled and some were executed (often, in brutal irony, by drowning) for their refusal to baptize their infants. These sentences were often carried out by fellow Protestants, including by Reformed Protestants such as Zwingli in Zurich.

That the refusal to baptize infants was considered to be an offense against the state illustrates another aspect of the objections to infant baptism, then and now. In addition to divorcing baptism from the articulation of personal faith in Christ, baptism could simply become a social rite, separated from discipleship. Particularly before the Enlightenment, which fractured the notion of a Christian state, automatic infant baptism could seem more like a mark of being "in Christendom" rather than of being personally "in Christ." In those countries where there is still a state church, there can be a perception that merely being born in a particular place means that someone is a Christian by default. Even in the United States, where the establishment of a state church is forbidden by the constitution, some fear that infant baptism is more likely to reflect social and church convention than to be a sign of true commitment to Christ.

Distinguishing a Reformed Approach from a Roman Catholic Approach

Clearly, then, the justification—and perception—of infant baptism raised genuine concerns from the Reformation era through the rise of the Baptist movements in the seventeenth and eighteenth centuries, and many of the same concerns remain. The early Reformers for whom pedobaptism was an important expression of the gospel had to articulate their adherence to infant baptism in the face of two opposite positions. On one side were those Protestants who declared that the Reformed had sold out the Scriptures for the sake of a corrupt theological tradition and the political status quo. On the other side, Roman Catholicism insisted on infant baptism for reasons that the Reformed could not accept. So they needed to distinguish a Reformed view.

Very briefly, Roman Catholicism had (and has) a very different understanding of the nature of the sacraments from that held by the majority of Protestants. In addition to having seven sacraments—five in addition to the two practiced by most Protestants (baptism and the Lord's Supper)—for Roman Catholics the sacraments convey a saving grace simply by being done (in technical terms, they are efficacious *ex opere operato*; lit., "from the work worked"). The particular saving grace conveyed in the act of baptism is the removal of the guilt of original sin. Of course, as the baby grows it will commit sins of its own, which will require participation in the other sacraments of the church, most notably reconciliation (confession) and the Mass.

Given that the Reformed reject the saving sacramental efficacy that accompanies the Roman Catholic understanding of baptism, and given the lack of explicit scriptural warrant for infant baptism, how did the Reformed in the sixteenth century—and how do the Reformed now—justify infant baptism? And why has it been so important to us?

Historical Reformed Justifications for Infant Baptism

Early Reformed theologians rightly point out that even if Scripture offers no explicit example of infant baptism, neither does Scripture forbid it. In his typically feisty way, Calvin points out that if the argument from silence on infant baptism were valid in and of itself, then "women should similarly be barred from the Lord's Supper, since we do not read that they were admitted to it in the apostolic age; but here we are content with the rule of faith. For when we weigh what the institution of the Supper implies, it is also easy to judge from this to whom the use of it ought to be granted. We observe this also in baptism. Indeed, when we pay attention to the purpose for which it was instituted, we clearly see that it is just as appropriate to infants as to older persons."[6]

6. Calvin, *Institutes* 4.16.8

In addition to pushing back against the argument from silence, this quotation from Calvin indicates a crucial question: Does the significance of baptism apply to infants as well as to adults? If the answer is yes (as we have already claimed), then infants should not be denied the outward sign. We will return to this very important point later. For the moment, more generally, the early Reformers did base their claims in Scripture, referring to passages that open the door to infant baptism, such as accounts of the baptism of entire households and of Jesus blessing the little children. The significance of these texts for infant baptism, and the scriptural and theological key to the Reformed defense of infant baptism, lies primarily in the continuities between the covenant God makes with his people in the Old Testament and the New, and in the respective outward signs; in other words, these Reformers saw a link between baptism in the New Testament and the Old Testament covenant rite of circumcision.

Zwingli is among the earliest in the Reformed tradition to emphasize this line of thought, in his disputes with the Anabaptists in Zurich. He ties baptism closely to the concept of covenant and highlights the ways Paul points to baptism as the equivalent of circumcision in the new-covenant community in Christ. Calvin picks up these themes, and they have remained prominent in the Reformed tradition ever since.[7]

A Scriptural Overview: Some Texts and Themes

The Reformed see one overarching covenant of grace at work throughout God's dealings with God's people. As a very brief summary, we understand that it is God's gracious initiative to call out Abraham, and through him the people of Israel, for a unique relationship with himself in order to further his purposes of blessing all nations through them (Gen. 12:1–3). It is God's equally gracious initiative to provide Israel with a way of living before God and relating to God in Torah (the Jewish Law) and the outward signs of the covenant, such as circumcision. From the outset, God acknowledges that Israel will not be able to fulfill its side of the covenant and offers provision for recognizing and responding to its inevitable failings.

---

7. For Calvin's treatment of baptism more generally, see *Institutes* 4.15. For his extended treatment of infant baptism, see 4.16. For an excellent secondary source on Calvin's theology of baptism, see Bierma, *Font of Pardon*. The following summary of the majority Reformed position owes much to our colleague James V. Brownson's outstanding account in *Promise of Baptism*, esp. Section 4, "The Case for Infant Baptism" (chaps. 17–20), and Section 5, "Disputes and Questions Surrounding Infant Baptism" (chaps. 21–24). Geoffrey Bromiley also gives a brief-but-substantial defense of this majority position in his book *Children of Promise*.

This narrative of God's gracious initiative, promise, and provision, and of God's covenant faithfulness in the face of the faithlessness of God's people, reaches its *telos*—its culmination and fulfillment—in Jesus Christ himself. Jesus is both sides of the covenant in person. He is the perfectly faithful covenant-keeping God come to his people; he does whatever it takes to fulfill God's promises to them and the whole world from the very beginning. He is also the perfectly faithful human covenant partner, Israel's representative Messiah, who embodies and fulfills everything Israel was set apart to be and to do in the purposes of God. After Jesus's death, resurrection, and ascension, being "in covenant" no longer equates to belonging to the people of Israel, with Torah and the outward signs and practices it enjoins. Instead, membership of the people of God is opened to all peoples on the sole basis of faith in Jesus Christ, as the way in which we appropriate his saving work. To be "in covenant" for Jew and gentile alike is to be "in Christ" by the Spirit through faith.

How does this relate to infant baptism, particularly given the centrality of faith in Christ for what it now means to be in covenant? For this, we must consider the pattern of God's covenanting from the beginning. As we noted above, covenant begins with God's gracious initiative. God calls out one person (Abraham) and through him one people (Israel). God's grace precedes and calls forth Abraham's response. As a sign of Abraham's faith in the promises of God, God summons Abraham to enact a sign and seal of this covenant relationship. That sign and seal is circumcision, for himself and for all the males in his household (Gen. 17:9–14, 23–27), including the command that all male infants should be circumcised on the eighth day after their birth. God's steadfast love and promises of blessing extend not just to the individual but to their children and families, even to the thousandth generation (e.g., Deut. 7:9).

Let us pause here and probe the multilayered significance of this. First, we should note that circumcision, as the sign and seal of belonging in the covenant community, is specifically commanded for infants, who, needless to say, can know nothing about God or God's covenant or what it means to live toward God. The infant's unknowing isn't a problem; it is a major part of the point. God's initiative establishes covenant relationship, and precedes any response of ours, such that our being brought into covenant relationship with God is a summons to become what he has called us to be. These infants are recipients of God's promises and belong within the sphere of God's covenant as members of the community in which God's promises and purposes are known, lived, and taught. As such, they are to receive the sign and seal of that membership and those promises precisely before they can know anything of them.

Second, we must note the significance of households within God's covenant community. When Abraham adheres to the Lord in faith, his whole household is included in that covenant relationship. All the males are circumcised, with no indication that they as yet have any personal knowledge of or faith in the promises of God. The culture of the Ancient Near East (and as we shall see, the presupposition in New Testament times also) was that the religious identity of the head of the household becomes the religious identity of every member of that household, including non-blood relations such as servants. This corporate approach to identity is a struggle for us to understand in our post-Enlightenment culture in general, which strongly emphasizes individual autonomy, and particularly for those of us who have been raised in the United States, where the overall culture extols "rugged individualism." This is also reflected in a US church culture that strongly emphasizes an individual's decision for and personal relationship with Jesus. Of course, just as for Abraham, personal faith and allegiance are vital to the fullness of covenant relationship with God and for salvation. But this is not, and never has been, the only aspect of receiving the outward sign of covenant membership in Scripture.

With this background we can turn to the New Testament and the implications of these themes for baptism as the sign and seal of belonging to the new covenant community in Christ. We will start with the second point first: the concept of the household. The New Testament understanding of the relationship between the head of the household and religious identity is essentially the same as that of the people of Israel in the Old Testament. The New Testament repeatedly indicates that as soon as the head of a household professes faith in Christ, the whole household is baptized (e.g., Acts 16:15, 31–33; 18:8). These households likely included infants, and few members of the household would have come to personal faith in Christ before joining the head of the household in the sacrament, which signified their entry into the new covenant people of God. In other words, we should not identify the act of baptism in the New Testament as uniquely and only for individuals who have professed personal faith in Jesus Christ as Lord. Baptism signifies more than just that.

These household baptisms suggest that the same pattern we see in the Old Testament of circumcising infants as covenant people can be applied to the baptism of infants when the head of the household becomes a Christian. This is reinforced by the continuation for Christians of the Old Testament declaration that the promises of God are "for you and for your children." Peter makes this point to the hearers of his Pentecost sermon (Acts 2:39), and Paul gives us a fascinating miniature case study in 1 Corinthians 7:12–16. In verse 14, we learn that even having only one believing parent means that the children are "holy"—they are set apart for God as members of his covenant people. The overall context in these verses concerns how a believing spouse also makes the unbelieving spouse holy. Tellingly, Paul makes no distinction between a wife or a husband in this regard, and he explicitly notes that an unbelieving husband is made holy by a believing wife whose faith also means that their children are holy. In effect, this makes the believing wife of an unbelieving husband the de facto spiritual head of the household, whose faith embraces the rest of her family.

In light of all of this, it could well be argued that one reason the New Testament does not specifically mention infant baptism is that there is no need to. We can assume that the same patterns we have seen in the Old Testament apply to the new covenant people in Christ.[8] The case could be made that it would require a clear command of Christ, or a clear prohibition elsewhere in the New Testament, to indicate that the inclusion of infants had now been abrogated by God. As James V. Brownson points out, when we understand the broader context, the burden is actually on those who advocate against infant baptism to show any change in basic understanding of the sign of entry into the covenant community between the Old Testament and the New in this regard.[9]

Beyond just inferring continuities between baptism and circumcision, we can see strong, direct connections between them within the New Testament, particularly in the Pauline epistles. Baptism is clearly depicted as the physical action that sets apart the people of the new covenant, as the sign and seal of their union with Christ in his death and resurrection, and their membership of the people of God in him (e.g., Rom. 6). Most specifically, however, Paul draws out the relationship between circumcision and baptism in Colossians 2:11–12, where he speaks of how the (gentile) Christians of Colossae have been circumcised in a new way ("a spiritual circumcision"); they die to their old, sinful nature with Christ in baptism and are raised to new life in him. Baptism is described as "the circumcision of Christ" (i.e., Christian circumcision) and, therefore, as the New Testament equivalent of the Old Testament covenant rite.[10]

With these general similarities and connections in mind, we can now turn to some ways infant baptism in particular may be considered to be the Christian

8. We might also note that there is also continuity here with the practice of Jewish proselyte baptism. When a gentile head of household converts, they and their entire household (including infants) are baptized, and once again, this is the case even if only one spouse converts.

9. Brownson, *Promise of Baptism*, 136, 141.

10. For a more detailed exegetical account of this, see Brownson, *Promise of Baptism*, 139–40.

equivalent of circumcision of male infants in Israel. The parallels are strong. As we have noted, the Old Testament is clear that God specifically desires— and requires—that the sign and seal of membership in the covenant community be given to those who have as yet no personal awareness of it. This is not an exception or a concession. It is normative and commanded. We might also note that where circumcision was given only to males, infant baptism is for both males and females, as is fitting for the sacrament that marks our entry into the household of God in which there is now "no longer Jew or Greek, there is no longer slave or free, there is no longer male and female; for all . . . are one in Christ Jesus" (Gal. 3:28). We might also add that the sign no longer involves pain and the shedding of blood, making it an even more fitting sign of entry into the new covenant community![11]

As with infant circumcision, infant baptism is about being brought into membership in the community where the promises of God are known, taught, and lived. This is why, as we noted above, the Reformed uphold the concept of *covenant* infant baptism. That is to say, we do not baptize any and all infants at the request of any and all parents. We baptize infants when one or both parents are professing members of the congregation.[12] This is also why the community of faith is integral to the significance of baptism, which is the sign of incorporation into the body of Christ, not simply in the abstract, but in the lived reality of a particular Christian community. Unless there are exceptional circumstances, baptism takes place within the context of a congregation gathered for worship. During the baptism, not only the baptized or their parents take vows and make promises; the congregation also makes promises to walk alongside and support the one being baptized in their growth in faith and discipleship. While Scripture indicates that the promises of God are held out to the children of believers, baptism is not primarily about the family of the person being baptized as such. It is the sacrament of our adoption and incorporation into the family of God, which gives the proper context for, but also relativizes, all earthly family bonds. Baptism signifies that there is no higher allegiance than the one we have to Jesus Christ, and there is no one else to whom we ultimately belong. No family loyalty can supersede it, and we can no more presume upon our familial descent for salvation in the

11. As the Belgic Confession puts it, Christ, by shedding his blood, has put an end to the shedding of blood as a sign of covenant relationship with God, so that "having abolished circumcision, which was done with blood, Christ established in its place the sacrament of baptism." Belgic Confession, 34 (*Our Faith*, 59).

12. In addition to the Belgic Confession, Article 34, see Westminster Confession, 28.4 (Dennison, *Reformed Confessions*, 4:267); Westminster Larger Catechism, Q 166 (Dennison, *Reformed Confessions*, 4:342–43); and Westminster Shorter Catechism, Q 95 (Dennison, *Reformed Confessions*, 4:366).

new covenant than the people of Israel could in their covenant relationship with God.

This brings us to another very important connection between infant circumcision for Israel and infant baptism in the community of Christ. In neither case is the outward sign of the covenant intended to be a guarantee of an individual's saving participation in the covenant. The stories of Ishmael and Esau make clear that physical circumcision is not a guarantee of actual covenant membership within the people of Israel, as do the prophetic laments about the small faithful remnant within the wider people of Israel in the context of the Babylonian exile and return. Paul picks up on this theme in Romans 2:28, where he notes the difference between inward and outward circumcision, and in his blunt summary of the Old Testament on this subject: "Not all Israelites truly belong to Israel, and not all of Abraham's children are his true descendants" (Rom. 9:6–7; see Rom. 9:6–13).

Likewise, there is no expectation that every baptized infant will come to personal faith. Both infant baptism and infant circumcision mark someone's entrance into the visible fellowship of God's people and summon those who receive this outward sign of the covenant to a life dedicated to the Lord. As Michael Green remarks, however, "Without faith you remain a 'baptized unbeliever.' . . . [You] bear upon your body the mark of how much God the Father cares for you, of what Christ did for you, of what the Holy Spirit could mean to you."[13] If someone baptized as an infant does not come to faith as an adult, they have not abandoned a profession they never made; rather, they have rejected a promise that God made to them.[14] Therefore, as we mentioned earlier, for the Reformed, the act of baptism does not guarantee anyone's salvation, infant *or* adult.

We now return to an issue raised by the quotation from Calvin above regarding the Anabaptist argument that since the New Testament nowhere specifically mentions infant baptism, it is therefore forbidden. Alongside his rather snarky but telling remarks about whether they will therefore forbid women to receive the Lord's Supper, the primary issue for Calvin is whether the significance of the sacrament applies to infants as well as adults. In that regard, Scripture is clear that infants can indeed be members of the household of God and recipients of salvation. That is part of the theological point of circumcision on the eighth day. The parallel point is made by Jesus, albeit not specifically in the context of Christian baptism (which had not yet been

13. Green, *Baptism*, 65. He offers the analogy that infant baptism is like the equivalent of a large check, which needs to be cashed before someone receives the sum it promises. Faith, in this analogy, is the equivalent of cashing the check.

14. Brownson, *Promise of Baptism*, 154.

instituted), when he insists on blessing the infants and children and on pointing to them as models of kingdom citizenship.[15]

As Brownson puts it, in this context, "Jesus publicly announces the salvation of children—even infants who are inherently incapable of expressing
faith. Those who can do nothing for themselves . . . can be saved by God.
Indeed, the disciples have something to learn from such as these."[16] This
does not imply that infants and very young children are saved on the basis of
foreseen future faith, or because of some notion of the innocence of babies.
We Reformed are clear that all of us, including infants, carry the debilitating
effects of sin within us and need the saving work of Christ. Infants are saved
in the same way as everyone else: on the basis of what Christ has done. This
is also why our historic standards are at pains to give assurance to parents
whose children die in infancy, whether or not they have been baptized. Unlike
the Roman Catholic understanding noted above, parents are not to place their
hope in the sacramental action and mediation of the church. Rather, they
are encouraged to rely on the saving work of Christ and the assurance that
the promises of God are not only for them but also for their children. So the
Canons of Dort includes a section offering comfort and assurance for parents
of infants who have died.[17] Uniquely among all of our historic standards, the
Westminster Confession of Faith also reaches out to parents whose children
(of whatever age) are unable, for any reason, to respond in ways that we have
come to consider normative: "Elect infants, dying in infancy, are regenerated
and saved by Christ through the Spirit, who worketh when, and where, and
how he pleaseth. *So also are all other elect persons who are incapable of being
outwardly called by the ministry of the Word.*"[18]

Again, therefore, as we think scripturally and theologically about the saving
work of Christ, what Christ has done applies as much to infants (and to those
with disabilities who may not be able to articulate their faith) as to adults
who are able to profess faith. In infant baptism, as well as infant circumcision, it is simply the case that for all those who will be saved, the outward
sign precedes the personal appropriation and public expression of the inward

15. This episode is found in all three Synoptic Gospels: Mark 10:13–16; Matt. 19:13–15; Luke
18:15–17. The Greek term in Luke's version of this episode specifically signifies "babes-in-arms."
16. Brownson, *Promise of Baptism*, 131; cf. 130–33.
17. "Since we must make judgments about God's will from his Word, which testifies that
the children of believers are holy, not by nature, but by virtue of the gracious covenant in which
they together with their parents are included, godly parents ought not to doubt the election
and salvation of their children whom God calls out of this life in infancy." Canons of Dort,
1.17 (*Our Faith*, 123).
18. Westminster Confession, 10.3 (Dennison, *Reformed Confessions*, 4:247; emphasis
added).

reality. The Belgic Confession puts it beautifully: "Truly, Christ has shed his blood no less for washing the little children of believers than he did for adults. Therefore they ought to receive the sign and sacrament of what Christ has done for them."[19] The Heidelberg Catechism similarly states that infants, no less than adults, "are promised deliverance from sin through Christ's blood and the Holy Spirit who produces faith."[20]

Wider Theological Considerations

All of this reminds us of the very important, wider theological point noted above. In Reformed theology, the sacrament of membership in the covenant community points first and foremost to what God has done and is doing. It is the sign and seal of God's promises, the covenant relationship he has established with us, and his unshakeable faithfulness to that covenant *before* it is the sign and seal of our personal response.

In effect, infant baptism sets before us a visible demonstration and enactment of how God works with all of us. It testifies to the truth that before any of us is ever aware of it, and in ways we can never fully grasp, God is at work in and for us, and it is always and only God's own leading and gift that enable us to appropriate that for ourselves. In technical terms, infant baptism is a witness to the *prevenient grace* of God; that is, God's grace always precedes our response. Infant baptism is, therefore, nothing less than the outward sign of the truth at the heart of the gospel: "God proves his love for us in that while we were sinners Christ died for us" (Rom. 5:8). The following quote from a French Reformed liturgy for infant baptism is a powerful expression of this truth: "Little child, for you Jesus Christ has come, he has fought, he has suffered. For you he has entered into the shadow of Gethsemane and the horror of Calvary. For you he uttered the cry, 'It is finished.' For you he rose from the dead and ascended into heaven and there he intercedes. For you, little child, although you do not know it yet. But in this way, the word of the gospel becomes true: we love him because he first loved us."[21] Here we see in a nutshell one of the major theological reasons why the Reformed, and many other Protestants, continue to baptize infants. Infant baptism and baptism upon profession of faith each particularly hold forth one side of the reality

19. Belgic Confession, 34 (*Our Faith*, 61).
20. This is part of the answer to Heidelberg Catechism Q and A 74, "Should Infants Also Be Baptized?" (*Our Faith*, 94).
21. An adapted and illustrated version of the full liturgy from which this quotation comes has been turned into a board book for very young children: Steenwyk and Witvliet, *At Your Baptism*.

of God's grace and our response to it. The prevenience of God's grace is emphasized in infant baptism, and in adult baptism we see the importance of personal response. Even so, it is still *the prior love and work of God* for and in us that leads an adult to profess faith in Christ.

Properly understood, both forms of baptism, therefore, signify the same thing. Whether it is for an infant or an adult, baptism is first and foremost about what God has done for us, and only secondarily about our response. While the danger in infant baptism is that it might seem to downgrade the response of faith, the danger in believers' baptism is that it looks like a ratification of someone's "decision for Christ" rather than a testimony to God's promises and God's work. There is also the danger of seeing faith as something we can come to all on our own, and as that which *effects* (accomplishes) our salvation. We will explore the relationship between faith and salvation in the following chapter, but for the moment, we will simply state that faith is not what saves us. *Christ* saves us, and faith is the means of appropriating the salvation that Christ has won. For these reasons, we might argue that infant baptism, far from sending the wrong message about the relationship between faith, baptism, and salvation, actually shows forth exactly the *right* relationship between faith, baptism, and salvation.[22]

Two Approaches Within the Reformed Tradition

As we've seen, infant baptism has been very important within our Reformed tradition from the outset, but there are many regular churchgoers today, and also some very prominent pastors and writers, who identify themselves as Reformed Baptists. That is, they consider themselves to be theologically Reformed, but they do not practice infant baptism in their churches and often do not recognize infant baptisms from other churches. This means that they will often "rebaptize" adults who were baptized as infants when they reach the point in their lives when they are ready to confess their personal faith in Jesus Christ as Lord and Savior.[23] When it comes to the early history of our tradition, the idea of being a Reformed Baptist is actually an oxymoron, a contradiction in terms. As we saw above, in the early Reformation era the Reformed and the Anabaptists were utterly opposed to each other. It is during the later seventeenth century, with the birth and growth of the English Baptist

---

22. Brownson, *Promise of Baptism*, 134.

23. As noted above with regard to the sixteenth-century Anabaptists, they would not call it "rebaptism," since their understanding is that infant baptism is not a legitimate Christian baptism in the first place.

movement, that we see the roots of the label *Reformed Baptist*. What this usually signifies is that someone has a strongly Reformed understanding of the doctrine of salvation, even though they reject infant baptism. In particular, it tends to signify that someone upholds an approach to election encapsulated in the acronym TULIP.[24] As we indicated in chapter 1, TULIP is a somewhat problematic summary of the seventeenth-century Reformed explanation of some disputed points about election in the Canons of Dort. The letters stand for *Total Depravity, Unconditional Election, Limited Atonement, Irresistible Grace*, and *Perseverance of the Saints*. We will examine some issues related to TULIP and the doctrine of election in the next chapter, but for the moment, the desire of many to identify as Reformed Baptists helps illustrate a wider tension in the question of what it means to be Reformed. Does refusing to practice infant baptism mean that you have to surrender your "Reformed card," even if you hold to a Reformed understanding of election, for example? Can we narrow down what it means to be truly Reformed to one doctrine, and then selectively opt out of other significant theological emphases in our tradition? Or does being Reformed mean recognizing and dwelling within a tradition that has something distinctive to say about a broad range of theological topics?

In this book we particularly want to resist narrowing down "Reformedness" to an approach to the doctrine of election, and we want to be clear that, from the very beginning, the Reformed have put a high priority on covenant infant baptism. But it is also important to acknowledge that there are two quite distinct streams when it comes to a Reformed understanding of the sacraments in general, and these two approaches have influenced disagreements within the Reformed family about whether or not there should be leeway with regard to the practice of infant baptism. Those who incline toward understanding baptism and the Lord's Supper as ordinances rather than sacraments will emphasize our actions toward God in these practices. In particular, they will see baptism as primarily about our own action of obedience to the Lord's "ordained" command. In this view, the central element of baptism and the Lord's Supper is not a gift to be received but a declaration of faith in Jesus Christ as Lord and Savior. They will often incline toward a credobaptist position today.[25] Those who see the primary movement of the sacraments as being *gifts* from God to us will consider that God is the primary agent in both baptism and the Lord's Supper, with our actions being a response to the grace that God

24. While the acronym TULIP is relatively recent, holding to a credobaptist position while strongly affirming a Reformed account of election and salvation stretches back to at least the seventeenth century, as witnessed by the London Baptist Confession of 1689.

25. It is important to note that while, historically, this "ordinance" view owes much to Huldrych Zwingli, he strongly defended infant baptism and vigorously persecuted those who did not.

holds out to us and the promises that God seals to us in the sacraments. They are much more likely to hold strongly to the importance of pedobaptism.

Some Pastoral Issues

It is very important to recognize, though, that whether or not to practice infant baptism is not simply a matter for discussion and debate over coffee. Many Reformed pastors and churches actively struggle with questions around baptism in the context of significant personal and pastoral issues. For example, some within or joining our Reformed churches actually hold a functional theology of baptism that is closer to the Roman Catholic understanding. Each of us is aware of instances in which parents have sought baptism for their infants on the assumption that this will somehow guarantee (or at least further) their salvation. Heartbreakingly, this often arises when parents ask their pastor to baptize their dead newborn in the hospital. As we noted above, a number of our confessions specifically address the issue of those who die in infancy (and this is usually taken to encompass miscarriage or stillbirth). A Reformed pastor who wishes to hold strongly to our historic tradition will not baptize the dead child but, instead, will gently offer the assurance that parents are often seeking when they ask for this: a funeral liturgy for the infant with the full assurance that this child of the covenant is beloved of the Lord, and now with the Lord, through the saving work of Christ.

Most of the time, however, people within or joining our churches are more aware of and comfortable with a credobaptist understanding. So parents might well ask their Reformed pastor for an infant dedication rather than baptism, explaining that they would like their children to make their own decisions about Jesus when they grow up and to be baptized then.[26] If we are to be consistent with our historic witness, we will not offer anything in worship that creates confusion about how we understand the meaning and purpose of baptism. To borrow Brownson's words, "From the perspective of Reformed theology, we do not *dedicate* our children in baptism; rather, God *claims and marks* them."[27]

This issue doesn't just concern parents and their babies, however. Some who have been baptized as infants, then drifted away or didn't sense enough personal faith to make a public profession in their teenage years, later come

26. As Brownson points out, the implicit theology of infant dedication is actually as discordant with a thoroughgoing credobaptist position as with a pedobaptist position. Brownson, *Promise of Baptism*, 202–3.

27. Brownson, *Promise of Baptism*, 203. For a scriptural and pastoral exploration of issues related to infant dedication versus infant baptism, see Brownson, *Promise of Baptism*, chap. 29.

to a vibrant and living faith. At that point they might well express a desire to mark their newfound personal relationship with Jesus through "a baptism that is actually meaningful to me, and that I choose to do, rather than it being chosen for me and done to me without me knowing anything about it," as one of my (Suzanne's) friends put it. Or perhaps someone joins a Reformed church after belonging to what they have come to think of as a false church, with teachings and practices that they now consider to be completely wrong. In light of their new understanding, they want to repudiate everything about their previous church, including what they no longer consider to have been a true Christian baptism.

A pastor will always want to wholeheartedly honor and affirm the deep transformation that someone has experienced and their passionate response to the work of God in their lives. But Reformed pastors ought not to rebaptize anyone who has already received water baptism in the triune name by someone duly authorized to perform it. This is very often spelled out in the polity of Reformed denominations.[28] This is because the validity of baptism does not depend on the moral, theological, or spiritual worth of the person performing the baptism but on God and God's promises. This is another instance in which it is extremely important to recognize that God is the primary agent in the sacraments, not the person enacting the liturgy or the person receiving the sacraments. With regard specifically to baptism, Scripture is clear that there is only one Christian baptism, as the sign of our adoption into the one household of God. All Christians are members of the one body of Christ, which is the communion across time and space of all those who profess Jesus Christ as Lord. This is true even though our divisions across denominational lines run deep, and our personal experiences of those divisions are often painful.

Just as the validity of baptism does not rest on the qualities of the person enacting it, neither does the validity of baptism depend on our response. It depends on the promise of God, and that promise is still valid even if, for a period of time, it is not fulfilled in the life of someone who has been baptized.[29]

---

28. The Presbyterian Church (U.S.A.), or PC(USA), and the Christian Reformed Church in North America (CRC) provide representative examples of this. In its *Book of Order*, the PC(USA) states that baptism is not repeated and that the denomination recognizes all baptisms by other Christian denominations "that are administered with water and performed in the name of the triune God." *Book of Order*, 96. Articles 57 and 58 of the CRC's *Church Order* refer, respectively, to administering baptism upon profession of faith for those who have not been previously baptized and to the validity of baptisms from other denominations if administered "in the name of the triune God, by someone authorized by that denomination." *Church Order*, 112.

29. Brownson, *Promise of Baptism*, 198. Brownson makes the analogy that someone could promise to give another person something if they come to the house to collect it. Even if the person does not come to the house, the promise remains valid. For an account of the key theological and pastoral issues around rebaptism, see Brownson, *Promise of Baptism*, chap. 28.

This is why we do not rebaptize someone who was baptized as an infant after they are led to affirm a personal, living faith in Christ. Baptism, whether of an adult or an infant, is the sign and seal of God's promises and the once-for-all act of initiation into the covenant people. The person who has come to the joyful realization of this later in life has come to appropriate for themselves the reality that has always been theirs. They are a member of God's people and have received God's promises. When this happens, it is indeed a matter for rejoicing! We need wonderful, creative ways to bear witness to and celebrate this beautiful, grace-filled reality in someone's life in the company of the people of God in worship. But the liturgical way of marking this should not be rebaptism, because what has happened in and for them is exactly what their baptism has already signed and sealed to them. They have come to know the reality of what God has accomplished for them, which carries them through the whole of life now and the life to come.

This is also why our Reformed tradition encourages us to reflect on our baptism throughout our lives, even though it was often enacted before we could know, feel, or experience anything of what it signifies. Our baptism is the source of our assurance, far more than our changeable responses to God in the various seasons of our lives. Our baptism points us to the solid ground we have beneath all the vagaries of our feelings and beyond all the ups and downs of our presenting circumstances: We have been signed and sealed with the unshakeable promises of God and what he has done for us, and we have received God's declaration about who we truly are.

4

The Mystery of Election: Predestination and Human Freedom in Reformed Theology

Key Question: Can a Reformed Approach to Election Really Be Good News?

For many people, election is *the* Reformed doctrine. Whether they love or loathe what they have heard about it, election has become the line in the sand for whether or not someone considers themselves to be Reformed, and aspects of Reformed teaching on the doctrine have been a lightning rod of controversy for centuries. Arguments often boil down to battles over the acronym TULIP (mentioned briefly in the previous chapter), and as we indicated in chapter 1, these disputes are often framed in terms of "Calvinism" versus "Arminianism." As we will explore more fully later in this chapter, the acronym TULIP is deeply problematic in a number of ways, and the terms *Calvinism* and *Arminianism* are misleading as well. Neither John Calvin, for whom Calvinism is named, nor Jacobus (James) Arminius, the theologian who gives his name to Arminianism, were alive at the time of the Synod of Dort when these matters were debated, and neither side in these debates fully reflected their views. Moreover, neither theologian's work can be reduced to five points on one topic! From our perspective, it is particularly unfortunate that many books purporting to introduce Reformed theology are nothing more than an exposition of a Reformed understanding of election in general, and TULIP in particular. While election is indeed an important doctrine for the Reformed, it is only one doctrine among many on which our tradition has a contribution to make. One of the reasons we have written this book is to help those within and outside our tradition encounter something of the breadth and depth of Reformed theology, rather than allowing it to be defined by one version of this one doctrine.

We must clarify several issues before we turn to the details of Reformed thinking on election. First, it sometimes seems as though only the Reformed have a doctrine of election. I (Suzanne) have heard any number of comments like, "Oh, I can't possibly be Reformed! I don't believe in election!" Election isn't simply a Reformed idea, though it is true that the Reformed have spilled more theological ink over it than many other traditions. *All* Christians and *all* theological traditions have a doctrine of election. Whether or not they acknowledge it or call it by another name, election is a central scriptural concept. We wouldn't be able to articulate what it means to be the church, or how we understand salvation, if we didn't have some account of the intersection of scriptural themes that make up what becomes known as a doctrine of election.

The Scriptural "Bigger Picture" of Election

A fully orbed scriptural account of election must deal with far more than just the question of how particular individuals are saved. Because of historical controversies, this is where our thoughts tend to go when someone mentions the doctrine of election—and indeed, many people think that individual election is all the doctrine is about. While election does indeed involve individual salvation, it is also about God choosing a people for himself and the purposes he intends to accomplish through them. In particular, we see in Scripture that election is about how the elect people of God are set apart to further God's promises and purposes for all of humanity and the whole of creation.[1]

The elect are not set apart primarily for their own sake, as if God is interested only in his "holy huddle" of chosen people and doesn't care about anyone else. On the contrary, the elect are set apart for an often costly role in the unfolding of God's wider purposes. A repeated theme from the outset

---

1. The broad scriptural account of election that follows owes a great deal to Bauckham, *Bible and Mission*; and McDonald, *Re-Imaging Election*. Two classic texts on the pattern of election in the Old Testament are Levenson, *Death and Resurrection*; and Kaminsky, *Yet I Loved Jacob*. See also van Driel, *Handbook of Election*.

is that the chosen one (whether that is an individual or a people) is set apart for the sake of furthering God's purposes to bless others. We see this pattern, of the one for the sake of the many, from beginning to end in Scripture. We find it, for example, in the foundational text in which God sets apart Abraham (and through him, the people of Israel) in Genesis 12:1–3, with its strong emphasis on bringing blessing beyond Israel to the nations. We see it in individual figures within Israel, such as Joseph. We see the culmination of this pattern in Jesus himself, the Chosen One who opens the way of salvation to all people, Jew and gentile alike.

As we described in the previous chapter, Jesus is both the covenant God come among us in person and the perfect human covenant partner, such that now, to be "in covenant" is to be "in Christ." To be in covenant is to be elect. We come to be "in Christ" and so are members of God's elect covenant people by the Spirit through faith. Those who are elect in Christ—all believers, in other words—are called to step into the same scriptural pattern of election. The church exists to be the one for the sake of the many. We are the community called together by God to further his purposes for the rest of humanity and the rest of creation, and to be the channel of God's blessing beyond ourselves.

This bigger scriptural picture of election helps us see it less as a doctrine of division and more as a summons to fulfill our calling as the people of God in and for the world. It also dispels the idea that the elect have a mandate from God to oppress and even destroy those who are seen as the "rejected" other. This approach has caused horrific harm down the centuries, from shaping the attitude of early settlers in America toward native peoples to the development of apartheid in South Africa. This distortion of election is sometimes at work in our churches today when some Christians effectively categorize those whose beliefs and lifestyles differ from theirs as people who are rejected by God. As we will see later, this is precisely what a properly Reformed doctrine of election forbids us to do.

For the moment, though, we will turn back to one aspect of what we have just described from the overall scriptural picture of election. We said that to be elect and to be in covenant with God are synonymous, and that this happens as we are in Christ by the Spirit through faith. Different ways of understanding how this comes about lie at the heart of the so-called Calvinists vs. Arminians debate. To anticipate something we will explore in more detail later in the chapter, the crucial question at the heart of all these disputes is, How does one come to faith in Christ? For Arminians, faith is something that, by the grace of God, everyone can come to for themselves. For the Reformed, sin has had such a debilitating influence on us that we could not possibly come to faith apart from the efficacious (effective) work of the Holy Spirit in us.

This view of the drastic effect of sin remains a constant, though Reformed theologians have come to different conclusions about aspects of election. The Reformed do not, in fact, have a monolithic understanding of the election of individuals. When people speak about the Reformed doctrine of election, they are usually referring to what they have learned about John Calvin's approach to it (although plenty of Reformed theologians other than Calvin had something to say about election in the sixteenth century), or to the seventeenth-century Reformed formulation of aspects of the doctrine in the Canons of Dort (which is not identical to Calvin's account of the doctrine).

What many of us think we know about a Reformed approach to election has actually been shaped by explanations of the misleading terms of TULIP. In what follows, we will explore some background to the historic Reformed understanding of election and seek to undo some of the damage caused by this unhelpful acronym. In the process we will also debunk some myths, such as that a Reformed approach to election is deterministic, denies freedom of the will, and takes away any impetus to evangelism.

A Reformed Approach to Election: Freedom of the Will and Grace

In order to understand how early theologians in the Reformed tradition came to their understanding of election, we must look behind election to some other key doctrines and to the early church. While the major elements of the historic Reformed tradition's view of election are indeed expressed by Calvin, and later expanded in the Canons of Dort, the roots of this position go back much further. Augustine articulated an almost identical position in his disputes with Pelagius in the fifth century. At their core, these disputes were about the nature of sin and the impact of sin on our capacity to turn to God. This gets us to the heart of questions about election and freedom of the will. Freedom is not about our choice of breakfast cereal, or even the career direction we take, or whom we marry. The crucial issue is whether, left to ourselves, we can turn to God in faith. Pelagius answers, "Yes, of course!" Augustine answers, "No, absolutely not!"[2]

For our purposes, we simply note the basic contours of the debate. Pelagius understood sin primarily in terms of wrong actions. Sin is the choice to do what is contrary to God and God's ways. For Pelagius, every human being is in an intrinsically neutral place before God, with an inherent capacity to choose for or against God. The witness of Scripture in general and the

---

2. For Augustine's understanding of the will and how this develops over the course of his theology, see Kantzer Komline, *Augustine on the Will*.

example of Jesus in particular show us the right path, and we either choose it or we don't. For Augustine, however, sin is best understood as the state of being out of right relationship with God, such that our disposition is to be turned away from God and God's ways. This is the condition that all human beings are born into after the fall, and it means that no one is in a neutral place in relation to God. We are already inclined away from God, or, to use more scriptural language, we are captives to and enslaved by sin (Rom. 6). In turn, this means that every aspect of who we are—including our minds, our desires, and our wills—is distorted. One outcome is that while we are free to choose whatever we want, we are not able to choose the one thing that is most important of all, which is to turn to God in faith and walk in God's ways.

The issue here is not the concept of freedom as such. Augustine would maintain, and Calvin follows him in this, that we all freely make choices. The key is our desires. We freely choose whatever we most want to do, but because sin infects and affects every aspect of us, we do not desire God or the things of God. And so, as Calvin explains, we sin by necessity but not by compulsion.[3] That is, we inevitably sin, but we sin freely. No one is forcing us to sin against our will. That is precisely the problem of sin. Our choices follow our desires, and our desires are turned away from God. As John Thompson puts it, left to ourselves, "our wills have a kind of freedom, but it's the freedom of an addict: an illusion we cling to."[4]

We could summarize this by saying that we all have free will (*liberum arbitrium*) in the sense that we all have the freedom to choose what we most want to do. But what we have under the condition of sin is a captive free will (*liberum arbitrium captivatum*). We freely choose to do whatever we want, but left to our own devices, we incline away from God. And above all, because we are captive to sin, *we cannot turn to God on our own*. Sin means we actually do not want to turn to God, and we cannot do anything for ourselves to change that. What we need is a liberated free will (*liberum arbitrium liberatum*). We need to be set free by God for God. The only way this can happen is by the work of the Holy Spirit within a person, setting them free from bondage to sin and enabling them to turn to God in faith. When the Holy Spirit effects this change of disposition, a person's desires are reoriented. When the Holy Spirit opens our hearts and minds to Christ, we joyfully, freely choose to turn to him. Faith is therefore both God's gift to us and our free response. Our turning to God is both enabled and free, such that faith is the first act of a liberated will.

---

3. Calvin, *Institutes* 2.3.5.
4. Thompson, "Saved Sola Gratia?"

To indwell this approach, however, means that we have to enter into a very different understanding of freedom than we are used to. This is especially the case for those of us brought up in the United States, where we have been taught since early childhood the idea that *freedom* means an unconstrained free choice between alternatives. This concept of freedom is closely associated with the rights of individuals to do whatever they want in pursuit of happiness, over and against any source of authority that might seek to restrict such freedom. Scripturally and theologically, however, freedom is never an individual's neutral poise between a range of alternatives with an uninhibited right to choose between them. Instead, Scripture indicates that true human freedom is freedom *from* sin and freedom *for* God. We are truly and fully free only when we are living in perfect love and obedience to God, and that will be the case only when we are with the Lord in glory, fully and finally redeemed, when all sin and causes of sin have been removed. Then, we will finally and unshakably realize the fullness of what we were created to be and to do: "to glorify God and enjoy him forever," to borrow from the opening question and answer of the Westminster Shorter Catechism.[5]

For the Reformed, then, election is all about God's extraordinary *grace*. For Calvin, the mystery and wonder of election is that God has chosen to come in Christ and to give the gift of faith through the Holy Spirit so that anyone can be saved, since all are equally deserving of God's condemnation for their sin. Election is unconditional; it never depends on any particular virtue or quality in those whom God chooses, and there is also no synergism in salvation. That is, we human beings do not have a co-decisive role in our salvation alongside God, as if God has played his part in Christ and now we need to add our faith into the equation in order to bring about our salvation. Rather, from beginning to end, salvation is God's work, and it is by God's grace and gift.

We therefore need to be careful about how we understand a popular slogan that summarizes the Reformation message in this regard. We most often hear that we are justified (or saved) by faith. This is the shortened version. The full version is that we are justified *by grace* through faith. Martin Luther was at pains to clarify this point. Faith is not something we can muster up for ourselves, which we then add to what Christ has done in order to be saved. That would turn faith into another kind of human "work" and would make the decisive factor in salvation our own. Instead, for Luther, as for Calvin and the Reformed tradition, faith itself is the gracious gift of God. It is not our faith that saves us as such. Rather, our faith is the means by which we *receive*

---

5. Westminster Shorter Catechism, Q and A 1 (Dennison, *Reformed Confessions*, 4:353).

the salvation of God in Christ. This is a point that our historic Reformed standards are very careful to articulate. For example, Article 22 of the Belgic Confession makes clear that it is the Holy Spirit who "kindles in our hearts a true faith" and, after clarifying that we are justified by Christ's work received in faith and not by any works of our own, it explicitly states: "However, we do not mean, properly speaking, that it is faith itself that justifies us—for faith is only the instrument by which we embrace the righteousness of Christ . . . [and] that keeps us in communion with him and with all his benefits."[6] For the Reformed, salvation is always and only by God's grace, from the eternal electing decision of God through the whole scriptural story of God's dealings with his people, to the saving work of the incarnate Son for us and the saving work of the Holy Spirit in us, to the consummation of salvation at the eschaton.

This insistence on election and salvation as entirely God's gift of grace leads straight to a conundrum. If it is possible to turn to God in faith only by the personal enabling of the Holy Spirit, and some people do not come to faith, it seems that God has chosen to save some people and not others. Calvin's account of this aspect of election is one of the few places in which he differs from Augustine. For Augustine, God actively wills to elect some to salvation but simply "passes over" the rest, leaving them to the consequences of their sin. This is an "asymmetrical" understanding of God's electing decision: The weight rests primarily on God's electing decision to save, with the negative corollary being that he passes over the rest. Calvin, however, took a "symmetrical" approach to the double decree, affirming that God is equally active in choosing to reject as well as to elect. The historic Reformed confessions, such as the Belgic Confession, the Canons of Dort, and the Westminster Standards, prefer to follow Augustine's asymmetrical approach.

Unsurprisingly, the Reformed have never been entirely comfortable with this. Calvin speaks of the reason God chooses some and not others as an impenetrable mystery. The Canons of Dort mention reprobation, but they do so relatively briefly, and with an abundance of pastoral caution.[7] This shadow side of the election of grace has led some Reformed theologians to see if different conclusions than those articulated by Calvin and the Canons might be reached from the same foundational premises. We'll return to this later.

---

6. For the relationship between faith and salvation, see Heidelberg Catechism, Q and A 61 (*Our Faith*, 90). For faith as the work of the Holy Spirit in us, see Heidelberg Catechism, Q and A 65 (*Our Faith*, 91).

7. See Canons of Dort, 1.6, 15 (*Our Faith*, 119–20); followed by immediate pastoral reassurance in 1.16 (*Our Faith*, 122).

The Canons of Dort

For now, we turn in more detail to the best-known articulation of the historic Reformed position on these issues, the Canons of Dort. Alongside the Canons, we also need to deal with the acronym TULIP, which has played such an outsized role in both the positive and negative appropriations of the historic Reformed understanding of election. It is very important for a proper understanding of the Canons in their own time, and for us now, to have a sense of their historical background and context. The Canons do not exist as a doctrinal statement produced in abstract isolation, even though they (and the acronym TULIP) are often thought of and used that way today.[8] In fact, the Canons were drafted as a response to a conversation between two groups, most often called the Calvinists and the Arminians.

As we noted above, although the two positions have ended up being referred to as Calvinism and Arminianism, both John Calvin (1509–64) and Jacobus Arminius (1560–1609) were long dead by the time the Synod of Dort met in 1618–19, and, self-evidently, neither engaged theologically with the other, since Arminius was only about four years old when Calvin died. Likewise, neither invented the ideas about election now associated with their names. As we have already indicated, with some minor differences, Calvin shares Augustine's understanding of election.[9] Similarly, the core of what comes to be known as Arminianism stretches back to the early church, through the medieval period, and into Reformation-era Roman Catholicism and also other branches of Protestantism (including Lutheranism, after Martin Luther's death in 1546).

By the seventeenth century, the vast majority of those who identified themselves as Reformed held to a doctrine of election that was substantially in accord with Calvin's and with further developments by other theologians within the tradition, such as Theodore Beza. Within the Dutch Reformed communion, however, Arminius argued that other interpretations of the Belgic Confession's statement about election were possible and would therefore be consistent with the Reformed tradition. After Arminius died, a number of his followers drafted a detailed document stating their objections to aspects of the majority Reformed understanding of election. They presented this five-point "Remonstrance" to the States General of the Netherlands (the Dutch government) in 1610. Major political figures became involved on both sides,

---

8. Much of what follows draws significantly from McDonald, "Canons of Dordt," reprinted here by kind permission of the *Calvin Theological Journal*. See also Muller, "How Many Points?"; Muller, *Calvin and the Reformed Tradition*, 51–69; and Billings, "The Problem with TULIP."

9. Thomas Aquinas also has a fundamentally Augustinian understanding of election. Levering, *Predestination*, 75–83. In the generation before Calvin, Luther forcefully maintained an Augustinian view of election, especially in his treatise *The Bondage of the Will*.

and the situation escalated to such an extent that these disputes over election threatened the stability of the Dutch Republic. Difficult as it is for most of us to believe in our current contexts, the close binding of church and state in the seventeenth century meant that once key political leaders took sides in this ostensibly theological dispute, the Netherlands began to slide toward civil war. So in 1617 the government called for a church council, the Synod of Dort. The synod met from 1618 to 1619, and the Canons of Dort are one of several important outcomes of the gathering.[10]

It cannot be emphasized too strongly that the Canons only exist in order to respond to the very specific and limited points raised in the Arminian Remonstrance. They are an entirely reactive document, and even their structure reflects their very circumscribed, polemical intent. The only reason the Canons have five points of doctrine (and, therefore, the only reason we have the so-called five points of Calvinism[11]) is because there were five points of Arminianism first.

As we pointed out in chapter 1, this means that the Canons of Dort are *not* a summary statement of what it means to be Reformed. The writers of the Canons themselves would be the first to correct that misunderstanding. They would send us instead to the Belgic Confession, which offers a Reformed understanding of all the key doctrines of the faith. The Canons of Dort are the equivalent of an explanatory footnote to Article 16 of the Belgic Confession, which is its brief statement on the doctrine of election. The very limited aims of the Canons also mean that they are not even intended to be a comprehensive statement of a Reformed doctrine of election. Calvin and other sixteenth- and seventeenth-century Reformed theologians had a great deal more to say about election than the issues raised by the five disputed points dealt with in the Canons.

The Theology of the Canons of Dort and Problematizing TULIP

This is all extremely important as we turn to the well-known but misleading acronym TULIP.[12] In addition to distorting the theology of the Canons,

---

10. The Synod of Dort also initiated the process of providing an official Dutch translation of the Bible and produced an official church order. It is also noteworthy that the Canons of Dort are the only one of the historic Reformed confessional standards put together and ratified by an international gathering of delegates.

11. As noted in chap. 1, the phrase *five points of Calvinism* is inaccurate and unhelpful in almost every way. It implies that election is the center of Calvin's theology—which it is not—and that everything about Calvin's theology can be reduced to a few points about this one doctrine. Moreover, many other Reformed theologians contributed to the Reformed understanding of election in the years leading up to the Synod of Dort.

12. See Stewart, *Ten Myths*, esp. chap. 3, for a history of the acronym and an account of some of its inadequacies.

TULIP has often been used in ways that are absolutely contrary to the intention of the Canons, as if these five points did indeed encapsulate everything that needs to be said about a Reformed doctrine of election, and as if they were a summary of the whole of what it means to be Reformed. The acronym itself seems to surface only in the early twentieth century—and, of course, it only works in English. Moreover, if we were to follow the actual order of the points as they are found in the Canons—dictated by the order of the five points of the Arminian Remonstrance—that would leave us with ULTIP. While this might seem a trivial objection, it gets to a more important matter. Just as the acronym distorts the structure of the Canons (and disguises the context of the Canons as occasioned by and structured around the Arminian Remonstrance), so the terms of TULIP, and what are very often bad explanations of them, distort the theology of the Canons.

A brief account of the terms of TULIP (in the order of the Canons themselves, rather than the spelling of the flower) will help us see this distortion at work and give a less misleading account of what the Canons teach. Through this brief sketch, we hope to offer a fairer account of the theology of the Canons than explanations of TULIP generally provide. We also hope to show a fairer account of the theology of the Arminian position to which the Canons object, since the Arminian position, too, is often distorted by Reformed advocates of TULIP to draw deeper lines of division between the two approaches.

The first point of doctrine in the Canons deals, in part, with the U of TULIP. This stands for *Unconditional Election*, and the first point of doctrine does indeed emphasize this theme. As Scripture makes clear, God's election has nothing to do with any merit or qualities in the ones God chooses. As Deuteronomy 7:7 indicates, God did not choose Israel because it was a numerous or powerful people. As Paul sums up in Romans 9:11–12, God's election does not depend on anything about us, but simply on God's choice and call. In terms of individual salvation, all are equally lost in sin, so that it is by grace alone that we are saved through faith, and faith is the gift of God.[13] The Canons name this in response to the first point of the Arminian Remonstrance, which argues that election is in fact conditional: God elects those whom he *foreknows* will come to faith. For the Reformed, however, as we noted above, to turn to

---

13. The focus here is on how the Reformed tradition understands the relationship between election and faith, in contrast to the Arminian position. It is important to note, however, that while the Reformed hold strongly to election as unconditional, the equally strong expectation is that saving faith will bear fruit in someone's life. We will reflect on aspects of the Reformed understanding of the relationship between faith and works in chap. 6, which discusses the relationship between justification and sanctification, and when we consider the last judgment in chap. 7.

God in faith is impossible without the personal and effectual enabling of the Holy Spirit. For the Reformed, therefore, election is the *source* of faith. For the Arminians, foreseen faith is the condition of election.

The second main point of doctrine in the Canons is about the salvation won by Christ. This is the notorious L of TULIP, so-called *Limited Atonement*. We earnestly wish that this term could be erased from everyone's theological vocabulary because it is so misleading as to be downright wrong. The Canons do not use these words (in fact, they do not use any of the TULIP terms specifically), and they do not teach what this phrase straightforwardly seems to imply. For the Canons, there is nothing deficient or limited about Christ's atoning work on the cross.

The Canons affirm a medieval (Roman Catholic) axiom to make sure that we grasp this point. Christ's death is *sufficient for all, but efficient (actually enacted) only for some*.[14] In other words, Christ's atoning work on the cross is enough to atone for all sins, past, present, and yet to come. It is the saving *efficacy* of the atonement that is limited. Both sides at the Synod of Dort agreed that not everyone will be saved. Both sides also agreed that the efficacy of Christ's saving death is limited to those who turn to him in faith. Two crucial questions get us to the heart of the differences between the two positions. The first we have already mentioned: How does someone come to faith? The second is, What does Christ's death mean for salvation?

To address this second question, the core of the second point in the Arminian Remonstrance is that Christ obtains universal *potential* redemption, which becomes *actual* if a person meets the condition of faith from their side. For the Canons, however, Christ's death does not simply hold out the possibility of salvation. That would make the decisive aspect of salvation our act, not Christ's. Instead, Christ's atoning work on the cross *achieves* salvation for particular people—for all whom God intends to save. As we indicated above, our faith is not an act that contributes to our salvation. Rather, the gift of faith is how we appropriate the salvation won for us by Christ. If we were to suggest another short phrase to replace *limited atonement*, then *particular redemption* might be a better way to capture what the Canons have to say on this question. Christ's death fully accomplishes the salvation of particular people.

To summarize the contrasting positions in these first two points: On the one hand, the Arminian Remonstrant position says that someone's election is conditional on God foreknowing that they will come to faith, and that Christ's death on the cross opens up the possibility of salvation, which is

---

14. See esp. Canons of Dort, 2.3, 8 (*Our Faith*, 126–27).

actualized by faith. On the other hand, the Canons say that election is not based on anything about us, and in particular not on foreseen faith, but on God's eternal sovereign choice to save some in Christ. Their sins are in actuality atoned for by Christ's death on the cross, and they appropriate that by God's gift of faith.

Both sides maintain that salvation is by grace through faith in Christ. The differences between them come down to the main focus of the next two points of doctrine and to the other crucial question we mentioned earlier: How does someone come to faith? Or, What is the source of faith? The decisive issue is whether we have the capacity to turn to Christ in faith without the personal and effectual enabling of the Holy Spirit.

It is very important to understand that both sides maintain that salvation is *by grace* through faith. It is all too easy for those of us who are Reformed to caricature the Arminian position on this. The third point of the Arminian Remonstrance makes absolutely clear that, because of sin, no human being could turn to God apart from the work of the Holy Spirit. By the grace of God, the Holy Spirit neutralizes the effects of sin for everyone in this one key respect, such that every person is able to choose for God in faith or not. This insistence that without God's grace and the work of the Spirit no one could turn to God in faith is the crucial distinction between the Arminian understanding of election and the position of Pelagius, which we mentioned earlier. From an Arminian perspective, someone's coming to faith is both graced and autonomous. It is only by the grace of God that someone could turn to God, and that grace has been extended to all, such that it is now up to each individual to choose autonomously for God in faith or not. In this context, the term *autonomous* signifies that the Holy Spirit has no further role in someone coming to faith than to give all people the capacity to turn to God if they so choose. Following from this, the fourth point of the Arminian Remonstrance is that some people will choose for themselves to do that, and some people will not. The Spirit's work to open up the possibility of faith for all can be and is resisted.

These issues are addressed in the combined third and fourth points of doctrine in the Canons (the T and I of the disordered TULIP). Like *Limited Atonement*, the terms *Total Depravity* and *Irresistible Grace* are so misleading that they can easily be thought to signify the opposite of what the Canons actually teach. *Total Depravity* does not mean that everyone is utterly wicked all the time. It also does not mean that nonbelievers are incapable of doing what is outwardly good and morally virtuous.[15] The core of this aspect of the

---

15. For the moral capacities of all people after the fall, see Canons of Dort, 3/4.4 (*Our Faith*, 130).

Canons is that our whole selves are affected by sin: our minds, wills, desires, emotions—everything about us. And the one key reason the Canons emphasize this is to answer that one central question that divides the Reformed position from Arminianism: How do people come to faith? The Canons insist that sin continues to affect all human beings such that we are not left by God's grace in a neutral place where we can then choose for God autonomously. Instead, the Canons insist that we need the personal, efficacious work of the Spirit in us to enable us to turn to God in faith.

This leads to the fourth point of the combined third and fourth points in the Canons, popularly known as *Irresistible Grace*. This unhelpful term is often taken to imply that we lose our freedom, as if the work of the Holy Spirit in us means that our wills are overridden by God in a divine takeover, and we have no choice in the matter. This is the last thing that the Canons imply. When the Holy Spirit enables someone to turn to God in faith, the Canons specifically state that "this divine grace of regeneration does not act in people as if they were blocks and stones; nor does it abolish the will and its properties or coerce a reluctant will by force, but spiritually revives, heals, reforms it."[16] The Holy Spirit does not trample on our freedom. The Holy Spirit sets us free from the bondage to sin, enabling us to desire faith, which without the Spirit's work we would not want.

Rather than *Irresistible Grace*, a better way to express what is meant by this point of doctrine in the Canons might be "the effectual call of the Spirit." This point is not meant to address all the ways the Spirit calls and prompts us in our lives, as if the Canons suggest the elect never resist the Spirit in any aspect of their lives. Of course they do, all the time, and the Canons testify to that reality. As ever, the Canons are making only a very specific and limited point in response to the Remonstrance, and the focus here is once again that no one can come to faith without the gift of the effectual work of the Spirit in them.

To clarify this concept, a contrast is often made between the *general call* of the Spirit—through preaching or the reading of Scripture, for example—and the *effectual call*, by which the Spirit opens someone's heart and mind to Christ such that they truly encounter the living Lord. Two people may hear the same testimony about Christ, and one is convicted while the other remains indifferent. Two people may read one of the Gospels, and one discovers in it the truth about God and themselves while the other finds it a mildly interesting account of an important figure from ancient times. Both have received the general call of the gospel, but the one who responds in faith has also received the effectual call of the Spirit, which enables them to receive the gospel.

---

16. Canons of Dort, 3/4.16 (*Our Faith*, 133).

This also helps us to see why, far from curtailing evangelism, the historic Reformed approach to election is a great impetus to and encouragement for evangelism. We have the assurance that all whom God has chosen to save will hear and respond in God's good time, and we have the encouragement that God has chosen to use various means to call the elect to the realization of their salvation. Calvin insists that we are to proclaim Christ to all people in all circumstances. Of all the historic Reformed standards, it is actually the Canons of Dort that explicitly encourages evangelism, with the powerful statement that we are to proclaim the gospel "without differentiation or discrimination to all nations and people."[17]

By the grace of God, any one of us might be the instrument through whom the Holy Spirit awakens someone to the reality of their election in Christ. This sets us free from performance anxiety when it comes to sharing the gospel and the fearful burden of wondering whether our inadequate words or imperfect actions are the reason someone has not come to Christ. The efficacy of the gospel call depends solely on the work of the Spirit within someone, not on our ability to be eloquent or persuasive, or on whether we have the "right" degrees or training. All of us are called to share the gospel—always being ready, as 1 Peter 3:15 puts it, to give an account of the hope that we have in Christ—but whether or not someone receives the gospel is not up to us.

The fifth and final point of doctrine in the Canons is the P of TULIP—*Perseverance of the Saints*. It is a response to the fifth point of the Arminian Remonstrance. For the Arminians, as with the decision of faith, where all human beings are in the graced position of being able to choose for faith or not, so also someone will either persevere in faith to the end or not, without the particular preserving work of the Holy Spirit. It will come as no surprise by now that the Canons insist that, left to ourselves, without the particular enabling work of the Spirit, we could never continue in faith—just as, left to ourselves, without the particular enabling work of the Spirit, we could never come to faith in the first place. Unless God preserves us, we could never persevere to the end. This is not presented as an encouragement to complacency, as if it does not matter how the elect live their lives. Rather, the idea of the perseverance of the saints is meant to be a source of comfort and assurance in difficult times. The Canons are as clear as the rest of the Reformed tradition that saving faith will bear fruit in the Holy Spirit's work of continuing to conform us to Christ. As Ephesians 1:4 puts it, the elect are chosen in Christ in order that they should be holy and blameless before him.

---

17. Canons of Dort, 2.5 (*Our Faith*, 127).

Later Reformed Thinking on Election: The Canons of Dort Do Not Have the Last Word!

As we noted earlier, all of the very robust and varied conversations about the doctrine of election within the Reformed tradition are clear that the core claim of the Canons against the Arminian position is correct. Left to ourselves, without the personal and effectual work of the Holy Spirit in us, no one could turn to God in faith. This leads to the difficult corollary mentioned above: If God gives the Spirit in this way only to some, then it seems that God has chosen to save some people but not others. This is the "double" nature of predestination. It becomes a major point of resistance within our tradition, and the catalyst for many of the later attempts to rework the doctrine. In response, a significant minority of Reformed theologians incline toward universal salvation in Christ, as a way of holding on to the sovereignty of God in salvation while avoiding the implication that God has denied the possibility of salvation to some people.

For example, in the nineteenth century, Friedrich Schleiermacher, who is sometimes called the "father of liberal theology," strongly defended core Reformed tenets on election in his contribution to debates on election in his time, and in his more detailed exposition of the doctrine in *Christian Faith*.[18] In his writings he holds to the classic Reformed insistence that election is not based on God's foreknowledge of faith, but rather that God's election is the source of faith. He is clear that it is only by the effectual work of the Holy Spirit in them that anyone can turn to God, and that God enables some to respond to the gospel during their lives and not others. However, he goes on to reject the historic Reformed tradition's interpretation of double predestination by anticipating the salvation of all human beings due to the continuing saving work of God after death for those who have not heard or accepted the gospel in this life.[19]

It is Karl Barth in the twentieth century, however, who offers the most important rearticulation of a Reformed doctrine of election since the sixteenth and seventeenth centuries. His monumental christological reorientation of election in his *Church Dogmatics* remains a milestone in the history of theology, and it continues to be a focal point of Reformed and wider reflection on the topic.[20]

---

18. See Schleiermacher's 1819 treatise, *On the Doctrine of Election, with Special Reference to the Aphorisms of Dr. Bretschneider*. Schleiermacher's full account of election can be found in Schleiermacher, *Christian Faith*, §§116–20.

19. For a fuller summary of Schleiermacher's doctrine of election, see McDonald, "Calvin's Theology of Election." For a much more detailed account, see Gockel, *Barth and Schleiermacher*.

20. For his mature doctrine of election, see Barth, *Church Dogmatics*, II/2. For a more detailed summary of Barth's mature doctrine of election, see McDonald, *Re-Imaging Election*, chap. 2.

Contrary to the historic Reformed understanding, Barth insists that the eternal electing decree of God is not the decision to save some individuals and not others, but rather God's decision to come among us to save in Jesus Christ. For Barth, the whole of election is concentrated in Christ. He is both the Electing God in person and also the one elect human being—and the purpose of his election is to bear our rejection. In Christ, God has chosen to take the negative side of predestination onto himself, such that any "No" that any human being could utter to God is taken on and taken away by Christ. As a consequence, the only word of God to human beings is now "Yes." In this way, Barth sees election as "the sum of the gospel." It cannot be a "mixed message of joy and terror, salvation and damnation." Instead, it is "the gospel *in nuce* [in a nutshell] . . . the very essence of all good news" because it is the ultimate expression of God-for-us.[21]

For Barth, unlike the historic Reformed tradition, all human beings are included in the election of Christ. Nevertheless, he continues to maintain the foundational Reformed understanding that no one can turn to Christ in faith without the effectual enabling of the Spirit. For Barth, some recognize the reality that all are elect in Christ and proclaim that reality to the rest of humanity. Those who do not hear the gospel, or who reject it, are only "apparently rejected."[22] They are not yet living in accordance with their real identity as elect in Christ, those whose condemnation has been borne by him. While Barth's account of the doctrine would therefore seem to lead to universal salvation, he rejects dogmatic universalism (the unequivocal assertion that all will be saved). He maintains that the rejection of some still remains an "impossible possibility" and sees universal salvation in Christ as something for which we may hope.[23]

Some Reformed "Bottom Lines" on Election

This very brief survey of two major alternative formulations of the doctrine of election within the Reformed tradition indicates that, as we noted earlier, there is no such thing as *the* Reformed doctrine of election. Nevertheless, there are some central themes that characterize all Reformed engagements with the doctrine. These can be summed up in four foundational affirmations with which all Reformed theologians down the centuries could agree:

21. Barth, *Church Dogmatics*, II/2, 13–14.
22. Barth, *Church Dogmatics*, II/2, 351.
23. For his refusal to accept dogmatic universalism, see Barth, *Church Dogmatics*, II/2, 417–18. Not surprisingly, the question of whether this is consistent with his account of election has been a matter of vigorous debate. For a wider critique of Barth's account of election, see McDonald, *Re-Imaging Election*, chap. 3.

1. *God's electing decision is eternal.* To borrow from the language of Ephesians 1:4, election, however the details are understood, is from before the foundation of the world. This is a point of agreement for all Christians. The next three points are distinctively Augustinian/Reformed.

2. *Election is unconditional.* Election is God's sovereign choice, not based on anything God foresees about those who are chosen.

3. *No one can turn to God without the Spirit's effectual enabling.* Our condition is such that we are incapable of turning to Christ in faith by ourselves. We need the Holy Spirit to personally, specifically, and efficaciously work in us.

4. *Christ's work achieves and secures salvation.* Christ's work achieves salvation, rather than simply creating the possibility of salvation that we then complete by mustering up faith in ourselves and sticking with it. Faith is the gift by which we appropriate the salvation Christ has achieved. When we say that Christ's work secures salvation, we mean that if we are united to Christ by the Spirit through faith, then nothing and no one can snatch us from his hand.

These points capture the essence of what Calvin and the Canons of Dort seek to maintain about individual election while leaving room to explore somewhat different conclusions, such as the two alternatives outlined above. These points are also a reminder that for the whole Reformed tradition, the glory and wonder of election is that it is grounded in the grace and gift of God, from eternity past, through all the twists and turns of the scriptural story and our personal stories, and into eternity future.

Some Pastoral Implications

As invigorating as the debates about views of election might be, we must never lose sight of the pastoral implications of the doctrine. The predominant note sounded in Scripture when it comes to election is that of assurance. We need to remind ourselves of this because the Reformed approach to election has sometimes led to deep spiritual anxiety, as people have wondered whether they—or those whom they love—are elect.

The historic Reformed tradition is deeply aware of this. The Canons have pastoral wisdom for those who are doubtful about their or someone else's election—perhaps because their own faith doesn't seem vibrant enough, or because they have stumbled in their life of faith, or because someone they know seems to have fallen away from the faith completely. The Canons remind us that we will inevitably face times of strength and weakness in our faith, times when we will be more or less overcome by temptations to sin. None of that, they declare, should plunge us into despair for ourselves or for others. None of it necessarily means that we or other people are rejected. The slightest inclination toward God, or desire to live more fully toward God, is already the work of God in us, and God has promised never to snuff out a "smoldering wick" or "break a bruised reed" (Matt. 12:20; cf. Isa. 42:3).[24]

The Canons also wisely urge us not to look primarily to ourselves, our present circumstances, or our feelings to gauge where we stand with God. Instead, we should look to God's promises in Christ and his steadfast mercy. Even when we feel discouraged, or not particularly connected to God at all, we are urged to continue with the ordinary means of grace—reading the Bible, attending worship to hear the Word preached and share in the Lord's Supper—because our standing before God does not depend on our circumstances or our feelings. It is rooted in his eternal promises, his saving work, and his faithfulness.[25]

There are many circumstances in which this kind of pastoral wisdom might apply. For example, all three of us authors know Christian parents who are deeply concerned for their adult children who seem to have walked away from the faith. There is deep comfort in this doctrine that, whatever someone's circumstances are now, they are not the only or last word in their child's salvation story. We can have hope, even for people who have done terrible things or who do not yet believe. Those whom God has eternally chosen he will draw to himself, and they will never stumble so as to ultimately fall. Christ's grip on his elect is far stronger than our wavering hold on him, and those whom the Father has chosen cannot ultimately be snatched from the Son's hand (John 6:37–40; 10:27–30).

We want to close this chapter by drawing out one more related pastoral point that connects to the larger scriptural picture of election that we outlined earlier. It also speaks into the terrible outcomes that ensue when those who consider themselves to be elect see this as a mandate to label others as rejected and to mistreat them accordingly. Election should *never* be expressed in terms of self-importance and superiority over others. One of the major scriptural themes of election is the often costly singling out of the one for the sake of being a channel of blessing to the many. Properly understood, the historic Reformed understanding of election should lead us to exercise the

---

24. See Canons of Dort, 1.16 (*Our Faith*, 122). See also Canons of Dort, 5.1–15 (*Our Faith*, 137–42).

25. Once again, much of this pastoral wisdom is to be found in Canons of Dort, 1.16 (*Our Faith*, 122); and Canons of Dort, 5.1–15 (*Our Faith*, 137–42).

judgment of charity toward everyone. It gives absolutely no one the right to write off another person—or group of people—as rejected by God. That is emphatically not our judgment to make. We cannot know when the Holy Spirit might illumine even the most seemingly unlikely person's heart and mind and set them free to confess Jesus Christ as Lord. As I (Suzanne) sometimes like to tell my students—somewhat provocatively—we are actually called to be "practical universalists." That is to say, while Scripture does suggest that not all people will be saved, we cannot make assumptions about any particular person from what we see of them and their circumstances. We have no right to assume anything other than that any person we encounter is someone whom God may draw to himself in God's good time.

5

Providence and the Problem of Suffering: Trusting the Lord's Rule in Lament and Gratitude

Key Question: Does Reformed Theology Teach Us to See God as a Controlling Tyrant or as a Loving Provider?

The doctrine of providence in Reformed theology is often a point of contention. Some see it as the prime reason to reject the Reformed tradition, while others embrace it wholeheartedly. We may enjoy debating determinism and free will in Shakespeare's plays or exploring themes of freedom and agency in films like *The Matrix* and *Interstellar*. However, for some Christians, Reformed theology appears to entail a theological version of *deterministic fatalism*—the notion that all things, including our every decision (whether our choice of a breakfast cereal, or a spouse, or a career direction), is predetermined by a higher force, whether fate, nature, or God. While we think this is not the case, the charge is serious and one among several we will consider in this chapter. This chapter is ultimately about how we confess God's character and ongoing action in relation to creation as a whole, in its history and future.[1]

---

1. Note that this chapter explores providence, a related-but-distinct doctrine from that of election (which was the focus of chap. 4). While both doctrines relate to God's agency regarding creatures, the doctrine of election focuses on *soteriology*, salvation. The crucial question

In common conversation, the term *providential* can just mean *lucky* or *fortunate*. You may hear someone say, "It was providential that I found a parking space because I was running late!" It may become more concerning, however, when this is extended to more direct references to God's agency: "God gave us the election!" Or perhaps, "God gave you cancer because he knew you would give a good testimony." What does it mean to frame events like these in terms of God's action?

The Reformed doctrine of providence emphasizes God's kingship and sovereignty over all creation. With this approach, the power and presence of the triune God, still active in creation, helps believers to cultivate gratitude in the midst of joy and hope in the midst of affliction, even when our circumstances would lead us to despair. However, critics argue that it fosters complacency, diminishes human responsibility, and makes it difficult to reconcile evil with a benevolent God. They contend that this view risks alienating people from God by claiming that calamities and tragedies are within God's will. They argue that we should say instead that God opposes evil and is with us, battling evil and seeking our rescue. This chapter reflects on how we can confess, in a way that is faithful and fitting in our world filled with both joys and tragedies, that the triune God is faithful in preserving, governing, and ordering creation.

After opening with some basic expositions of the sources and overall role for a doctrine of providence, this chapter considers several significant objections to the doctrine. We seek to both disentangle the doctrine from misunderstandings and address shortcomings about some expressions of the doctrine by Reformed Christians. In all of this, we aim to show how a Reformed way of inhabiting the catholic Christian tradition on providence can be a gift to the church and the world. Drawing on Scripture and the Reformed confessions, the Reformed tradition testifies to God's ongoing providential work and highlights the practice of praying the psalms, including the psalms of lament.

Providence and Scripture's Testimony to God as King

A healthy Christian doctrine of providence is not the result of empirical observation of the world. It does not claim to be part of a universal cultural story that humans tell about the world—as obviously good or evil, or in dominion or freedom. It emerges in response to the testimony of God and his work found in Scripture. Drawing on Scripture, a Reformed theology of providence narrates

---

there is whether or not, left to ourselves, we can turn to God in faith. This is distinct from the doctrine of providence, which is concerned with God's ongoing action in ruling, sustaining, and directing creation to its final end.

the power and presence of the triune God who sustains, governs, and orders all that is not God—that is, all of creation. In the words of the Westminster Shorter Catechism,

> Q. What are God's works of providence?
> A. God's works of providence are his most holy, wise, and powerful preserving, and governing all his creatures; ordering them, and all their actions, to his own glory.[2]

In Scripture, the Lord freely speaks creation into being, yet he does not passively sit back and simply observe the creation like a clockmaker whose handiwork functions independently after being constructed. The Lord continues to be active as the source of life and being, preserving and governing creation toward a particular end.

The Reformed doctrine of providence relates not only to creation but to a God-given analogy presented widely and deeply in the scriptural narrative, God as the true and rightful king of creation:

> Clap your hands, all you peoples;
>   shout to God with loud songs of joy.
> For the LORD, the Most High, is awesome,
>   a great king over all the earth. (Ps. 47:1–2)

The psalmist rejoices in the kingship of God, looking with expectation and, at times, fear to the royal judgments of the Lord. In fact, the declaration that God is the one true king is a theme that extends through the whole biblical canon, from Genesis to Revelation.

God's kingship is also key for trinitarian theology, reflecting the faith of those baptized in the name of the Father, the Son, and the Holy Spirit, confessed in the early church catechisms and creeds. In early baptismal creeds, God's sovereign (i.e., kingly) providence over all, as the creator, was acknowledged with the confession of God as Father. The Apostles' Creed says, "I believe in God, the Father almighty, creator of heaven and earth."[3] And the trinitarian theology of the Nicene Creed clarifies how the work of the Father in creation is the work of the one God, thus fully shared with the Son and the Spirit, for "through [the Son] all things were made," and the Spirit is confessed as "the Lord, the giver of life."[4]

---

2. Westminster Larger Catechism, Q and A 18 (Dennison, *Reformed Confessions*, 4:302).
3. Apostles' Creed (*Our Faith*, 13).
4. Nicene Creed (*Our Faith*, 14, 15).

Thus, there is a trinitarian character to God's providential work. A Christian doctrine of providence should testify not to a vague and impersonal fate but, rather, to creaturely life as given by God the gracious Father, through the beloved Son, by the power of the Spirit. This is of particular importance for Reformed Christians, who care deeply about the doctrine of creation and trinitarian theology. Providence ultimately fits within a larger drama of the triune God's work in creation, such that the goodness of creation is not destroyed but healed and restored through the work of the triune God. As noted in chapter 1, this is a key Reformed theme, expressed succinctly by Herman Bavinck. It is "the reality that the creation of the Father, ruined by sin, is restored in the death of the Son of God and re-created by the grace of the Holy Spirit into a kingdom of God."[5]

The trinitarian character of providence may be a helpful reminder that God is not a tyrant, exercising power from the sky, so to speak. Yet, in catholic Christian theology, this does not in any way downplay the image of God as the one almighty king. As the Athanasian Creed clarifies (in an archaic but illuminating translation), "The Father is almighty, the Son almighty, and the Holy Spirit almighty. And yet they are not three almighties, but one almighty." Of course, to have "three almighties" would be a contradiction in terms. But that is precisely the point: God is eternally Father, Son, and Spirit, and we are incorporated into God's saving life by the Holy Spirit, in Christ, as children of the Father. Yet we still need to speak of God as the king who rules creation. There is one almighty, not three. Providence, then, is a particular example of the triune God's action as almighty king of the whole of creation.

The Meaning and Place of Providence in Reformed Theology

The doctrine of providence is an extension of a Christian doctrine of creation, bearing witness to the ongoing action and presence of the triune God in his good creation that has been corrupted by sin. Even apart from the fall into sin, providence would be a reality, for the God of Scripture freely spoke creation (that which is not God) into being, and creation depends on his ongoing presence and power. For creatures like us, each breath and each day comes to us as a gift.

Yet, both Scripture and our experience remind us that we do not live in paradise. There is evil, alienation, and deep brokenness. How could this be? For the Reformed confessions, a doctrine of providence is not an attempt to solve the problem of evil in a theoretical way, to account for how an almighty

5. Bavinck, *Reformed Dogmatics*, 1:112.

and benevolent God could allow horrendous evil in the world; moreover, it is not an attempt to make God's purposes transparent to us, so that we could understand why a tragedy has taken place.

To rightly confess this mystery is quite different from saying that we fully comprehend it. Sometimes Christians debate providence as if it were a trivia game, where having the most "answers" means you win. If that was what the doctrine of providence was about, the Reformed confessions admit defeat from the outset. After proclaiming God's ongoing governance of the world—and that God is, nevertheless, not the author of sin—the Belgic Confession declares,

> We do not wish to inquire
> with undue curiosity
> into what God does that surpasses human understanding
> and is beyond our ability to comprehend.
>
> But in all humility and reverence
> we adore the just judgments of God,
> which are hidden from us,
> being content to be Christ's disciples,
> so as to learn only what God shows us in the Word,
> without going beyond those limits.[6]

Although the Reformed tradition makes use of human reason and philosophy in the course of its exposition of the doctrine of providence, the overall question that providence addresses is deeply doxological: Given that God is God and we are not, how can we faithfully offer praise to the Lord, the source of all good gifts?

Theological reflection on providence also helps believers recognize the benefits of belonging to the triune God, being incorporated into his household by the Spirit as adopted children of the Father in Christ. Thus, God's ongoing work in creation in our daily lives can reflect various forms of his fatherly care. The opening question and answer of the Heidelberg Catechism addresses this point eloquently. After confessing that the Christian belongs, body and soul, to their "faithful Savior, Jesus Christ," whose cross and resurrection bring forgiveness and new life, the answer continues:

> He also watches over me in such a way
> that not a hair can fall from my head

6. Belgic Confession, 13 (*Our Faith*, 37).

without the will of my Father in heaven;
in fact, all things must work together for my salvation.
Because I belong to him,
Christ, by his Holy Spirit,
assures me of eternal life
and makes me wholeheartedly willing and ready
from now on to live for him.[7]

This passage in the Heidelberg Catechism is both beautiful and, for some hearers, potentially misleading. It does not deny the power of alienation in the world, the work of the world and the devil, and the loss that comes with sickness and death. While it reflects the truth of Romans 8:28, "We know that all things work together for good for those who love God, who are called according to his purpose," it gives a gloss that clarifies: "for my salvation." It does not claim that when terrible things happen to Christians, all will work out for good by our own standards or within this mortal life. The good is salvation, living into our adopted identity as children of the Father, belonging to Christ by the Spirit, who offer our lives back to God as an offering of praise. This is the good that no "hardship, or distress, or persecution, or famine, or nakedness, or peril, or sword" (Rom. 8:35b) can separate us from, the life that comes to us "from the love of God in Christ Jesus our Lord" (Rom. 8:39).

Especially for affluent Christians today, this comfort in life and death can actually be hard to hear. As the Heidelberg Catechism goes on to say, God's providence is

the almighty and ever present power of God
by which God upholds, as with his hand, heaven
and earth and all creatures, and so rules them that leaf and blade,
rain and drought, fruitful and lean years, food and drink,
health and sickness, prosperity and poverty—
all things, in fact, come to us not by chance
but by his fatherly hand.[8]

This may or may not sound reassuring to audiences today. God upholds and rules all of creation so that all things come not by chance but by his fatherly hand. The "all things" includes joys as well as crushing losses. When the Heidelberg Catechism addresses the question of how knowledge of God's creation and providence helps us, it states this explicitly:

7. Heidelberg Catechism, Q and A 1 (*Our Faith*, 69–70).
8. Heidelberg Catechism, Q and A 27 (*Our Faith*, 77–78).

> We can be patient when things go against us,
> thankful when things go well,
> and for the future we can have
> good confidence in our faithful God and Father
> that nothing in creation will separate us from his love.
> For all creatures are so completely in God's hand
> that without his will
> they can neither move nor be moved.[9]

God's love is steady and powerful; no event or power in creation can "separate us from the love of God" (Rom. 8:39). This applies not only when things go well but also when they go "against us." Although drought, lean years, sickness, and poverty may make it *seem* like God has abandoned us, that we have slipped through his hands, this is not the case. If we were to simply look at our circumstances, we could easily conclude that things are as they appear—an irredeemable mess, bereft of God's love and provision. But, as a gift of sight received through revelation in Scripture, we can recognize that things are not as they presently appear.

Our situation may appear to be a failure by the standards of the world. Indeed, it may appear to be a failure by the standards of much Christian piety today, which teaches that God desires our success and prosperity (in a way that *we* would recognize as success and prosperity): "God wants you to live abundantly!" "Unlock God's blessings with faith!"[10]

Instead of pursuing this direction, the Heidelberg Catechism cultivates "good confidence" in our God and Father—a confidence that, as we will see in a later section, is essential for living a life of both rejoicing and lament before God. The Spirit assures us of eternal life—beginning now, according to the Heidelberg Catechism, and continuing into the future, when our true lives will be on display. For while our present lives now are "hidden with Christ in God," as Paul says, "when Christ who is your life is revealed, then you also will be revealed with him in glory" (Col. 3:3b–4). The end toward which the providential Lord is directing history will show how our deepest flourishing and restoration comes in our identity "with Christ in God" in the age to come.

---

9. Heidelberg Catechism, Q and A 28 (*Our Faith*, 78).

10. According to a Pew study, most people who believe in God in the United States (56 percent) affirm that "God will grant good health and relief from sickness to believers who have enough faith." Rates among Christians of a multiplicity of denominations affirming this in several other countries average as high as 85 percent. Pew Research Center, "Spirit and Power."

Facing Objections with David Bentley Hart: A Heartless Doctrine, Producing Callous Hearts?

On the day after Christmas in 2004, the earth shook. With waves up to one hundred feet that raced across the ocean at high speeds, an Indian Ocean tsunami claimed between 230,000 and 280,000 lives of women, men, and children. The unexpected catastrophe devastated coastal communities across fourteen countries, including Indonesia, Thailand, India, and Sri Lanka. One of the deadliest natural disasters in recorded history, it left vast regions in ruins, displacing millions.

Five days after the tsunami, theologian David Bentley Hart wrote a column for *The Wall Street Journal* titled "Tremors of Doubt." He followed up in later months with other articles and reflections, which were eventually published in the 2005 book *The Doors of the Sea: Where Was God in the Tsunami?* The book became widely read and discussed, as people both with and without faith discussed the horrors of the tsunami and the puzzling responses. While Hart is not a specialist in Reformed theology, his book offers a forceful distillation of an objection to a Reformed doctrine of providence—that it is heartless and inhumane, presenting an equally heartless God.

Hart observes the reactions to the tsunami from two different quarters. First, many agnostics and atheists saw the tsunami as an indication that Christian belief in God is self-contradictory. In Hart's rendering, they claimed, "Here we have an instance of empirical horrors too vast to be reconciled with belief in a loving and omnipotent God, and that upon this rock the ship of faith must surely founder and sink and leave nothing but fragments of flotsam to wash up into the shoals of the future."[11] The overwhelming horror of the tsunami vividly demonstrated the problem of natural evil—the problem of reconciling the fact that immense suffering results from natural events, like tsunamis, with the belief in a good God whose providential ordering of events extends to all that occurs in our world. To some, the tsunami provided a compelling demonstration that an almighty and benevolent God simply does not exist.

On the one hand, Hart pushes back against the hubris on display when authors summarily dismiss the Christian faith based on the tsunami. They display profound naivete about the history and teaching of the Christian tradition that they reject: "It seems a curious delusion—but apparently it is one shared by a great number of the more passionate secularists—to imagine that Christianity has never at any point during the two millennia of its

---

11. Hart, *Doors of the Sea*, 7–8.

intellectual tradition considered the problem of evil, or confronted the reality of suffering and death, or at any rate responded to these things with any subtlety."[12] The Christian tradition has probed these questions much more deeply than its critics tend to assume. Indeed, not just in Christian history, but in the eras that generated the books included in the Old and New Testaments, many forms of horrific evils were much more common than they are in our own era.

On the other hand, as Hart read comments and notes from Christians after the tsunami, he found that they often "rationalize[d] the catastrophe in ways that" unintentionally confirmed the suspicions of the atheist commentators that the Christian God does not *really* love his creation.[13] Hart lists a number of responses of Catholics and Protestants, and quite a few were like the responses of Job's friends to his suffering. Job was afflicted with the loss of fortune, family, and health, even though he was "blameless and upright, one who feared God and turned away from evil" (Job 1:1). His suffering was not punishment for his wrongdoing. Yet Job's friends reasoned retroactively from the calamity and assumed that it *must* have been a consequence of wrongdoing. Similarly, many claimed that the tsunami was a fitting act of divine judgment for especially egregious sins, which must have been committed by people in the affected countries.

Hart's narration suggests that some are just ill-informed about their own theological tradition. But when it comes to an outspoken author that he refers to as a "Calvinist pastor," Hart assumes that he is a spokesperson for the Reformed tradition. With particular ire, Hart reports that "a Calvinist pastor, positively intoxicated by the grandeur of divine sovereignty, proclaimed that the Indian Ocean disaster—like everything else—was a direct expression of the divine will, acting according to hidden and eternal counsels it would be impious to attempt to penetrate, and producing consequences it would be sinful to presume to judge."[14] The pastor displays confidence that this catastrophic tsunami is exactly the way things are supposed to be, because God is king. To Hart, this is both preposterous and offensive.

As the book progresses, Hart presents his alternative view, drawing on medieval scholastic distinctions like primary and secondary causality and the active will of God versus the permissive, which we will discuss further below. He frequently critiques the "Calvinists" who, in his view, fall into fatalism, neglecting to lament the "tens of thousands of dead children" and displaying

12. Hart, *Doors of the Sea*, 9.
13. Hart, *Doors of the Sea*, 26.
14. Hart, *Doors of the Sea*, 27.

an "exuberant callousness regarding the dead."[15] This, he argues, distorts both their doctrine and piety.

Toward the end of his book, Hart acknowledges that he has made Calvinism the "bête noire" (detested thing) of his argument, though this wasn't his original intent. He explains that he kept returning to it because, after his column was published, "those who reacted with the greatest belligerence and most violent vituperation to any suggestion that God might not be *the immediate cause of all evil in the world* were all Calvinists of a particularly rigorist persuasion."[16] Hart adds that this reaction highlights "the reality that between Eastern Orthodox [his own tradition] and Reformed theology there are some differences so vast that no reconciliation is possible." Reflecting on John Calvin specifically, he laments, "I only wish it had been historically possible for him (and for other of his contemporaries) to take the subtleties of high scholastic theology more seriously, and the riches of patristic thought more to heart."[17]

While Hart's account misconstrues the Reformed tradition in some ways that we will clarify, his most salient point relates to a distortion in *piety* (reverence) in relation to divine providence. The "Calvinist pastor" did not display genuine grief or lament before God and others. In essence, the pastor asserted that the horror and carnage of the tsunami makes perfectly rational sense. It is an expression of God's royal decree.

We agree with Hart that this is a very problematic distortion of Christian piety. It appears in all different Christian traditions, but it can be especially common within parts of the Reformed community.

Complaint, Compassion, and the Lord's Hidden Ways

Hart looks to Ivan Karamazov, a character in Fyodor Dostoevsky's *The Brothers Karamazov*, to express what was right about the response of non-Christians who felt both compassion and horror in the wake of the tsunami. Ivan rejects the Christian faith, raising a powerful protest against God's creation. If horrors are to be used by God in order to create, in the end, a higher harmony in heaven, then that is "too high a price on harmony; we can't afford to pay so much for admission. And therefore," Ivan says, "I hasten to return my ticket." Ivan gives an example of a child who dies of terrible abuse,

---

15. Hart, *Doors of the Sea*, 93–94.
16. Hart, *Doors of the Sea*, 94 (emphasis added).
17. Hart, *Doors of the Sea*, 94.

saying that, especially when involving the innocent, he rejects any notion of a justifying "higher purpose" for suffering.[18]

Ivan's claims may simply sound impious and irreverent to some. But with Hart, we agree that Ivan's protest has moral value. In fact, in some ways, Ivan's anguish echoes the raw lament of Job in the Bible, who protests to the Lord, demanding answers for his unexplained suffering. Job boldly and repeatedly complains to God that his affliction is unjust. He laments in protest to the Lord that he wishes he had never been born:

> Why did you bring me forth from the womb?
>   Would that I had died before any eye had seen me,
> and were as though I had not been,
>   carried from the womb to the grave. (Job 10:18–19)

In a sense, in his bold complaints, Job is suggesting that he wants to "return [his] ticket." Whatever this affliction could purchase in terms of some later redemptive result, it's not worth it. It would have been better if the Lord spared him from life altogether, he complains.

Likewise, lament psalms often complain to the Lord with a tone of anger and even protest. In Psalm 102, the psalmist cries out in his affliction,

> For I eat ashes like bread,
>   and mingle tears with my drink,
> because of your indignation and anger;
>   for you have lifted me up and thrown me aside.
> My days are like an evening shadow;
>   I wither away like grass. (vv. 9–11)

The psalmist is afflicted to the point of death. He asks why the Lord, who is "enthroned forever," will not hear his cry. Instead of responding and bringing relief to his anguish, the Lord, he says, "has broken my strength in midcourse; he has shortened my days" (vv. 12, 23).

However, there is a major difference between the questions and complaints within these biblical texts and those of Ivan. They both accuse God of neglecting the creation, of hiding his face rather than being present in the midst of calamity. The difference is that the psalmists keep God in the room, so to speak. They keep lamenting. They keep praying. They trust God enough to keep coming back to God, especially when they don't understand the reasons for their suffering.

---

18. Dostoevsky, *Brothers Karamazov*, 245.

In contrast, within the context of Dostoevsky's novel, Ivan simply rejects God as a reality, seeking to live as if there is no God. Although Ivan compassionately identifies with the suffering of an innocent child, he eventually comes to the conclusion that if there is no God, then "everything is permitted."[19] He is unable to continue the lament or protest because it was a belief in God that assured him the suffering was indeed horrific. Without this grounding, he eventually becomes complicit in the death of his own father. As Albert Camus describes it, "From the moment that [Ivan] rejects divine coherence and tries to discover his own rule of life, [he] recognizes the legitimacy of murder. If all is permitted, he can kill his father or at least allow him to be killed."[20]

What Ivan misses, when he declares God guilty of his accusation, is the reality that the ways of the Lord in providence are truly hidden from us. This recognition does not lead to stoic acceptance of horrific realities like the tsunami as "the way things are supposed to be." The psalmists repeatedly remind us of this. But Job also vividly shows how the answers to our most pressing *why* questions are beyond *"the limits of human wisdom."*[21] In the climax of the book of Job, after Job has repeatedly said that he wants to make his case before the Lord, the Lord finally appears. The encounter is majestic and awe-inspiring:

> Then the Lord answered Job out of the whirlwind:
> "Who is this that darkens counsel by words without knowledge?
> Gird up your loins like a man,
>   I will question you, and you shall declare to me.
>
> "Where were you when I laid the foundation of the earth?
>   Tell me, if you have understanding.
> Who determined its measurements—surely you know!" (Job 38:1–5)

Job receives his request, to see the Lord himself, so that he can make his case. But the encounter does not answer any of Job's questions. God changes the subject. In four chapters (Job 38–41), the Lord declares his freedom in creating the world and points to the vast distance between God's viewpoint and human understanding. God doesn't explain why suffering happens to Job or to humans in general. Even by the end of the book of Job, we as readers still don't know.

Likewise, as we see in the psalms of lament, the psalmists do not claim to know *why* the Almighty has permitted the calamity that they face. They

---

19. Dostoevsky, *Brothers Karamazov*, 589.
20. Camus, *The Rebel*, 58.
21. Bechtel, *Touching the Altar*, 181 (emphasis original).

lament, wrestling with God's promises. But they do not accept that the suffering in their midst is just the way things are supposed to be. They come to
the Lord in trust and hope, based on the covenant promise that he will be the
Lord of his people, shine his face upon them, and be present with them. For
even if the psalmist makes his bed in the dark pit of Sheol, the Lord is there
(Ps. 139:8). The psalm continues:

> If I say, "Surely the darkness shall cover me,
>   and the light around me become night,"
> even the darkness is not dark to you;
>   the night is as bright as the day,
>   for darkness is as light to you. (Ps. 139:11–12)

As noted earlier, the Reformed confessions insist that while we can trust in
God's benevolence and power, much about God's providence is simply "hidden
from us."[22] If the Lord is king, why was there a horrible tsunami on December
26, 2004? We do not know, nor do we "wish to inquire with undue curiosity
into what God does that surpasses human understanding and is beyond our
ability to comprehend."[23] To blame the countries impacted by the disaster,
to develop a theory for how the tragedy is all for the good—this is to give in
to the temptation that the Reformed confessions caution us against. God is
God, and we are not. As we respond in compassion toward the weeping, we
can join the psalmists in complaint and lament.

Avoiding Lament and the Problem of the Anger of God

The disfigured Christian piety that Hart points to, which refuses to lament, has
a complex relationship to the Reformed tradition. Reflecting the Reformed emphasis on God's kingly, sovereign power, the Westminster Confession speaks
of providence in terms of God's "decree" and that which is "ordained" by
God.[24] Both terms, *decree* and *ordain*, had been common in academic theology
(among Roman Catholics and Protestants) for centuries. Taken in its full
context, which we will examine below, this is *not* an affirmation of fatalism,
or that tragedies like the tsunami are immediately caused by God, as Hart
worries. But to modern ears, that language can certainly sound like fatalism,
which should lead us to a stoical response.

---

22. Belgic Confession, 13 (*Our Faith*, 37).
23. Belgic Confession, 13 (*Our Faith*, 37).
24. Westminster Confession, 3 (Dennison, *Reformed Confessions*, 4:238–39).

I (Todd) recall a friend who reached out to a Christian couple shortly after they experienced a miscarriage. He noticed that their faces were expression-less. "Well, it's what God has decreed," the husband said. Between the lines, the assumption seemed to be, "We can't complain or be angry at God for the loss of our child; it's what God has ordained." In this case, they had been reading books by some Reformed authors who emphasized divine sovereignty in a way that had no place for lament.

When I was diagnosed with an incurable cancer in 2012, I returned with renewed energy to the psalms, to the overall witness of Scripture, and to Chris-tian theology. I wrote a book on providence and lament, making a case for how believers need to lament with the psalmists as an act of trust and hope in the covenant Lord. In my own prayer life, I moved beyond cherry-picking to find the happy psalms. I realized that I had been missing out on a treasure by skipping over a third of the psalms, the psalms of lament. Drawing on Calvin, who approached the psalms as an "anatomy of the human soul," I began to see the psalms as a divine pedagogy for bringing our whole life, with all of our emotions, before the Lord.[25]

But as I spoke to congregations and students at colleges and seminaries, I found a major obstacle to biblical lament: Some saw it as sinful and impious to express anger at God. This is sometimes explicitly taught; at other times, it is simply modeled by the studious avoidance of lament psalms in worship, whether in public prayer or in song.

At these events, it was clear that Christians of many traditions felt the force of this objection. But as I dug more deeply, I discovered that some of the figures who argue most directly that it is sinful to be angry with God are also seen as representatives of the Reformed tradition, figures such as John Piper and R. C. Sproul.[26] While Piper and Sproul have made valuable contributions on a variety of topics, I came to see that their approach was not sufficiently bibli-cal on this point and that it departed from key Reformed exegetical insights.

Piper makes his case with some helpful distinctions, which were not always present when I would hear this objection. He suggests that anger can have

25. See Billings, *Rejoicing in Lament*, chaps. 4–5. Calvin quotation from Calvin, *John Cal-vin's Bible Commentaries*, 19.

26. Both Sproul and Piper make this case in a variety of contexts. See Sproul, "Locus of Astonishment"; and Sproul, "Is It a Sin to Be Angry with God?" The most concise of Piper's accounts are Piper, "It Is Never Right to Be Angry with God"; and Piper, "Is It Ever Right to Be Angry at God?" Two more recent books are Piper, *Lessons from a Hospital Bed*, and Piper, *Providence*. Although the psalms are frequently quoted, lament psalms are notably absent, with Piper discouraging complaints to God, not allowing for the possibility of a faithful complaint. In contrast, Timothy Keller, without referencing Sproul or Piper, offers a sharply contrasting response to the question of anger at God in *Walking with God*, chap. 12.

a place in prayer, as bringing our anger toward others before God can be an act of faithfulness. But directing anger toward God is always wrong, a "sinful emotion."[27] Why? Because, Piper writes, anger should be directed only toward those who are sinful, fallible: "Anger at a person always implies strong disapproval. If you are angry at me, you think I have done something I should not have done."[28] However, God's ways are perfect. Even if God chooses to permit Satan to "hurt us and our children," as in the case of Job, we should not disapprove of God or his work. Thus, Piper argues that being angry at God is never right. "It is wrong—always wrong—to disapprove of God for what he does and permits."[29]

Piper is right to see that, at times, complaint and anger at God can be sinful in a biblical account. In some biblical narratives, anger toward God leads to an exit—a *cutting off* from fellowship with God to serving other gods. The books of Exodus and Numbers give numerous instances of the "grumbling" of the Israelites after their deliverance from Egypt on the long journey to the land the Lord had promised. They turn away from God's promise to them as covenant people. In their impatience and anger, they berate Moses and even turn their devotion to a golden calf of their own devising. In these biblical examples, Piper's point about anger at God being sinful is on target. If we are angry at God in a way that leaves us wallowing in self-pity or serving gods other than the Lord, we need to repent of this failure to love the Lord our God.

But Piper's approach misses the second major biblical trajectory, which gives us a path for faithfully expressing complaint, anger, and even protest to God. In this approach, God's people do not turn *away* from their covenant Lord in anger; they turn *toward* him. In this regard, Piper would have been wise to learn from Reformed authors who have stated this distinction with great power.

When approaching lament psalms, even the most strident and vehement ones, many Reformed and Puritan authors embraced the notion that a complaint to God, with anger at God, could be faithful. For an example, consider one of the most desolate laments, Psalm 88, which excludes the conventional declaration of trust in the Lord that concludes most lament psalms. Instead, it concludes with words of deep grief, anger, and protest:

> Your wrath has swept over me;
>   your dread assaults destroy me.
> They surround me like a flood all day long;

27. Piper, "Is It Ever Right to Be Angry at God?"
28. Piper, "Is It Ever Right to Be Angry at God?"
29. Piper, "Is It Ever Right to Be Angry at God?"

> from all sides they close in on me.
> You have caused friend and neighbor to shun me;
>   my companions are in darkness. (Ps. 88:16–18)

How could this be a pious prayer for a Christian to pray? This is not an easy question to answer. In his commentary, Calvin develops several strategies for faithfully praying psalms of lament, and his comments on Psalm 88 (along with those of other Reformed commentators) illustrate one of these strategies used in a variety of psalms, that of *faithful* complaint.[30] Calvin writes that this Psalm "contains very grievous lamentations, poured forth by its inspired penman when under very severe affliction, and almost at the point of despair."[31] Yet, he notes that total despair does not bring these afflictions to God. Rather than his complaint and protest to the Lord displaying a *lack of faith* in the Lord and his promises, Calvin concludes that the opposite was true: "Whilst struggling with sorrow, [the psalmist] declares the invincible steadfastness of his faith" precisely in the persistence of his lament.[32] "These lamentations at first sight would seem to indicate a state of mind in which sorrow without any consolation prevailed; but they contain in them tacit prayers."[33] Bringing anger before the Lord can be an act of trust, for even the accusations are "tacit prayers."

If anger at God can lead some in the biblical narrative to disobedience, what sets faithful lament apart? The difference isn't in expressing anger or protest toward God; it's that, in the psalms, even provisional disapproval is voiced within prayer, maintaining fellowship with the Lord. The term *provisional* is key here. As noted earlier, Piper argues, "It is wrong—always wrong—to disapprove of God for what he does and permits."[34] We agree that such disapproval is wrong if it pivots us away from seeking the presence of God. If we declare God guilty, in a final way, we no longer come to God in prayer. But this is precisely why the psalms of lament are such a gift. Through these psalms, the Spirit shapes a Christian piety that wrestles with God's providence while remaining in fellowship with the Lord.

---

30. For more on these strategies, and a response to some recent misinterpretations of Calvin on lament psalms, see Billings, "Laments as Christian Scripture," 58–82. Wolfgang Musculus (1497–1563), a Reformed professor in Berne, and Puritan authors such as Thomas Wilcox (ca.1549–1608), give powerful comments on Psalm 88 that parallel Calvin's exegetical approach. See Musculus, *Psalms of David*, and Wilcox, *Exposition upon the Psalms*, in Selderhuis, *Psalms 73–150*, 101–2.

31. Calvin, *Commentary on the Book of Psalms*, preface to Ps. 88.

32. Calvin, *Commentary on the Book of Psalms*, preface to Ps. 88.

33. Calvin, *Commentary on the Book of Psalms*, comments on Ps. 88:14.

34. Piper, "Is It Ever Right to Be Angry at God?"

The complaints within the psalms are bold but also open-handed: "How long, O LORD? Will you forget me forever? How long will you hide your face from me?" (Ps. 13:1). Rather than stomping away like a jilted lover, psalms like this bring anger at God *to* God—focusing not on our own ideas of how a deity should serve our interests but on the covenant promises we have received from the Lord. Again and again, God says he will always remember his people, and he will shine his face on his people. Yet those promises don't appear to be coming to fruition in the midst of the psalmist's calamity. Thus the psalms turn God's covenant promises into the interrogative, asking the Lord, Where are you and your promised works in the midst of this calamity?

In a sense, the lament psalms champion the assumption of the "Calvinist pastor" in Hart's account—the assumption that God is the true and only king of creation. But rather than leading to a callous heart in the face of great calamity, the lament psalms believe that God's sovereign power gives us all the more reason to shed tears with the suffering, in lament. In the words of one Old Testament scholar, "It is faith in *a sovereign God* that causes confusion" in psalms of lament. "Why does an all-powerful king suddenly and inexplicably no longer bless, no longer order life, and no longer hold things together? If a person did not believe that God was sovereign, there would be no cause for lament."[35] It is precisely out of trust that God is sovereign that the psalmist repeatedly brings laments and petitions to the Lord. If God is not the sovereign Lord, then the rationale for complaining to God collapses, as preventing or overturning the calamity would not be within his power anyway.

One of the great gifts of the Reformation in Geneva was a fruit of the work of biblical scholars and musicians: the Genevan Psalter, all 150 psalms in the vernacular that could be sung and prayed, whether in corporate worship or in the fields, in the marketplace or by the bed of a church member who was dying. Its influence was widespread, for it was a "publishing phenomenon that broke all the records in those still early days of printing and publishing. Within just a few years, it was available in nine languages and in more than a hundred thousand copies."[36] It was a gift of the Reformed church to the church catholic.

We believe that recovering the practice of praying (and singing) the psalms, including psalms of lament, can help prevent the deformed piety that Hart noticed in response to the tsunami. Rather than avoiding anger and grief before the Lord, in the midst of great calamity, our willingness to complain

35. Pemberton, *Hurting with God*, 93 (emphasis added).
36. Brink, "Reformed Approach to Psalmody," 20.

with the psalmist brings this into the Lord's presence. In the end, biblical lament is a hopeful act, an act of testimony to God's kingship and extravagant love for creation.

It is also an act that is intimately connected to following the path of Jesus himself. As Musculus points out, when Jesus cried out through the direct complaint from Psalm 22 on the cross, it was a prayer of desolation, yet also covenantal trust: "My God, my God, why have you forsaken me?" (Matt. 27:46).[37] Jesus was not controlled by a fear that this question was irreverent or would offend the majesty of God. Instead, Jesus himself prayed God's Word back to the Father—lamenting in trust. As those who are in Christ, we are invited to join the psalmist's lament as well, by the Spirit. When we feel abandoned by God, we can and should still call out to the Lord, "groan[ing] inwardly" by the Spirit as we ache and long for Christ's return and the glory that will be revealed on that day (Rom. 8:18–25).

Recovering the Catholicity of a Reformed Theology of Providence

In this section, we will focus on how scholastic distinctions clarify a Reformed doctrine of providence, countering the stereotype that it is fatalistic. We will begin by briefly examining Hart's objection to Calvin and the "Calvinists," then we will show how these distinctions function within Reformed theology, particularly in the context of tragedy.

In *The Doors of the Sea*, Hart seeks to clarify the Christian doctrine of providence by drawing on distinctions that were developed in biblical interpretation, especially in the medieval era; these are *primary and secondary causality* and the *active and permissive will* of God. Hart seeks to hold together two realities: the transcendence of God as Lord and the contingency (dependence) of creation. The distinctions provide a way to avoid the mistake of seeing God as actor in the world—either as the immediate cause of the tsunami or as a deity who is helpless in the face of creaturely tragedy. God is Lord and King, *and* creation depends on God for its continuation.

Hart's basic approach here is illuminating. However, he incorrectly frames the Reformed tradition as sharply divergent from these ideas. After criticizing the "Calvinist" pastor who said the tsunami was the direct and immediate expression of God's will, Hart attacks Calvin's theology of providence, describing it as an "oddly pantheistic expression of God's unadulterated power."[38]

---

37. Selderhuis, *Psalms 73–150*, 102.
38. Hart, *Doors of the Sea*, 91.

He laments that Calvin and other Reformed theologians miss out on "the subtleties of high scholastic theology . . . and the riches of patristic thought."[39]

Ironically, in affirming the scholastic distinctions that he proposes, Hart is in the company of most sixteenth- and seventeenth-century Reformed confessions on providence. Yet, Hart clearly thinks that Calvin dramatically misconstrues the doctrine, and he then casts other theologians within the Reformed tradition in that mold.

In this, Hart gives an extremely faulty account of the Reformed doctrine of providence, but he is far from unique in doing so. This is partly because Hart (like many others) makes two key assumptions that lead to misinterpretations: that Reformed theology basically derives from one "great thinker" (i.e., Calvin) and that predestination was a central doctrine in Calvin's thought, such that his theology is derived from the starting point of this "central dogma."[40]

Hart advocates distinguishing primary and secondary causality to avoid viewing all events as direct expressions of God's will; yet, ironically, he overlooks that Calvin and Reformed confessions of the time use this very distinction.[41] Hart then gives a lengthy criticism of Calvin for rejecting the distinction between God's active and permissive will. While this is a legitimate objection, it is largely irrelevant to his claims about later "Calvinist" and Reformed theology, since the Reformed confessions quite consciously and consistently diverge from Calvin on this point.

This leads us to question: How do these scholastic distinctions, derived from the earlier catholic Christian tradition, function within a Reformed theology of providence? Can they show that the Reformed doctrine of providence avoids fatalism, which Hart rightly names as an important concern?

When introducing this to students, we first note that these conceptual distinctions are not "theological magic" designed to solve the problem of evil or to make difficult questions about providence disappear. Rather, they serve

39. Hart, *Doors of the Sea*, 108–9.

40. The great-thinker model and its inadequacy is discussed in chap. 1. A central-dogma way of interpreting Calvin's theology mistakenly assumes that it functions as a deductive system, rather than as a set of biblically grounded doctrinal topics. On the problems with approaching Calvin's theology in this way, see Muller, *Calvin and the Reformed Tradition*, esp. 62–64.

41. Tellingly, Hart does not quote Calvin's *Institutes* on providence, his topic of critique, but only on predestination, given his central-dogma approach to Calvin. Thus, he misses Calvin's exposition of the primary and secondary causality distinction within his chapter on providence. In opening a section using the distinction, Calvin asks for readers to affirm that God is "the principal cause of things," yet this needs to be balanced by giving "attention to the secondary causes in their proper place." See Calvin, *Institutes* 1.17.6–9. Calvin clearly denies that events within creation are the unmediated expressions of God's will, and Calvin's view is distant from the "oddly pantheistic" view that Hart describes.

as guardrails to help Christians avoid two opposing extremes while receiving Scripture's testimony.

What are these two extremes? The first is that God would "abandon" creation "to chance or fortune."[42] The second is that God is the only truly active agent in the unfolding of events, making God the "author" of sin who could be "charged with" the sin occurring in the world.[43] Notably, to truly join the psalmist in lament in the face of a tragedy like the tsunami, one must avoid these extremes. If God created the world but has left its ongoing survival and direction to chance, then we serve a *deistic* God who is not worth crying out to in lament. If God is the only meaningful cause in the unfolding of events and therefore the author of sin, then God is malevolent and untrustworthy. It would be foolish to expose one's grief, anger, and petitions to such a deity.

What does it mean to occupy the space between these two options? It is a mysterious middle that theologians call *divine concurrence*: God is the almighty Lord and King, the source and end of creation's life and history; *at the same time*, creation is contingent, and creatures have genuine agency that is upheld by God. At the center of this mystery is an extraordinarily beautiful yet counterintuitive reality: Divine and creaturely agency are not competitive. Agency is not a zero-sum game. A creature's being moved by God does not make that creature less its own, but more. In denying the two extremes, Bavinck says, the Christian "confesses that the world and every creature in it have received their own existence, but increase in reality, freedom, and authenticity to the extent that they are more dependent on God and exist from moment to moment from, through, and to God. *A creature is the more perfect to the degree that God indwells it more and permeates it with his being.*"[44]

The extremes of the hands-off God, on the one hand, and the God who is the only true agent, on the other, are explicitly excluded by Reformed confessions. To readers today, it can *sound like* the seventeenth-century confessions (including the Westminster Confession) slip into one extreme or the other, but in fact, they hold a clear middle ground. We need to examine a key example from the Westminster Confession to unpack the role that the scholastic distinctions play: "GOD from all eternity, did, by the most wise and holy counsel of His own will, freely, and unchangeably ordain whatsoever comes to pass: yet so, as thereby neither is God the author of sin, nor is violence offered to

42. Belgic Confession, 13 (*Our Faith*, 37).
43. The technical term for this second extreme position is *monocausality*. Belgic Confession, 13 (*Our Faith*, 37).
44. Bavinck, *Reformed Dogmatics*, 2:608 (emphasis added).

the will of the creatures; nor is the liberty or contingency of second causes taken away, but rather established."[45]

The first two lines may *sound* quite jarring, as if God is the only meaningful agent in the universe, since God ordains "whatsoever comes to pass." Indeed, in the last century the textbook account of this view of providence has often been framed as a form of modern *compatibilism*, within *compatibilist* versus *libertarian* debates about creaturely freedom. According to this view, God's providential determination is compatible with human freedom only in the sense that the creaturely will is not coerced. But in reading this paragraph from the Westminster Confession as a whole (alongside similar passages in that confession), something different comes into view, in light of the technical use of scholastic distinctions: God ordains all that comes to pass, but he does so in a way that does not threaten the freedom and contingency of creatures; rather, he does so in a way that establishes and upholds creaturely freedom and contingency. Creatures are contingent and free, but theirs is a *dependent* freedom, dependent on God's providential power.[46]

Thus, for the Westminster Confession, in the words of John Fesko, "whatever God ordains comes to pass, but it can and will come to pass contingently."[47] Creatures are not robots, or mere automatons. Certainly, creatures are completely dependent on God in his primary agency, which enables creaturely life and freedom. Creatures are contingent. But what does this contingency entail? For the Westminster Confession, it "does not mean that something does not have a cause. . . . Rather it means that something *could be otherwise*."[48] In this account, note that while creatures are *dependent* on God, the primary and secondary causes are still distinct, for creatures act in a contingent way that is not overturned by God as primary cause but is upheld by him. Moreover, to emphasize the reality of creaturely agency even more emphatically, the Westminster Confession joins earlier Reformed confessions in affirming a distinction between the active will and the permissive will of God—for

45. Westminster Confession, 3.1 (Dennison, *Reformed Confessions*, 4:238).

46. For an overview of how this point in seventeenth-century Reformed theology is often misunderstood, see Fesko, *Theology of the Westminster Standards*, chap. 3; and Muller, *Divine Will and Human Choice*.

47. Fesko, *Theology of the Westminster Standards*, 102–3.

48. Fesko, *Theology of the Westminster Standards*, 103 (emphasis added). On this precise point, Jonathan Edwards diverged from the Westminster Confession. For Edwards, contingency meant the absence of a cause—an absurdity in his view—and was therefore ruled out entirely. In its place, he articulated a stricter form of divine determinism that leaves no room for contingency. As a result, many theologians shaped by Edwards—especially in the United States—have embraced a more constrained view of human freedom than that of the Westminster Confession, which affirms contingency within God's providential use of secondary causes. See Fesko, *Theology of the Westminster Standards*, 96–110.

example, noting that God freely chose to permit the sinful action of Adam and Eve to disobey the Lord in the garden. Even in permitting creaturely agency acting against his revealed will for creation, however, the Lord can "order it to his own glory."[49] In the words of Bavinck, "Human persons speak, act, and believe, and it is God alone who supplies to a sinner all the vitality and strength he or she needs for the commission of a sin. Nevertheless, the subject and author of the sin is not God but the human being."[50]

If your head is beginning to spin, a concrete biblical example may help. In Genesis 37–50, we learn the story of Jacob's beloved son Joseph, who is envied by his brothers and sold into slavery, yet he eventually serves Pharaoh's court in Egypt. His brothers, seeing "him from a distance, . . . [conspire] to kill" him, and they throw him into a pit (Gen. 37:18–24). After debating their options, they ultimately sell Joseph into slavery and deceive their father by claiming that a wild animal has killed him. This is a free and contingent choice—they have other real options they might take, but they choose betrayal through selling Joseph into slavery.

Years later, during a famine, Jacob sends his sons to Egypt to buy grain. Unknowingly, they encounter Joseph, who is now in Pharaoh's court. After a series of events (Gen. 42–45), Joseph reveals his identity to his brothers, testifying that God has worked through their betrayal. Elevated to a position of power, Joseph provides for his family, stating, "God sent me before you to preserve for you a remnant on earth, and to keep alive for you many survivors. So it was not you who sent me here, but God" (Gen. 45:7–8). Although his brothers' act was wicked, another "sending" was at work: the sovereign Lord sending Joseph to Egypt for his own purposes, working those purposes even through human betrayal. The Second Helvetic Confession reflects on Joseph's brothers' wicked action, highlighting God's extraordinary providence with Augustine's words: "What happens contrary to [God's] will occurs, in a wonderful and ineffable way, not apart from his will."[51]

Thus, in this narrative, even in the same event, there are two spheres of action taking place: the sovereign action of God *and* the responsible, contingent actions of creatures. As hearers of the Joseph story, we are reminded that *God's ways are not our ways* (Isa. 55:8–9). What looks like a terrible tragedy (the selling of Joseph) is indeed a terrible tragedy, a deeply sinful betrayal by his brothers. The brothers are responsible for enacting their wicked scheme. Yet, the Lord of the universe is not a deistic God who abandons his creatures

---

49. Westminster Confession, 6.1 (Dennison, *Reformed Confessions*, 4:241).
50. Bavinck, *Reformed Dogmatics*, 2:615.
51. Second Helvetic Confession, 8 (Cochrane, *Reformed Confessions*, 236).

"to chance or fortune."[52] He also does not force the brothers to betray Joseph and sell him into slavery; they freely choose this course of action, and they are morally responsible for it. How can we make sense of this?

The technical distinctions within the Reformed confessions help us to testify to this mystery in providence, even as they do not fully answer our questions of why God would work this way. In affirming *both* divine sovereignty and creaturely responsibility together, they show what it means to understand God through Scripture by way of *analogy*, because God is not reducible to an object or a cause among a chain of causes in the world. Rather, as Michael Horton explains, "God is directing all of history toward his purposes without in any way canceling the ordinary liberty, contingency, and reality of creaturely causes."[53] God's action does not *compete* with human action; God sovereignly directs history toward his purposes, and yet human beings are responsible.

Conclusion

Does Reformed theology teach that God is a controlling tyrant, or a loving provider? The journey within this chapter suggests that while the answer is the realm of the latter, a Reformed theology of providence is also textured and layered. The gifts of life and breath come from the Lord, our provider, and he loves us with a steady, covenant love. But within our good-yet-fallen creation, this love and provision do not necessarily come to us in the way we would expect or prefer. We trust in the provident Lord, but there is much that is hidden from us.

Reformed theology embraces the royal imagery of God as the one king and Lord of creation with great seriousness. With the psalmist, it testifies that "the LORD sits enthroned as king forever" (Ps. 29:10). At times, it can seem that we have been abandoned to chance, for some "persecute the poor" and "murder the innocent" (Ps. 10:2, 8). They assume this world has no sovereign king, for "they think in their heart, 'God has forgotten, he has hidden his face, he will never see it'" (Ps. 10:11). In contrast to these functional deists, the Reformed tradition joins the psalmist's acclamation that "the LORD is king forever and ever" (Ps. 10:16). Even when the wicked prosper, when innocent children die in a tsunami, and other events take place in which there is no visible victory for this Lord of love and justice, we trust that this Lord is the true king; for "the earth is the LORD's and all that is in it" (Ps. 24:1).

52. Belgic Confession, 13 (*Our Faith*, 37).
53. Horton, *Christian Faith*, 362.

Even so, our trust in God as king also makes us ache and lament. By the Spirit, we join "the whole creation [which] has been groaning in labor pains until now," until the final redemption comes in fullness (Rom. 8:22). With the psalmist, we see that justice is often not done, and our suffering and rebellious world often does not *appear* to be governed by a just and loving king. But in lament and hope, we can join the psalmist in calling out in complaint and petition, "How long, O LORD?," while trusting in the Lord's "steadfast love" (Ps. 13:1, 5).

Within Reformed theology, when disaster hits, we can trust that the sovereign God is present and active, even when things seem out of control. We cannot embody this truth in abstractions or easy clichés; we embody it by joining with the suffering, bringing our tears of grief and anger to the Lord in faithful lament. This is God's world, and although God permits creaturely agents to rebel from his ways, "God indeed hates sin."[54] Whether we face the wreckage of creaturely life amid abuse and oppression, or through the loss and grief of a tsunami or cancer, we are invited to abide in Christ as we walk in his way: with anger at injustice, as Jesus did toward those who profiteered from pilgrims visiting the temple; with grief amid loss, as Jesus was "greatly disturbed in spirit and deeply moved" and joined Mary in weeping when she told him Lazarus had died (John 11:33–35). In all things we give thanks to God for his covenant love and daily provision. In prayer and action, we are called to bring anger and grief into God's presence, for in hopeful-yet-earnest lament we express trust in God's sovereign power and his steadfast love. God is almighty and loving, and terrible things happen. We don't know why. But we do know where to direct our trust: toward the Lord who has pledged himself to us in covenant, such that "[we] are not our own, but belong—body and soul, in life and in death—to [our] faithful Savior, Jesus Christ."[55]

54. The Bremen Consensus (1595) emphatically corrects a possible misunderstanding of God's "permission" of sin in providence, making it clear that this distinction in no way implies endorsement of sin, injustice, or wickedness. "However, *God does not ordain evil in the same way* that He ordains good, that is, as something pleasing to Him, but *rather as something that He hates*; though He knowingly and willingly decrees it, *permits* it to be in the world, and in a wondrous manner uses it for good" (paragraph 6; emphasis added). For "God indeed hates sin" (paragraph 8). "Divine Providence," in Bremen Consensus (Dennison, *Reformed Confessions*, 3:668–69).

55. Heidelberg Catechism, A 1 (*Our Faith*, 69).

6

Reformed Theology and the Church's Mission: Faith, Justice, and the Gospel

Key Question: Do Reformed Christians Care About Evangelism and Social Justice?

When I (Alberto) engage the topic of the church's mission and work in the world with students, we address the history of the church's work in cultivating social justice.[1] This is not a new priority for the church; it has been vital to its calling and witness for centuries. I lead students through a discussion of the Didache, a second-century text that gives an important role to caring for the poor and the oppressed; we discuss John Chrysostom's homilies rebuking political corruption and the necessity of giving to the poor; and we reflect on Basil of Caesarea's fourth-century hospital,

---

1. The phrase *social justice* can mean many things to many people. In this chapter, the term refers to the work of cultivating a more fair and equitable society that cares for the most vulnerable. For Christians, the call to cultivate social justice is rooted in the very character and nature of the triune God of love, mercy, and justice. As the prophet Micah writes, the people of God are called by God "to do justice, and to love kindness, and to walk humbly with . . . God" (Mic. 6:8).

among other sources.[2] Then we turn to the Reformed tradition and discover John Calvin's role in establishing the French purse, a relief fund that provided for thousands of French refugees seeking asylum in the city of Geneva. Calvin developed a robust theology of justice and equity as a key component of his doctrine of sanctification. As one scholar describes it, Calvin's theology of neighbor-love calls "believers to show the same love, compassion and self-sacrifice to others that God has shown to them in Christ."[3]

More than three centuries after Calvin, the Reformed legacy of social justice can also be witnessed in the Barmen Declaration's rejection of political ideologies that seek to replace Christ as the true head of the church;[4] the witness of the Belhar Confession to reconciliation, unity, and justice in apartheid in South Africa; and numerous other callings of Reformed Christians around the world today.[5] The Reformed tradition has a long history of cultivating a more just society as a form of witness to Jesus Christ. This history is rooted in the early church's commitment to caring for the poor, the oppressed, and those on the margins. In one class session, a student raised their hand to ask a critical question: "Obviously, it's good for Christians to care about the poor, the needy, and the oppressed, but isn't it more important for the church to be concerned with the conversion of unbelievers? Isn't that the true nature of the church's mission in the world?"

This question displays a tension and growing rift among many Christians today: those who feel the church's primary mission should be to cultivate social justice in the world and those who see evangelistic witness as the church's primary mission.[6] This tension is not only rooted in theological debates but is also fueled by an increasingly polarized political climate. Pastors and people

---

2. The Didache, also known as "The Teaching of the Twelve Apostles," offers a window into the most important matters to some of the earliest Christians. Its brief and rich content admonishes believers repeatedly to care for the poor and the oppressed (Didache 1:5; 4:5–8; 5:2; 15:4). John Chrysostom, the fourth-century bishop of Constantinople, preached a series of sermons in AD 388 on the parable of the Rich Man and Lazarus (Luke 16:19–31) in which he admonished his listeners to give alms to the poor because to withhold from the poor is to deprive them of what they need to live and therefore is sin (First Sermon on Lazarus and the Rich Man). For the Didache, see Kleist, *Didache*. For Chrysostom, see Chrysostom, *On Wealth and Poverty*. For an overview of these themes, see Rhee, *Loving the Poor, Saving the Rich*.

3. Haas, *Concept of Equity*, 123.

4. See chap. 2, above, for more on the context that led to the drafting of the Barmen Declaration.

5. In the Reformed tradition, the whole cosmos is seen as the sphere of God's redemptive work, and thus a wide range of Christian callings relate to justice in God's world. Two books that highlight the expansive vision of justice in the Reformed tradition are Hoang and Johnson, *Justice Calling*; and Keller, *Generous Justice*.

6. This division is often starker in classrooms where students are from the Global South. Indeed, this debate is not unique to North America; the church is wrestling with this across the globe.

in the pews alike are shaped by political pundits who give them an either/or choice: You can be a social justice warrior, or you can be a Bible-thumping Christian. They seem to think that love for justice and love for the Scriptures just don't go together.[7] In light of these tensions experienced by many in the twenty-first-century church, what resources does the Reformed tradition have to offer? Do Reformed Christians care about witnessing through evangelism *and* cultivating social justice in the world?

As this chapter will show using Scripture and the Reformed confessions, when the hope of the gospel is understood as loving communion with the triune God and—through the triune God—with all of creation, we can obtain a more integral understanding of the Christian life and the church's mission, including witness through social justice and witness through evangelism. This chapter affirms that the church carries forth an *integral mission*, a theological concept coined by Latin American evangelical missiologists like René Padilla, Orlando Costas, and Samuel Escobar in the 1960s and '70s. Though the term *integral mission* is recent, the theological reality to which it points has deep biblical roots and has been embodied throughout the history of the church.[8]

The Gospel as Loving Communion with the Triune God

What is the gospel that Christians proclaim? When I pose this question to students and parishioners, a common answer goes something like this: "The good news of the gospel is that Jesus died on the cross for my sins, so that if I believe in him, I can have eternal life." Another common answer might be: "The good news of the gospel is that Jesus has come to liberate us from the social, political, and economic chains that oppress us, transforming us into a loving and kind people who care for the least among us." Both answers are true, yet both also miss critical components of the gospel.

For example, in both it would seem that Jesus alone is necessary for salvation, rendering the Holy Spirit's work superfluous at best or somehow the

---

7. Among Reformed churches, this tension about the church's mission is exacerbated by certain misguided interpretations of the doctrine of election. Should Christians be concerned with preaching the gospel if God has already elected who will be saved? The implications of a Reformed doctrine of election for evangelism are clarified in chap. 4. This chapter focuses instead on the dichotomy today between the church's callings to cultivate social justice and to engage in evangelistic witness.

8. In the classic collection of essays *Mission Between the Times*, René Padilla traces the development of *integral mission* from its first breakthrough onto the world scene in the 1974 International Congress on World Evangelization, in Lausanne, Switzerland, to its more recent realization in the Micah Network. Padilla also shows how the notion of the church's integral mission is deeply rooted in Scripture and the Protestant theological tradition.

aftermath of salvation.[9] Moreover, it is not clear in either answer how all parts of Jesus's life—from his taking on flesh, to his death, resurrection, and ascension—are for us and for our salvation. One example places all the emphasis on Christ's death and the other on his ministry. Yet, in his letter to the Corinthians, the apostle Paul makes perfectly clear that if Christ has not been resurrected, then the power of his death on the cross is nullified (1 Cor. 15). In Romans 8:34, he further explains how Christ's ascension to intercede for us is also a critical component of our salvation. Yet, none of this would save us from the predicament of sin if Christ, the eternal logos, had not taken on flesh and lived among us. Finally, the answers also fail to bear witness to the cosmic scope of the gospel by limiting the good news of salvation to the realm of humanity. The gospel is good news not just for humans but for every square inch of creation, since, as the apostle Paul notes, "the whole creation has been groaning in labor pains," awaiting the redemption that comes from Jesus (Rom. 8:22), the "firstborn of all creation" and the one through whom "God was pleased to reconcile to himself all things, whether on earth or in heaven" (Col. 1:15, 20).

The root of the problem in both accounts of the gospel outlined above is confusing a *benefit* of salvation—eternal life or liberation from oppression— with *the central gift* of the gospel—intimate and loving communion with the gift-giver, the triune God. This is not a plea for explanations of the gospel to be more spiritual or to drag on with theological details that lose the listeners; rather, it is a plea for Christians to see and know that the grounding of the gospel, the core of the good news that Scripture testifies to, is nothing less than intimate and loving communion with the Father through the Son and the Spirit. As we are reconciled to the Father through the Son and the Spirit, we gain access to a fountain of blessings awaiting us in the New Creation.[10]

As the Spirit unites us to Christ, our sins are forgiven, and we receive eternal life, for as the psalmist writes, the Lord "is the fountain of life" (Ps. 36:9); and indeed, it is Jesus Christ who grants us access to this fountain, promising that "those who drink of the water that I will give them will never be thirsty. The water that I will give will become in them a spring of water gushing up to eternal life" (John 4:14). Moreover, as those who "once were far off" yet

9. Jesus affirms the necessity of the Spirit for salvation when he admonishes Nicodemus with these words: "Very truly, I tell you, no one can enter the kingdom of God without being born of water and Spirit" (John 3:5). It is the Spirit who joins us to Christ so that we might participate in his life, death, resurrection, and ascension.

10. Writing to the Corinthian church, Paul proclaims, "So if anyone is in Christ, there is a new creation: everything old has passed away; see, everything has become new! All this is from God, who reconciled us to himself through Christ, and has given us the ministry of reconciliation" (2 Cor. 5:17–18).

"have been brought near by the blood of Christ," we gladly receive the promise that, in Christ, God has "broken down the dividing wall, that is, the hostility between us" (Eph. 2:13–14). Though we are estranged siblings from every nation, in being joined to Christ by the Spirit, we are invited to be healed from our histories of oppression and brutal violence as we are made members of one household, the church.[11] Indeed, as we enter into the holy presence of the Lord of Hosts, we are reconciled with all of creation and restored to our place as "a royal priesthood," called to mediate between God and creation as those who "continually offer a sacrifice of praise to God, that is, the fruit of lips that confess his name" (Heb. 13:15).[12] So, the hope of the gospel is nothing less than life with the triune God, the source of "every generous act of giving" (James 1:17) and the one from whom all blessings flow.

However, when the benefits of salvation are detached from the core of the gospel, which is union with the triune God of love, then not only do the gifts lose their coherence and unity, but these benefits can even become idols. Detached from a vision of the riches and goodness of life with the Creator, churches can manipulate the very real fear of death that is in all of us mortals by offering a vision of salvation as merely a kind of eternal life insurance policy or a ticket to heaven. Fear of death can and often does bring people to God, yet the hope of the gospel is much greater and more glorious: In Christ and through the Spirit, not just death but all our suffering is overcome, and indeed, all our earthly longings are satiated.[13] In the United States during the past fifty years, belief in God has drastically decreased, but belief in an afterlife

11. This promise is uttered by the prophet Isaiah when he sees the end of history and proclaims, "He shall judge between the nations, and shall arbitrate for many peoples; they shall beat their swords into plowshares, and their spears into pruning hooks; nation shall not lift up sword against nation, neither shall they learn war any more" (Isa. 2:4). See also Ephesians 2:17–19: "So he came and proclaimed peace to you who were far off and peace to those who were near; for through him both of us have access in one Spirit to the Father. So then, you are no longer strangers and aliens, but you are citizens with the saints and also members of the household of God."

12. As we've argued in other chapters in this book, that salvific work of God entails a restoration of all of creation and not just of human sinners. Yet, humans do have a critical role to play in that redemptive work, and at least part of it is through our participation in Christ's priesthood: "Through him, then, let us continually offer a sacrifice of praise to God, that is, the fruit of lips that confess his name" (Heb. 13:15). See also 1 Pet. 2:9: "But you are a chosen race, a royal priesthood, a holy nation, God's own people, in order that you may proclaim the mighty acts of him who called you out of darkness into his marvelous light." As a royal priesthood, we praise and bless the Creator for the gifts of creation, thus acting as mediators of praise between the creation and the Creator.

13. The Heidelberg Catechism states clearly that "eternal life" is something that starts now, even as it will bring us into the eschaton, where it finds culmination. Its exposition of the Apostles' Creed is quite beautiful: "Even as I already now experience in my heart the beginning of eternal joy, so after this life I will have perfect blessedness such as no eye has seen, no ear

has increased. People long for the defeat of death and eternal life, even if they do not think that it will be accomplished by a personal God.[14] However, when Christians claim that the gospel means the overcoming of all injustice and oppression, this is not a deistic fantasy about a world that will finally run perfectly on its own. A perfectly just society cannot exist apart from right relationship with the triune God. If a church professes that Christianity can offer liberation from political and economic systems of oppression, without rooting that liberation in the freedom that is won in Christ through the Spirit, that church offers a truncated gospel. These eschatological promises given to the faithful—the promise of eternal life and the promise of liberation from oppression—are good and true, but they become idols if they are detached from communion with the triune God. The risk here is turning God into a means to an end, an instrument to receive the things we desire and long for, when in truth an intimate relationship with the triune God, and through God with all creatures, is the unrelenting hope to which all of Scripture points.

When the heart of the good news of the gospel is not life with the God of love, we end up with multiple gospels, each pursuing a different benefit of salvation. This theological confusion tills the soil for the contemporary debates about the mission of the church and sows the seeds of the conflicts we find ourselves in today. So how have Reformed Christians held together the gracious gifts of God offered to us in Christ and by the Spirit?

The Double Grace of the Gospel[15]

Thus far, we have described the gifts that those who are in Christ through the power of the Spirit will receive in the age to come; yet aspects of these gifts are already present in this life. Despite the great struggles and injustices that we face in this current age, this life is also a preparation of believers for the age to come, a time of repentance and growth in anticipation of Christ's return that will inaugurate the new heavens and the new earth. For Calvin, the shorthand for the great gifts for this life received through our union with Christ is the *duplex gratia*, the double grace of justification and sanctification. As Calvin notes, "Christ was given to us by God's generosity, to be grasped and

---

has heard, no human heart has ever imagined: a blessedness in which to praise God forever." Heidelberg Catechism, Q and A 58 (*Our Faith*, 89).

14. Fox, "Fewer Americans Believe in God."

15. Parts of this section are indebted to the chapter "The Gospel and Justice: Union with Christ, the Law of Love, and the Lord's Supper" in Billings, *Union with Christ*, which also may interest readers seeking to explore the connections between a Reformed sacramental theology and justice.

possessed by us in faith. By partaking of him, we principally receive a double grace: namely, that being reconciled to God through Christ's blamelessness, we may have in heaven instead of a Judge a gracious Father; and secondly, that sanctified by Christ's spirit we may cultivate blamelessness and purity of life."[16] According to Calvin, as the Holy Spirit dwells in the believer, granting them the gift of faith, the believer is enabled to participate in Christ's life, death, resurrection, and ascension. Those who are in Christ through the Spirit's grace thus receive the gift of adoption into God's household; they are no longer strangers but now children of the Father, "and if children, then heirs, heirs of God and joint heirs with Christ" (Rom. 8:17). This double grace constitutes the Christian life as an integrated whole and fuels the church's mission in the world.[17] Before we turn to the church's mission, let's unpack the implications of the double grace of justification and sanctification for the Christian life.

As an article of faith, the doctrine of justification gives believers assurance that those who are in Christ through the Spirit have been declared to be in right relationship with God. According to the doctrine of justification, God freely pardons sinners, on the basis not of their righteousness but of Christ's righteousness. In the words of the Belgic Confession, "The Holy Spirit kindles in our hearts a true faith that embraces Jesus Christ, with all his merits, and makes him its own, and no longer looks for anything apart from him."[18] The believer can "possess" Christ's righteousness only because the Spirit's grace enables and empowers them to "embrace" Christ and thus be made one with him. As people made one with Christ and his righteousness by the Spirit, we are declared justified and thus pardoned of sin by the Father, foreshadowing our final judgment at the end of this age.[19] This has profound implications for the Christian life, for Christ's righteousness "is enough to cover all our sins and to make us confident, freeing the conscience from the fear, dread, and terror of God's approach."[20] Reconciled to the Father in Christ by the grace of the Spirit, the believer rests on the grace of God and can thus live a life of gratitude, having done nothing to earn God's grace. The grace of justification is what makes the Christian life and the church's evangelistic mission not an endless anxious striving but a joyful work of gratitude and love that flows from the very heart of God, revealed to us in Jesus Christ (John 1:18).

---

16. Calvin, *Institutes* 3.11.1.

17. "With good reason, the sum of the gospel is held to consist in repentance and forgiveness of sins. . . . For when this topic is rightly understood it will better appear how man is justified by faith alone, and simple pardon; nevertheless actual holiness of life, so to speak, is not separated from free imputation of righteousness." Calvin, *Institutes* 3.3.1.

18. Belgic Confession, 22 (*Our Faith*, 46).

19. Billings, *Calvin, Participation, and the Gift*, 15.

20. Belgic Confession, 23 (*Our Faith*, 47).

Along with the gift of justification comes the gift of sanctification. In the words of the Belgic Confession, sanctification is "the work of the Holy Spirit," in which the Spirit "regenerates us and makes us new creatures, causing us to live a new life, and freeing us from the slavery of sin."[21] Sanctification is the gift of new life in and through the Spirit that results in "holiness of life" and a life of "repentance."[22] It is important to remember that sanctification is the work of the Spirit in the believer once they are united to God in Christ, not a condition for being united to God. Unlike justification, which according to Calvin is an irrevocable change in status before God based on Christ's righteousness, sanctification is a prolonged process that takes up the entirety of the believer's lifetime and remains incomplete in death. As the believer is sanctified by the Spirit, they are enabled to participate in God's ongoing redemptive work in the world, a work that includes the undoing of sin and its effects in every part of the created order.

From a Reformed perspective, sanctification is not extra credit for particularly passionate Christians who have already been saved by justification. Sanctification is not an add-on to the gospel. Sanctification and justification are distinct-yet-inseparable elements of salvation. To use a tree analogy, they are like the two main branches that grow out of a single trunk—that is, union with God. As Calvin vividly (and jarringly) claims in his Romans commentary, the "gratuitous remission of sins" in justification "can never be separated from the Spirit of regeneration; for this would be as it were to rend Christ asunder."[23] In Christ, by the grace of the Spirit, we are justified and sanctified, forgiven and offered the gift of newness of life in the Spirit.

In Reformed theology, the doctrine of sanctification is also related to how we understand God's law and its role in the Christian life. In his sermons on the Ten Commandments, Calvin preaches that the law contains commandments "whose purpose is to unite us to our God. And that [union with God] constitutes our happiness and glory."[24] Calvin refers to this—what is known as the "third use of the law"—as an instrument by which God draws believers into deeper communion with himself.

Calvin affirmed what were called the first "two uses" of the law in his day: God's law as a teacher, revealing our need for Christ, and God's law as a means to curb human wickedness and promote justice in civil society.[25] However,

---

21. Belgic Confession, 24 (*Our Faith*, 48).
22. Calvin, *Institutes* 3.3.1.
23. Calvin, *Institutes* 3.16.1.
24. Calvin, *Ten Commandments*, 39.
25. These three uses of the law are rooted in the apostle Paul's exhortation to the Galatians found in Gal. 2:15–4:7.

although it was controversial among some Protestants, Calvin and the early Reformed tradition also taught a third use of the law: God's law as providing guidance for believers "to learn more thoroughly each day the nature of the Lord's will to which they aspire," showing believers the shape of the Spirit's work in sanctification.[26] Crucially, this involves receiving God's commands *in light of* the grace of justification. That is to say, to fully see the grace of the law, we first need the light provided to us by the grace of our justification in Christ.[27] In recognition that we are adopted children of God in Christ and therefore justified before our Father, our conscience can "rise above and advance beyond the law, forgetting all law righteousness."[28] Calvin does not think that we can acquire salvation in our fallen state through striving to obey the law. However, freed from the urge of striving to save oneself through works, those who are in Christ can "hear themselves called with fatherly gentleness by God, [and] they will cheerfully and with great eagerness answer, and follow his leading."[29] As adopted children of God, believers are enabled by the Spirit to see the law as a gift that draws them deeper into intimacy and communion with the living God.

The basic components of this third use of the law are taught in a variety of Reformed confessions, from the Reformation era to the late twentieth-century Belhar Confession. One of the most vivid presentations of the third use of the law is found within the third section of the Heidelberg Catechism. The Heidelberg Catechism is organized around a three-part structure: First, it explores our inability to fulfill God's law, displaying our "sin and misery" and thus our need for God. Then it explores how we are "set free" from our sin and misery through the grace of the triune God. Its final, and very substantial, section explores sanctification based on the notion of receiving the law (in this case, the commands to love God and neighbor and the Ten Commandments) as concrete instruction for a life of gratitude.[30]

The Heidelberg Catechism teaches that new life by the Spirit calls the believer to "do whatever I can for my neighbor's good, that I treat others as I would like them to treat me, and that I work faithfully so that I may share with those in need."[31] For the Heidelberg Catechism, pursuing equitable and fair

---

26. Calvin, *Institutes* 2.7.12.

27. "We should, when justification is being discussed, embrace God's mercy alone, turn our attention from ourselves, and look only to Christ." Calvin, *Institutes* 3.19.2.

28. Calvin, *Institutes* 3.19.2.

29. Calvin, *Institutes* 3.19.5.

30. Heidelberg Catechism, Q and A 2 (*Our Faith*, 70).

31. Heidelberg Catechism, Q and A 111 (*Our Faith*, 110). Also see Q 107: "Q. Is it enough then that we do not murder our neighbor in any such way? A. No. By condemning envy, hatred, and anger God wants us to love our neighbors as ourselves, to be patient, peace-loving, gentle,

social relationships through justice isn't an addition to the Christian calling; it's an essential part of the Spirit's work in the Christian life. "Christ, having redeemed us by his blood, is also restoring us by his Spirit into his image, so that with our whole lives we may show that we are thankful to God for his benefits."[32] Our participation in this restoration is the path of sanctification. For the Heidelberg Catechism, sanctification involves growing in love for our neighbor and practicing justice, as emphasized repeatedly in its exposition of the Ten Commandments, which presents the Christian life as one marked by acts of justice.

Christians often separate the calling of reconciliation in Christ from that of evangelism. However, within Reformed theology they go hand in hand, as one could not grasp reconciliation "without at the same time grasping sanctification also," as Calvin notes.[33] Justification, which requires reconciliation to God, and sanctification, which requires cultivating the virtue of justice and evangelizing, "are joined together by an everlasting and indissoluble bond" so that those who are reconciled are irrevocably mandated to do the work of justice as they share the good news.[34]

Some theologians have worried that "justification by faith" rather than "works" would displace the importance of a fruitful life of good works, a life of loving God and neighbor. However, holding on to the notion of the double grace of justification and sanctification, Reformed theology can overcome this tension. In the words of Calvin, "We are justified *not without* works yet not *through* works, since in our sharing in Christ, which justifies us, sanctification is just as much included as righteousness."[35] In receiving the proclamation of the gospel, we never receive one gift (forgiveness of sins) detached from the other (new life in the Spirit). They are, in other words, a *double grace* inseparably received in union with Christ by the Spirit. "Christ justifies no one whom he does not at the same time sanctify. These benefits are joined together by an everlasting and indissoluble bond."[36] Understanding the gospel as union with God in Christ and through the Spirit means that we can hold together the gifts of justification and sanctification. So what implications does the Reformed understanding of double grace have for the Christian life?

---

merciful, and friendly toward them, to protect them from harm as much as we can, and to do good even to our enemies" (*Our Faith*, 109).

32. Heidelberg Catechism, Q and A 86 (*Our Faith*, 101).
33. Calvin, *Institutes* 3.16.1.
34. Calvin, *Institutes* 3.16.1.
35. Calvin, *Institutes* 3.16.1.
36. Calvin, *Institutes* 4.16.1.

After speaking of how salvation comes through faith in Christ, the apostle Paul asks, "But how are they to call on one in whom they have not believed? And how are they to believe in one of whom they have never heard? And how are they to hear without someone to proclaim him? And how are they to proclaim him unless they are sent? As it is written, 'How beautiful are the feet of those who bring good news!'" (Rom. 10:14–15). The church is *sent* to joyfully make the good news of God in Christ known to the world, both in word and in deed. As we saw in chapter 4, the Canons of Dort state, "It is the promise of the gospel that whoever believes in Christ crucified shall not perish but have eternal life. This promise, together with the command to repent and believe, ought to be announced and declared without differentiation or discrimination to all nations and people."[37] Indeed, although a myth persists in some circles that the Reformed tradition has little interest in the evangelist aspect of global mission, the significant place of Reformed Christians in the history of mission tells a different story.[38]

At the same time, as ambassadors of Christ's reconciliation, we are called not only to announce the good news but also to live out this reconciliation as we participate in God's powerful work of uniting all of creation, across the walls of difference and indifference, through Christ and the Spirit (Eph. 2:14). This reconciliation demands attending to unjust structures and systems that keep people in the world separated not only from God but also from one another and from the rest of creation. The life of growing in loving communion with God *and with our neighbors* is central to the gospel. The Christian life is a life of pursuing love of God and neighbor, the sum of the law that Christ gives us (Matt. 22:36–40; Mark 12:28–34; and Luke 10:25–28). Displaying God's love in the world through building hospitals, advocating for the welfare of vulnerable people in our communities, and caring for creation is not mere decoration for the gospel. It is important work. But even more than that: Insofar as working for justice is an aspect of our sanctification, it is core to the gospel of salvation. Justice in all its forms is a fruit of the Spirit's gift of new life.

As a result, both the proclamation of the gospel through evangelism *and* concrete works of justice and love are integral to living gospel lives. Through sharing the good news of Christ with those who don't know him and caring for and loving our neighbor, we demonstrate that we are living into our adopted identity as children of the God who seeks to restore communion with us and the whole of creation. Calvin was emphatic about this, moving directly from

37. Canons of Dort, 2.5 (*Our Faith*, 127).
38. See Stewart, *Ten Myths*, chap. 5.

our calling to love God and neighbor to the necessity of a Christian commitment to justice and equity, not simply within the church but to all persons, who are our neighbors.[39] Today we may expand Calvin's words to include not only our human neighbors but also our other creaturely neighbors who, living under the conditions of the curse, groan as they await the renewal of the heavens and the earth (Rom. 8:22).

In sum, there is no gospel without sanctification and justification. Therefore, there is no church mission that doesn't entail both the evangelistic witness of the forgiveness of our sins in Christ and the cultivation of justice in our souls and in the cities in which we live. Both are gospel gifts not to be separated or prioritized one over the other. The true gospel to which Christians are called to witness entails not only our justification by grace through faith but also our *sanctification* by grace through faith.

Integral Mission and the Reformed Tradition

This integral understanding of the double grace of justification and sanctification corresponds with what Latin American theologians and missiologists like Escobar, Padilla, and Costas describe as the church's *integral mission*. In the 1970s, a group of evangelical pastors, missiologists, and theologians out of Latin America brought a powerful witness to an evangelical world that was wrestling with what it meant to promote the gospel in the turmoil of the twentieth century.[40] Their witness was this: The call of the gospel is not just to believe in God and be forgiven from our sins but also to repent from sin and live a life of righteousness seeking justice. In other words, they said that the church's mission ought to be *integral*, entailing both evangelistic witness to the gospel and the cultivation of social justice in the world. To be a missional church not only means door-to-door evangelism—though telling people about the good news of Jesus Christ is an important aspect of the church's calling. It's also getting involved to seek the welfare of the city in which the church is planted, through economic, political, and social advocacy on behalf of the vulnerable, the marginalized, and the oppressed. In doing both, by God's grace, the church fulfills its mission and call to proclaim in word and deed the good news of Jesus Christ and the kingdom of God he has come to establish.

Though well-grounded in Scripture and in the history of the church, this understanding of mission as integral represents a departure from the modern

---

39. See Billings, *Calvin, Participation, and the Gift*, 151–70.
40. This group of Latin American pastors, theologians, and missiologists convened to form the Fraternidad Teologica Latinoamericana/Latin American Theological Fraternity.

missionary movement as embodied by many evangelical churches in North America and Europe. Padilla writes that the evangelical church in the West had embraced a view of missions in which "the purpose of missions was to save souls and to plant churches, mainly in foreign countries."[41] Padilla recognizes that the Spirit has used this traditional missionary model to bring many people to Christ, and moreover, that many missionaries who participated, and still participate, in this traditional approach are devoted Christians who deserve our respect for their faithfulness in serving God. However, he says, this mode of mission remains incomplete at best and can lead to the cultivation of churches that do not fully live out their calling.

Padilla offers four problematic divisions that the traditional model of missions creates.[42] First, Padilla argues that the traditional missionary model creates a "dichotomy between churches that send out missionaries (generally located in the Christian West) and churches that receive missionaries (almost exclusively in countries in the so-called Two-Thirds World: Asia, Africa, and Latin America)."[43] This trend appears to be slowly reversing in recent decades. Nevertheless, the dichotomy between sending and receiving churches manifests a powerful problem for our understanding of mission. The task of fulfilling the church's mission becomes that of the "sending" churches, and "receiving" churches are regarded merely as beneficiaries, not full participants in and agents of God's mission in the world. This creates the illusion that missionary-receiving countries and churches are, proverbially, the "mission field," places where the gospel has yet to take root or mature. This kind of infantilizing narrative often obscures the deep historical roots of the gospel in many places in the majority world and creates the false sense that the church is more at home, or exhibits greater maturity, in Western nations.

Padilla identifies a second dichotomy that grows out of the first: For many lifelong missionaries, their sending country remains their "home," and the country in which they do their ministry never ceases to be "the missionary field."[44] This creates two powerful and interrelated distortions. First, to do missionary work for the church entails leaving to go somewhere else, and rarely, if ever, is mission related to living out the Christian calling in one's own neighborhood or city. Second, the places where missionaries live and minister for decades—often with their families and, therefore, where their most intimate relationships are found—never fully become home. The wound that this leaves is often left untreated and leads to experiences of rootlessness and an

41. Padilla, *What Is Integral Mission?*, 5–6.
42. Padilla, *What Is Integral Mission?*, 5–11.
43. Padilla, *What Is Integral Mission?*, 6.
44. Padilla, *What Is Integral Mission?*, 7.

incapacity to feel like one fully belongs anywhere. This wound is present not only in the missionaries themselves but also in their families.

Third, Padilla notes that the traditional model delegates the task of living out the church's mission to missionaries who are specially trained for "foreign missions." Mission is then not treated, as it should be, as an aspect of every Christian's vocation and calling.[45]

Fourth and finally, and related to the rendering of missionary work as the special task of certain individuals, Padilla notes that the traditional missionary model creates a dichotomy between "the life and the mission of the church."[46] Missionary work becomes a branch of the church's programming, distinct from the church's other tasks, such as planning and executing Sunday worship, offering social services to the community, and discipling the youth.

By contrast, integral mission understands the mission of the church not just as another church program but as the beating heart of everything the church does. That is because the mission of the church is not first and foremost a task of the church; it is the church's participation in the redemptive work of the triune God in the world. As missiologist Darrell Guder notes, "We have come to see that mission is not merely an activity of the church. Rather, mission is the result of God's initiative, rooted in God's purposes to restore and heal creation."[47] As believers live out the church's mission through being gathered and sent each Sunday morning, through the work of evangelism and the cultivation of social justice, and in bearing witness to God's goodness through their daily work as lawyers, farmers, teachers, and every other profession, believers are not merely "doing their job" as Christians but are simultaneously being conformed to Jesus Christ and, ultimately, by the grace of the Spirit, being drawn into the very life of God.[48] The church's mission is thus nothing less than our active communion, intimacy, and belonging with the triune God, as those sent by God to be a channel of God's blessing to others and called to live faithful, hopeful, and loving lives with our neighbors.

Therefore, whether we live in Europe or Latin America, whether we reside at home or abroad, whether we have received formal theological training or have simply embraced the life of faith in Jesus Christ, and indeed, whether we serve God as clergy or as faithful church members, we are all called to

---

45. Padilla, *What Is Integral Mission?*, 7.
46. Padilla, *What Is Integral Mission?*, 7.
47. Guder and Hunsberger, *Missional Church*, 4–5.
48. "From a theological perspective, pastors and worship leaders do not invite workers into the mission of God. The workers in the pews have been laboring within the *missio Dei* all week long. Gathered worship should not only acknowledge the worker's participation in God's mission but also bless it. The work of the people is integral to the mission of God, not incidental." Kaemingk and Wilson, *Work and Worship*, 47.

live out the mission of God in every moment of our lives, in whatever we do or say. As Padilla puts it, "Integral mission is the means designed by God to carry out, within history, his purpose of love and justice revealed in Jesus Christ, through the church and in the power of the Spirit."[49] The mission of the church is therefore not limited to the proclamation of the gospel to unbelievers; it is a whole life given in service to God and in love of neighbor.

Today, some who identify with the Reformed tradition have embraced the more traditional account of mission rather than this integral view. For example, Kevin DeYoung and Greg Gilbert define the church's mission this way: "The mission of the church is to go into the world and make disciples by declaring the gospel of Jesus Christ in the power of the Spirit and gathering these disciples into churches, that they might worship the Lord and obey his commands now and in eternity to the glory of God the Father."[50] According to this definition, the church's mission is, at its core, evangelism and discipleship. While doing acts of justice and obeying God's commands are important, they are not the church's central mission. This chapter has offered an alternative account of mission, one that values evangelism and discipleship but embraces an integral understanding of the church's mission in which the church is called to proclaim the gospel, disciple into maturity, and love our neighbor in cultivating justice, all in presenting our lives as an offering of thanks to God in Christ (Rom. 12:1).

In expositing this view, we have drawn on a more robust and classically Reformed understanding of the church's mission that sees both the root of the church's work of cultivating social justice and her proclamation of the good news of Christ as the love of God for all of creation. The love of God creates, restores, heals, unites, and binds up a broken and hurting creation. The love of God gathers us and heals us. It is the good news that we proclaim, and it is what fuels the church's work of justice and evangelism. The love of God is the beating heart of the good news of the kingdom of God that Jesus inaugurates. It is what he teaches across his home region of Galilee and in Jerusalem, and it is why he sends his disciples to go throughout the nations to teach and proclaim this gospel.

Today, the witness of people like Padilla, Escobar, and Costas continues to be felt globally through various groups of Christians around the world who are committed to the church's integral mission in each of their own contexts.[51]

---

49. Padilla, *What Is Integral Mission?*, 9.
50. DeYoung and Gilbert, *What Is the Mission of the Church?*, 62.
51. One example of a group of evangelicals forged around the notion of integral mission is the Micah Network, formed in 1999 and now called Micah Global. Micah Global today includes hundreds of Christian institutions and members whose vision is forged around Mic. 6:8: "He

Integral mission is an account of the church's mission that Christians rooted
in the Reformed tradition—with its claims about the gospel as a double grace
received in union with Christ through the Spirit—can and should embrace.
So what examples can we find in the history of the Reformed tradition of
people living out the church's integral mission in the world?

The Belhar Confession: Calling for Unity, Reconciliation, and Justice in South Africa's Apartheid

The Belhar Confession, accepted in 1986 by the Dutch Reformed Mission
Church, speaks to the issues of the church's unity, reconciliation, and justice in direct opposition to both the South African government's apartheid
and the South African Reformed churches' separation of communions on
the basis of race. We briefly mentioned the Belhar Confession in chapter 2
as one among many global Reformed confessions that display multivalent
catholicity, but because this confession is especially significant to the topic
of this chapter, we are engaging the Belhar Confession here as an example
of a Reformed theology of justice and witness. While it was written in South
Africa, it has been adopted by a number of Reformed communions in Europe
and the United States and can provide insights to the Reformed tradition
as a whole.

Dirk J. Smit, a South African theologian and one author of the Belhar
Confession, writes, "The story of the Reformed faith in South Africa is indeed
intimately interwoven with the story of apartheid and the struggle against
apartheid."[52] This was true for good and for ill. The story of the Belhar
Confession begins well over a century before it was written, when the Dutch
Reformed Church made a fateful decision to *dis*integrate its gospel. Their
reasons for doing so are quite telling.

In 1857 the General Assembly of the Dutch Reformed Church (DRC) received a request from some white members for permission to celebrate the
Lord's Supper separately from Black members of the church. This request
was clearly against the Reformed polity of the DRC, which emerged from the
Synod of Dort.[53] Moreover, the 1857 Synod searched and found no biblical
grounds for the separation of communion based on race.

---

has told you, O mortal, what is good; and what does the LORD require of you but to do justice,
and to love kindness, and to walk humbly with your God?"

52. Smit, "Reformed Faith, Justice and the Struggle Against Apartheid," 27.

53. Indeed, an earlier request for separate communion had been rejected by the Dutch Reformed Church, for the Lord's Supper was to be administered "without distinction of colour."
See Smit, "South Africa," 17.

However, in its own self-understanding, the DRC assembly decided to be "flexible." They gave a pastoral accommodation that, "due to the weakness of some" (the white members who made the request), communion and worship could be organized for separate celebrations based on race.[54] Unfortunately, this pastoral accommodation "gradually became common practice" and later the "norm for the order and structure of the church."[55] This 1857 decision led to the establishment of a separate, racially based denomination, under the ownership of the DRC, for Coloured members in 1881 (the Dutch Reformed Mission Church) and later, in 1951, one for Black members (the Dutch Reformed Church in Africa).[56]

Lest we think that this movement emerging from the 1857 DRC decision is utterly foreign to today's concerns, at the time it was framed as a way to be flexible and missional rather than rigid and traditional. John de Gruchy notes that "despite the fact that this development went against earlier synodical decisions that segregation in the church was contrary to the Word of God, it was rationalized on grounds of missiology and practical necessity. Missiologically it was argued that people were best evangelized and best worshiped God in their own language and cultural setting, a position reinforced by German Lutheran missiology and somewhat akin to the church-growth philosophy of our own time."[57]

Indeed, de Gruchy is correct in making connections to church-growth philosophy. Donald McGavran (1897–1990), one of the twentieth century's most influential missiologists, founded the church-growth movement. While he did not argue for separation based on race, one of his central ideas was that the churches most likely to grow are the ones with an affinity, specifically a "homogeneous unit." As church leaders in the United States heard this, many embraced the idea that if you wanted to be a missional, growing church, you needed to focus on a homogeneous unity, whether in shared ethnic identity, socioeconomic status, or belonging to the same generation. Whether this was a cause for, or simply an endorsement of, deeply segregating forces within the United States, this vision is clearly apparent in the congregational landscape today.

Whether in South Africa or the United States, the gospel of one new humanity in Christ can easily be sacrificed at the altar of church growth. Evangelism

54. Smit, "South Africa," 17, 33.

55. Smit, "South Africa," 33.

56. In South African racial classification under colonial and apartheid systems, *Coloured* referred to people of mixed racial ancestry, and *Black* referred to indigenous Africans. In the nineteenth century, these racial categories were socially enforced and increasingly formalized in church and state institutions, laying the groundwork for their legal codification under twentieth-century apartheid.

57. De Gruchy, *Liberating Reformed Theology*, 23–24.

and the resulting church growth can be a fruit of the Spirit's work. But when this is engineered in a way that bypasses reconciliation and justice, we end up with a truncated gospel. The good news does not always look attractive for those who are pragmatic or missionally minded if *mission* primarily means adding numbers to the church. Having a pious heart or an ambitious mission program is no assurance that one is faithfully responding to the good news of the gospel, which overcomes walls of cultural hostility in Christ.

As the decades passed from the nineteenth to the early twentieth century, what began as a pastoral accommodation without any clear biblical justification was eventually developed into an elaborate theology that sought to ground the separation of the races in creation. Due to this theological understanding, the DRC became an avid public advocate of apartheid as a government policy beginning in 1924, claiming that "competition between black and white on an economic level leads to poverty, friction, misunderstanding, suspicion and embitterment."[58] The DRC, and its new ideology emerging from its broken theology of the Lord's Supper and justice, became a major source for the political ideology that led to the system of apartheid.

What exactly was apartheid? Apartheid "literally means apartness, separateness," as Smit points out.[59] While it became the official political system in South Africa in 1948, starting in the 1960s it was labeled by its advocates as *separate development*. Politically, it "sanctioned strict racial segregation and political and economic discrimination against all people legally classified as 'nonwhite.'"[60] But as the label *separate development* implies, its justification was based on a particular way of seeing race and ethnicity, which was applied to the notion of *nations* in Scripture and claimed to value human distinctness. Yet it did so coercively and in a profoundly unjust way, directing most of the country's financial and educational resources to the country's white population, which was the minority overall.

In the face of this separation within the church, then enforced by the government, the threefold emphasis of the Belhar Confession directly confronts the problem: unity, reconciliation, and justice. The church's *unity* is "both a gift and an obligation for the church of Jesus Christ."[61] While the DRC had said that they were "spiritually united," even though separated based on race, the Belhar Confession rejects this and any doctrine "which professes that this spiritual unity is truly being maintained in the bond of peace while believers of the same confession are in effect alienated from one another for

58. Pitikoe, "Ecumenical Address," 169.
59. Smit, "Reformed Faith, Justice and the Struggle Against Apartheid," 27.
60. Smit, "Reformed Faith, Justice and the Struggle Against Apartheid," 27.
61. Belhar Confession, 2 (*Our Faith*, 146).

the sake of diversity and in despair of reconciliation."[62] Instead, for the sake of living into the Spirit's work, and in witnessing to the gospel in the world, "this unity must become visible so that the world may believe that separation, enmity and hatred between people and groups is sin which Christ has already conquered."[63] On *reconciliation*, the Belhar Confession denounces any doctrine endorsing the "forced separation of people on the grounds of race and color."[64] They confess that "God's life-giving Word and Spirit has conquered the powers of sin and death, and therefore also of irreconciliation and hatred, bitterness and enmity"; thus the church is called "to live in a new obedience which can open new possibilities of life for society and the world."[65] And on *justice*, the Belhar Confession calls "the church as the possession of God" to "stand where the Lord stands, namely against injustice and with the wronged."[66]

The ground on which the Belhar Confession stands to decry racial segregation in the church and society is nothing less than the gospel. So long as the white South Africans refused to meet with their Black siblings, so long as they refused to cultivate a common life in church and society, they bore false witness to the gospel of Christ through whom God promises to reconcile all peoples, nations, and tongues across the walls of enmity and difference that divide them. The very gospel that the DRC proclaimed on Sundays in their racially segregated services witnessed against them. For it was impossible to claim that those who are baptized in Christ through the Spirit are adopted children of God's one household while, in their everyday lives, South African Christians lived as rival houses. The very body of Christ was being torn in two.[67] Therefore, the Belhar Confession renders racial segregation in the church, and by extension in society, to be *status confessionis*, an issue that threatens the integrity and veracity of the very gospel that the church confesses. The gospel demands the undoing of systems of racial segregation and oppression and the reconciliation of all peoples everywhere in the world in the name of Jesus Christ. The world tells one story. The gospel tells another. The church's job is to leave the world's story and to be transformed to the story of the gospel, thus moving from lives marked and wounded by disunity and oppression into lives of unity and reconciliation. And this gospel claim

62. Belhar Confession, 2 (*Our Faith*, 146).
63. Belhar Confession, 2 (*Our Faith*, 146).
64. Belhar Confession, 3 (*Our Faith*, 147).
65. Belhar Confession, 3 (*Our Faith*, 147).
66. Belhar Confession, 4 (*Our Faith*, 148).
67. One of the benefits of being in Christ through the Spirit is being joined to one another as well. The vertical (relationship with God) has implications for the horizontal (relationships with others, creation, and one's own self). Justification has implications for sanctification.

is what we inhabit and inherit in the Christian rites of the Lord's Supper and baptism.

Baptism calls us not only to remember and receive the promise of our union with Christ through the Spirit but also summons us to live lives that correspond to such a truth. In baptism we receive the promise of membership in the household of God and a unity grounded in our shared belonging to God. In turn, the Lord's Supper is a meal wherein believers are reminded of our story as people gathered and sent in Christ. In the Lord's Supper, the Spirit calls people from all tribes, tongues, and nations to share a common table where they enjoy what Calvin calls a "spiritual banquet," wherein it is Christ on whom believers feed in faith. In common fellowship around the body and the blood of Christ, believers are joined to God and to one another, thus playing out the very drama of the gospel through the elements of bread and wine. Baptism and the Lord's Supper are signs and seals not only of being clothed with Christ's righteousness and thus justified before God but also of our communion across racial and ethnic markers through a shared identity in Christ by the power of the Spirit.[68] In a way, the very liturgy that the DRC practiced was an affront to and a witness against any story that prompted division and disunity, whether along racial, ethnic, or economic lines. Their baptism and their celebration of the Lord's Supper was a summons to embrace the double grace of justification and sanctification, to proclaim their salvation in Christ, and to condemn any worldly ideology that denied the reconciliation between peoples. The vertical and horizontal, the good news of reconciliation with God and with neighbor in Christ through the Spirit, are always at play in the gospel, in the Christian liturgy, and, therefore, are always integral aspects of the church's mission.

If the gospel is reduced to justification *without* sanctification, and therefore the mission of the church is only to make converts who believe they have been justified, then the fateful decision to separate congregations or denominations based on race might seem defensible. But if the gospel purports an integral mission grounded in justification and sanctification by grace through faith, forgiveness of sins, and the reconciliation of all things in Christ, then the church and her mission are also fundamentally to be integral, always and unequivocally summoning people to be reconciled to God and to one another through the proclamation of the good news and the cultivation of social justice.

---

68. For further exploration of how a Reformed theology and practice of the Lord's Supper has wide implications for living into the God-given "household of God," with its racial and ethnic diversity, see Billings, *Remembrance, Communion, and Hope*, esp. chap. 7.

The Heidelberg Catechism: Christian Identity in the Face of Division

This chapter has argued that understanding the gospel as loving communion with the triune God and with our neighbors generates an integral understanding of the church's mission wherein evangelistic witness and cultivating social justice are distinct-but-inseparable works of the church. In making such a claim, we do not wish to enter the fray of people trying to dictate what the right kind of Christianity is or what the right kind of Christian life looks like. Questions about calling, vocation, and the nature and shape of the Christian life are ageless. Although we are not the first generation to ask them, this generation is asking these questions at a time in history characterized by deep polarization in which warring political factions are fighting over who is *truly* Christian. Against the temptation to define ourselves or the church's mission by a political ideology or contemporary cultural current—whether conservative or liberal, fundamentalist or progressive, mainline or evangelical—let us learn from what our earliest Reformed siblings discovered at a time when the church in Europe was suffering deep division and strife.

The Heidelberg Catechism was written when Christian identity was deeply fraught. Protestants and Roman Catholics entered into violent disputes over whose version of Christianity was true. Yet the fight was not only between Protestants and Roman Catholics. Even among Protestants, contentious and divisive debates exploded throughout the sixteenth and seventeenth centuries about whose brand of Protestantism was the right one. Some followed Luther and Melanchthon and others Zwingli and Calvin. Into this fray, the Heidelberg Catechism sought to offer an account of the Christian life that called the church into unity.[69] The very first question and answer of the Heidelberg Catechism offers us a powerful statement about the nature of the Christian life that can serve as a proper starting point for our own debates today. The catechism begins with this fundamental statement of Christian identity: "What is your only comfort in life and in death? That I am not my own, but belong—body and soul, in life and in death—to my faithful savior, Jesus Christ."[70]

Fundamental to a Reformed understanding of the Christian life is that the core of the Christian life is not self-referential. The object of our lives is

---

69. Though the Heidelberg Catechism is known as one of the most ecumenical of the Reformed catechisms and confessions, the addition of Q and A 80 in its third edition—labeling the Mass "condemnable idolatry"—introduces challenges for ecumenical dialogue. Most translations note this as a later addition, and Reformed communions vary in how they address this issue.

70. Heidelberg Catechism, Q and A 1 (*Our Faith*, 69).

not to point to ourselves at all, neither to our accomplishments nor to our defeats, nor is it about pointing to our theological heroes or favorite political ideologies. Instead, the core of the Christian life is about pointing to God's love for us revealed in Jesus Christ through the Spirit. This is one of the deep mysteries of the Christian faith, that the more we correspond our lives to Jesus, such that our lives are measured by Christ's own life, the more truly we become ourselves. Put another way, the more we imitate Christ, the more authentically *us* we become.[71] However, conforming one's life to Christ is not something that can be accomplished merely by hard work. Being conformed to Christ is about opening ourselves up to the Holy Spirit's work in our lives. It is the Spirit who, by dwelling in us, conforms our lives so that we bear witness to Christ. This means that gratitude, not merit, is at the foundation of the Christian life. Whether we are doing door-to-door evangelism or serving food at a local soup kitchen, we do so not out of a sense of anxiety but out of deep gratitude. For the church in mission depends fully on the Spirit descending on our lives and filling us with the presence of Christ, so that those who are witnessing our work and hearing our testimony may be drawn closer to Christ and the Spirit, who are at work reconciling all things to God the Father.

71. This is what Paul meant when, in Eph. 4:22, he spoke of putting away the "old self," the false self.

7

Eschatology: In the End, What?

*Key Question: What Does Reformed Theology Teach
About the End Times?*

When I (Suzanne) teach on eschatology, many of my Reformed students say that this is their first formal teaching of any kind on issues related to the end times. They have often grown up in church, been through youth and adult Christian education, and some have gone to Christian schools, but almost never, in preaching or teaching, has anyone broached the topic of eschatology. Staid Reformed folks tend not to talk about the "end times" very much. An outsider coming into a Reformed community might well wonder: Is there a Reformed approach to eschatology? Or does the Reformed tradition somehow opt out of this Christian teaching?

In this chapter we explore how biblical eschatology does have a crucial role in Reformed theology, even if it is a neglected topic in some Reformed churches. Indeed, it relates to what the Westminster Catechism states as the "chief end" of humankind: "to glorify God and enjoy him forever."[1] Perhaps eschatology is neglected because the moment anyone mentions a topic like the return of Jesus, for example, many people's minds go straight to celebrity preachers who have predicted the date of Christ's return, were utterly mistaken, and turned Christianity into a laughing stock (often making a good deal of money in the process). Or they think of preachers, bloggers, or

---

1. Westminster Shorter Catechism, Q and A 1 (Dennison, *Reformed Confessions*, 4:353).

songwriters who encourage us to live in anticipation of the rapture and try to fit every major national and international event or natural disaster into a timetable for the coming tribulation. Many assume eschatology is about predicting the time of Jesus's return, not wanting to be left behind, and anticipating the end of the world.

The historic Reformed tradition most definitely believes in the return of Jesus Christ in glory and gives an important place to eschatology in the broad biblical sense. Like Christians throughout the ages, the Reformed affirm with the Apostles' Creed that the resurrected Christ has ascended to "the right hand of God the Father almighty. From there he will come to judge the living and the dead." Thus, in light of the Spirit's work in salvation, believers look forward to "the resurrection of the body, and the life everlasting."[2] In the end, just as in the beginning, God the Creator loves his finite and small creatures extravagantly and desires to have fellowship with them as the covenant Lord. In eschatology, we gladly confess that the Creator of the universe has not abandoned his creation, even in its rebellion, but promises to come again in Christ to judge, cleanse, and renew it. While our historic confessions do not have much to say about eschatology in relation to the whole of creation, the Reformed tradition upholds the New Testament teaching that Christ's redeeming work is not simply for human beings but for the whole of creation.[3] All creation is groaning, awaiting the fullness of its redemption alongside the fullness of the redemption of the people of God (Rom. 8:19–23). Just as all things were made by, through, and for Christ, and in him all things hold together, so also the victory Christ won on the cross is for all things (Col. 1:15–20). This Colossians text is not about *soteriological universalism* (the claim that all people will be saved). Rather, it is about the creation-wide scope of redemption in Christ. At the eschaton, therefore, sin and evil and death, and all the consequences of sin and evil and death, will be removed for us and for the whole of creation, and we along with all creation will glorify God.

Reformed theology teaches this good news with vigor! It is a shame that many within Reformed churches today have little familiarity with it. Unfortunately, what goes under the name *eschatology* today—end-times predictions correlated with contemporary politics, undergirded by a conviction that the church will be "raptured" from an earth headed only for destruction—is unscriptural and deeply misleading, from a Reformed standpoint. At times, since Reformed Christians do not want to be associated with such movements, we

---

2. Apostles' Creed (*Our Faith*, 13).

3. For an early example of this, see John Calvin's understanding that the whole of creation will participate in the eschaton. Tyra, *"Neither the Spirit Without the Flesh,"* chap. 6.

don't even know how to begin to have a conversation about eschatology. This silence on eschatology in our churches is both disappointing and dangerous.

It is disappointing because when we neglect to speak of eschatology we are not providing witness to the fullness of the story of God, or the fullness of the gospel as we find in Scripture. The whole of Scripture, from Genesis to Revelation, is oriented toward the future consummation of all things. It is not just a few books, or a few chapters of books taken in isolation, like Revelation and parts of Daniel, Ezekiel, and Zechariah. According to the Old and New Testaments, the arc of time itself bends toward the coming Day of the Lord—God will appear, the contamination of sin and brokenness will be cleansed, and God will dwell with his creation in fullness. As Christians, we can boldly petition for this Day of the Lord in hope, for none other than Jesus Christ himself will return, bringing the fullness of salvation and the coming kingdom.

Neglecting eschatology is dangerous because all of us rightly have questions about what God will do "in the end." If eschatology is not preached, taught, and discussed, people will understandably turn elsewhere for less-than-helpful answers. It is also dangerous because what we think will happen "in the end" shapes how we live our lives *now*, even if we aren't aware of it. Bad eschatology leads to bad discipleship.

A Reformed eschatology does not claim to have new information about the end of the world that has just been disclosed in the last ten or twenty years—or the latest news cycle. While a Reformed approach to eschatology has some distinctive emphases, our approach belongs in the mainstream of the historic Christian tradition as a shared *catholic* doctrine, found in the Apostles' and Nicene creeds and drawing on extremely deep reservoirs of biblical testimony. In the next section, we will take a short dive into a central storyline from the Bible that underlies Reformed eschatology.

The Pit, the Temple, and the Coming of the Lord

When we pray the psalms, we enter into the geography of our life with God and creation—geography that a biblical eschatology puts to use in surprising ways. Praying with the psalmist, we do not approach God and the world in a detached way; we cry out in our need:

> O God, you are my God, I seek you,
>   my soul thirsts for you;
> my flesh faints for you,
>   as in a dry and weary land where there is no water. (Ps. 63:1)

We know from Genesis that we are created for communion with God—to walk and talk with him. We are meant to dwell with God and creation, as in the garden of Eden. But right now, with the psalmist, we thirst and ache in a desert land. The communion of creation has been disrupted. While the psalmist declares "How very good and pleasant it is when kindred live together in unity!" (Ps. 133:1), we know that often our lives don't reflect this call. We live in fellowship with, but also in alienation from, one another. In a world of abuse and contempt and enmity, we cry with the psalmist for deliverance from our enemies (Ps. 139:19–24). Truly, God made our bodies, this earth, and its many creatures to testify to his glory. And as God's creation, they are still good. "Oh Lord, how manifold are your works! In wisdom you have made them all; the earth is full of your creatures" (Ps. 104:24). But communion with God and others has been poisoned by alienation and hatred.

Thus, rather than communion with God in the garden, we cry out to God from a deep and miry pit—one of the most widespread and significant landscapes in the geography of the psalms. The pit is in darkness, where the psalmist fears being overcome by the silence of death, by the terror of his enemies, by distance from God's presence.

However, the pit also relates to another part of the geography of the psalms: the temple.[4] The temple is the opposite of the pit; it is the dwelling place of God—the place of light, of God in his life-giving presence. At the center of the temple is the Holy of Holies, carefully designed by divine instructions given in Exodus to be the throne room of the king of the universe.[5]

From the pit, the psalmist aches for the presence of the Lord in the temple:

> One thing I asked of the Lord,
>   that will I seek after:
> to live in the house of the Lord
>   all the days of my life,
> to behold the beauty of the Lord,
>   and to inquire in his temple. (Ps. 27:4)

What does all of this have to do with eschatology? Many biblical scholars have pointed out how God's creation in Genesis uses temple imagery. God creates the cosmos as a place for his own dwelling; Eden is a garden-temple.

---

4. Jon Levenson describes how the pit of Sheol is the antinomy of the temple in this biblical geography: "To move from Sheol to the Temple is to move from death to life." Levenson, *Restoration of Israel*, 97; see chap. 5 for a development of this theme.

5. For a Christian account of how the temple shapes the eschatological horizon in Scripture, see Richter, *Epic of Eden*, chap. 5.

Likewise, the new creation is portrayed in temple terms in the New Testament. When Revelation says of the new creation, "Death will be no more; mourning and crying and pain will be no more" (21:4), this is framed not as the main *purpose* of the new creation but as a *consequence* of the temple-like fellowship God will have with his people: "See, the home of God is among mortals. He will dwell with them; they will be his peoples, and God himself will be with them" (21:3).

Moreover, the tabernacle (a portable temple) and the temple are absolutely central to how God's dwelling among us in Jesus Christ is described in the New Testament: "The Word became flesh and lived [or, *tabernacled*] among us" in Jesus (John 1:14). Jesus claims that he himself, in his body, is the true temple (John 2:19–21). He is the true presence of God, the true priest and the true sacrifice for sin (Heb. 4:14; 10:12). Of course, the biblical imagery for the temple must reckon with a real problem: sin and alienation. Cain killed his brother Abel; people gathered to make a name for themselves at the Tower of Babel; with the psalmist, we too cry out from the pit—humanity, in ancient times and today, lives in idolatry and alienation. God in his holiness and beauty cannot fully dwell with sinful creation, just as oil and water cannot truly commune. But rather than abandoning creation, the Lord lovingly gives a place where heaven and earth can come together and the holy God and creation can dwell in harmony, even if in the limited space of the temple. Thus, the Lord commands the Israelites, through Moses, "Make me a sanctuary, so that I may dwell among [you]" (Exod. 25:8). This sanctuary of the tabernacle was accompanied with the gift of God's law, giving Israel a path toward obedience and a sacrificial system to atone for their ongoing sin. God's purpose in creation was for the whole of creation to be his dwelling place. In accommodation to sin, he chose a people (Israel) and a place (the temple) to testify to his kingship that humanity, in rebellion, had denied.

Thus, it should not surprise us that when Christ comes, as the perfect dwelling place of God, the temple in his own person, he not only brings the loving presence of God but also takes on our alienation and sin. Because God won't abandon us to our sin, Jesus himself must be not only the *priest* of the temple but also the *sacrifice*. And in his resurrection, Jesus is the "first fruits" of the prophesied new creation, in which the temple of the cosmos is judged and cleansed, and God again dwells in fullness with his people. Christ, as our priest and our righteous sacrifice, ascended to the Father, bringing his human body with him—a pledge that we who live in frail human bodies can dare to hope for everlasting life, belonging to him. Until the day he appears again to initiate this final and full temple-like fellowship, we cry, "Come, Lord Jesus." Come to us, Lord, in your holy and loving presence.

As we can see from this big canonical storyline, if we want a biblical theology of eschatology we also must have a theology of beginnings—of creation, of Israel, and of God's reconciling work in Christ. In the beginning God made bodies and the material world as his good dwelling place. That matters for eschatology. God doesn't create the earth and our bodies to be thrown away; he intends to dwell in them. But humanity turned away from God and his commands and toward sin and contamination. As a result, they find themselves helpless, in a pit, far from the light of God's temple. Even so, in an astonishing act of love, the Lord promises in covenant to come to Israel in the temple, and to come to the cosmos in Jesus Christ, so that communion with God and creation can be restored. We're not there yet. This communion will not take place until Christ's kingship is uncontested by sin, death, and the devil—by the "cosmic powers of this present darkness" (Eph. 6:12). Until Christ comes again, we pray, "Your kingdom come. Your will be done, on earth as it is in heaven" (Matt. 6:10). Our prayer will not be *fully* answered until the *eschaton*—the consummation of all things when Christ comes again.

Thus, eschatology is not just about one point in Christian doctrine; it is a dimension of all theological topics and of the whole life of faith. This is because we are living in what New Testament scholars call the in-between time—the time between Jesus's victory over sin and death and his return in glory. This tension, between what Christ has already done and what has not yet been fully consummated, means that every doctrine awaits and points us toward eschatological fulfillment. So, our Christology is not complete if we reflect only on the birth, ministry, death, resurrection, and ascension of Jesus. All of this will find its consummation in his return in glory. Baptism and the Lord's Supper are not simply about what God in Christ has done and is doing; they also point us toward and give us a genuine foretaste of what he will do at the time when our union and communion with the Father in the Son by the Holy Spirit is complete. The purpose of election from all eternity is that we will finally be fully conformed to the image of the Son, which will take place when we behold him face-to-face in glory. We could point to the future, eschatological dimensions of every topic we have covered in this book, and any other theological topic too.

Our approach to eschatology shapes the way we live in the in-between time. When we see it as the culmination of all of God's promises and purposes, and when we understand that God is already bringing anticipations and foretastes of the fullness of the coming kingdom, then we see that part of our calling as the people of God means to walk now in the trajectory of this future that has already broken into our present. We are called to participate now, by grace, in those hints and foretastes of a future that is already at work in the world.

We are to live as the new creation we already are in Christ (2 Cor. 5:17), in anticipation and expectation of what it will mean when Jesus Christ returns in glory to set all things right and make all things new.

This aligns well with the Reformed tradition, particularly neo-Calvinism, which encourages engagement with every aspect of life for transformation in Christ. We live within the dynamic space of creation and re-creation, as the sovereign Lord directs history toward its intended end.[6] Our eschatology calls us to witness to Christ, the coming king, treating others and creation in ways that reflect and anticipate the fullness of his kingdom, with a longing for justice, mercy, righteousness, peace, restoration, and renewal. We do this knowing that our attempts will be partial and flawed, knowing that it is not up to us to bring in the kingdom of God. That is God's job, not ours—thanks be to God! Christ himself will bring the kingdom in fullness when he comes again in glory. Even so, the content of our eschatological hope should shape our discipleship—and the context of everyone's eschatological hope shapes their discipleship, whether they realize it or not. If our hope for the future boils down to little more than waiting for God to set us free from our bodies and pluck us away from this evil world, then our attitude toward and engagement with the issues that confront us in this world are likely to look very different.

The Intermediate State

With these broad contours in mind, we are now ready to turn to some of the key future aspects of eschatology. The first of these is what happens after death. While we might find ourselves thinking about this in the abstract, it becomes viscerally real for us when we are grieving the death of someone we love, or when we are facing our own death. The general understanding many of our students express is that after believers die they go to heaven to be with Jesus. They are often surprised to learn the technical name for this, which is the *intermediate state*. This is important because, as we will see shortly, "going to heaven to be with Jesus" is not the *final* state. It is not the fullness of our hope. For the moment, though, the Reformed tradition joins with most theologians across denominations and down the centuries to affirm the existence of this intermediate state between the end of our earthly life and the second coming of Christ, when the dead will receive their resurrection bodies.[7]

---

6. See Sutanto and Brock, *Neo-Calvinism*, chap. 9.

7. The scriptural witness to the intermediate state is limited, and the nature of the intermediate state (and indeed, whether there *is* an intermediate state) has been and continues to be deeply contested. For an overview of some of the issues, see Cooper, *Body, Soul, and Life Everlasting*.

The phrase seems abstract and cold for a beautiful reality and a wonderful source of assurance. For believers who have died, their souls, along with those of all who have died in the faith, are with the Lord in the intimacy of his loving presence. If you find yourself wondering where your believing loved one is after they have died, you can be assured that they are with the Lord. They are held in his love in ways that are so far beyond what we can experience in this life that it is almost impossible for us to imagine.[8]

The Heidelberg Catechism states this teaching concisely and elegantly, even as it points ahead to the fullness of our hope in the resurrection:

> Q. How does "the resurrection of the body" comfort you?
> A. Not only will my soul be taken immediately after this life to Christ its head, but also my very flesh will be raised by the power of Christ, reunited with my soul and made like Christ's glorious body.[9]

Death does not separate the believer from the love and presence of Christ, even as we await the fullness of our salvation in the Day of the Lord, when Christ will return and bring about the bodily resurrection through the Spirit.

All of this points to a major problem that has arisen in eschatology: confusing the intermediate state with the final state. We see this tendency in old hymns, contemporary songs, and in much common language about eternal life. With all the talk about Jesus "saving souls" and our souls being with God "in heaven" forever, it can seem as though our bodies (and the rest of creation) basically disappear from view. Bestselling books claiming to give eyewitness accounts of heaven hinge on a similar confusion between heaven and eternal life in the new creation. Books such as *Heaven Is for Real* and *90 Minutes in Heaven* recount near-death experiences in which a person revived after a close encounter with death speaks about leaving the body, moving toward the light, and experiencing "heaven" before returning to their earthly life. While such stories may have inspirational value, they are not divine revelation about the age to come.

We cannot emphasize enough that Christians do not believe simply in the immortality of the soul but also in the resurrection of the body. Scripture is absolutely clear that the final destiny of believers is not to remain disembodied

---

8. We sometimes find that our students conflate the idea of the intermediate state with the concept of purgatory. Purgatory is a Roman Catholic doctrine and is understood to be a place where the sins of believers that have not been fully expiated in this life will be purged, so that they can subsequently enter the presence of God in heaven. The Reformed (along with the vast majority of Protestants and the Orthodox tradition) reject purgatory but maintain the understanding of the intermediate state outlined above.

9. Heidelberg Catechism, Q and A 57 (*Our Faith*, 88).

souls in a nonmaterial heaven but to receive glorified resurrection bodies and dwell eternally in the transformed creation that is the new heavens and the new earth. We will have more to say about this later in the chapter, but for the moment, this means that Jesus does not simply save our souls; Jesus saves our bodies too. This is extremely important, not just for our vision of what eternal life with the triune God will be like but also for how we live now. If we think God cares only about our souls and has no planned future for our bodies, it will affect how we treat our own bodies (and other people's) now and also how we think about health care, end-of-life issues, and myriad other concerns that relate to our present physicality.

The Return of Jesus: What Will It Be Like?

Before we reflect further on the fullness of resurrection life as our eternal destiny, we turn to the event that brings the intermediate state to an end and ushers in the final state: the return of Christ, or his second coming. Like *intermediate state*, the phrase *second coming* is not used in Scripture, but it is a useful summary of what we expect—that Jesus will come among us a second time, physically and visibly. This does not imply that although Jesus came once long ago and will come again sometime in the future, right now he is basically disengaged, uninvolved, or on some kind of extended vacation. Jesus is the active and reigning Lord now, and we wait for the full manifestation of that lordship when he comes again in glory.

While we might not hear it very often, the word used most in the New Testament for this second coming, and the one that theology has adopted as a technical term, is *parousia*. The word *parousia* means *arrival* or *presence*, and the nexus of ideas around it gives us a very strong sense of what New Testament writers like Paul want us to understand about the return of Jesus. It is often translated as *coming*, but it might be better to think of it in terms of something like *powerful presence*. The word *parousia* has two key connotations. First, it was used by Jews and non-Jews to describe the mysterious and powerful presence of God (or, in the case of non-Jews, the gods), often in healing, deliverance, or salvation. Second, it was the term used when a ruler came to a region to reign in person. In that kind of situation, *parousia* was the word for *royal presence*. This made it an ideal word when the New Testament writers wanted to convey that Jesus will one day be bodily present to the whole world as reigning Lord in transforming power. When the true Lord of lords (as opposed to sinful and temporary earthly rulers) comes to rule the world in person, in the fullness of the saving power and presence of

God, and to bring final deliverance from evil, sin, and death—that will be the parousia of parousias, so to speak.

What will it be like? Here, we run up against more questions than we are given answers. Although none of this is easy to get our heads around, what we can say from Scripture is that Jesus will return once, physically, visibly, and in glory, in such a way that nothing and no one will be able to miss it. We cannot say, though, exactly how this can be, or when it will happen. Jesus himself warns us against attempts to predict when he will return, although that has not prevented many from trying. We are to live discerningly in the present in light of the coming kingdom, in the expectation that Jesus will return. It is not for us to try to construct a blueprint for the end times.

As we seek to live well in light of Jesus's coming again, we also must be honest about the hardest question of all. The most profound and difficult issue for the whole of Christian eschatology is not the "how" questions that usually come to our minds (e.g., How will Jesus return in such a way that everyone will see him? How will we get our resurrection bodies? How will this world be transformed?). It is the agonized *"How long?"* of the psalms, of the souls under the altar in Revelation 6:9–10, and of each of us as we grapple with the consequences of injustice, illness, suffering, the groaning of creation, and all the ongoing manifestations of sin, evil, and death. If Jesus has triumphed over all these things in the cross, resurrection, and ascension, why is it taking so long for his return in glory to consummate that victory?

This means that the implications of Christian eschatology for the present are not just comfort (though thanks be to God, there is that!) but also a deep and ongoing lament until Christ's reign comes in fullness. Second Peter 3:4–9 briefly addresses some of these issues, reminding us that, with the Lord, a day is as a thousand years and a thousand years as one day, and that the Lord is patient in giving time for more people to turn to him. Even so, this is not an easy answer. Ultimately, we place our trust in the promises of what God *will* do based on what he *has done*, and particularly, what he has done in the cross and resurrection of Jesus.

What About the "Millennium" and the "Rapture"?

Reformed believers down the centuries have understood that, when the parousia does happen, this event will inaugurate the fullness of the eschaton. With Christians through the ages, we testify that Jesus "will come again in glory to judge the living and the dead, and his kingdom will have no end."[10]

10. Nicene Creed (*Our Faith*, 14).

The return of Jesus will set in motion the culmination of God's promises for the age to come: the resurrection of all the dead, the last judgment, and the new creation.

This brings us to highly disputed territory regarding what we mean by Jesus's "thousand-year reign" (also called the "millennium"), mentioned only in Revelation 20:1–6. Interpretations of this and other related texts vary, and Reformed believers have held a range of views, including what have become known as historic premillennialism, postmillennialism, and amillennialism. Very briefly, *historic premillennialism* considers that Jesus will return to inaugurate a thousand-year reign on earth. During that time, sin and death will still exist, but at the end of the thousand years, Satan will finally be defeated, and the fullness of the eschaton will commence. *Postmillennialism* considers that Christ will return after the millennium. This millennium is not a literal thousand years, but rather the time between Christ's ascension and parousia when he reigns in heaven but not yet on earth. During this time, a "golden age" of peace and prosperity and supernatural abundance for the whole of creation will gradually emerge on earth as more and more people convert to Christianity. Christ will then return to inaugurate the fullness of the eschaton. *Amillennialism* is the most common Reformed position (and the one implied in our historic confessions). This view also considers that the millennium is the time of Christ's heavenly rule between the ascension and the parousia. On this view, though, there is no gradual dawning of a golden age, and there may well be an intensification of sin and evil (the "tribulation") just before Christ returns. When he does return, the fullness of the eschaton is inaugurated: Sin and evil and death are destroyed, the dead are raised, Christ inaugurates the last judgment, and the new creation is born.[11]

One additional view, which arose in the nineteenth century and has become extremely prominent in the United States, is known as *dispensational premillennialism* (or simply *dispensationalism*). This view shares with historic premillennialism the idea that Jesus will return to inaugurate his thousand-year reign on earth, but it adds a number of distinctive details, probably the best known of which is the "rapture." This is the idea that Jesus will initially return invisibly, causing true Christians to be whisked into the air and up to heaven, while others are left behind to endure the tribulation.[12] This is the basis of the perennially popular *Left Behind* book series, with spin-off movies,

---

11. For a classic Reformed account of all four millennial views in the context of a biblical case for amillennialism, see Hoekema, *The Bible and the Future*, chaps. 13–16.

12. This is the classic pre-tribulation rapture. However, since Jesus is clear that true Christians will endure the eschatological tribulation (e.g., Mark 13:19–20), some dispensationalists have adopted the idea of a post-tribulation rapture.

video games, and so on. Seven years after the rapture, Jesus will return once again, this time visibly and in glory, to inaugurate his thousand-year reign on earth from Jerusalem.

There is much more to dispensational premillennialism than we can possibly name here, but most people recognize the basic framework: the rapture, the tribulation, the first great battle when Jesus returns, his thousand-year reign on earth, and the destruction of Satan in another great battle at the end of that time; then the world is destroyed, and the saved go to heaven for eternity. Along with this is an approach to interpreting Scripture that sees direct correlations between what are considered to be end-times prophecies in Scripture and contemporary world events. These become signs to predict when end-times events might happen. The basic elements of dispensational eschatology are taken for granted by many evangelicals in the United States and in the broader culture. If all of this sounds familiar to you, it is a testimony to the immense cultural influence of dispensationalism in American evangelicalism, and through American influence, in other parts of the world.

Along with the rest of historic Christianity, Reformed theologians regard the rapture as a serious misinterpretation of the very few scriptural texts that might suggest it. Foremost among these is 1 Thessalonians 4:13–18. This text gives us the term *rapture*, which comes from the Latin translation of the Greek word for *caught up*: Believers will be "caught up" in the air to meet the Lord on his return (v. 17). The key verb in this text, however, is not *caught up* but *meet*, and the meaning of this word decisively rules out the concept of the rapture as it is popularly understood. The Greek word for meeting the Lord is the term used for when you go out to meet a visiting dignitary to escort that person back to where you have come from. To give another scriptural example, when Paul is being taken to Rome as a prisoner, the Christians in Rome go out from Rome to meet him, in order to escort him back with them into the city (Acts 28:15–16). This overall picture is reinforced by Paul's use of the term *parousia* to describe the return of Jesus in 1 Thessalonians 4:15. As we mentioned earlier, *parousia* is the term used to describe a ruler coming to reign personally in a territory. From all of this (not to mention the archangels and trumpets in v. 16, which signify the public, powerful, and eschatological nature of this event), it is very clear that Paul is not describing an invisible return of Jesus in which Christians are taken up into the sky and off to heaven. Rather, Paul is describing the once-for-all return of Jesus in glory to the earth, with believers meeting Christ to escort him back down to reign.[13]

---

13. In addition to rejecting the rapture, the Reformed tradition also rejects the other distinctive beliefs of dispensationalism, from the above-noted approach to biblical interpretation

The General Resurrection and the Final Judgment

We now turn to the key events that follow the return of Jesus. The first of these is known as the general resurrection. Those who have died before the return of Jesus, and so are experiencing the disembodied intermediate state, will be reunited in their souls and their now transformed and glorified resurrection bodies. Those who are alive at the return of Jesus, Scripture implies, will be immediately transformed in body (1 Cor. 15:50–54; 1 Thess. 4:17). Many of the details about our resurrection bodies are beyond us, but the Reformed tradition affirms that what we can know from Scripture of Jesus's resurrection and our own indicates there will be both continuity and discontinuity between our bodies now and our bodies then. It really will be us, each of us in our particularity, in our resurrection bodies, and yet we will also be very, very different. In 1 Corinthians 15, which is the most extended reflection on the resurrection in the New Testament, Paul uses the analogy of a grain of wheat that is planted and the stalk that emerges (vv. 35–38). We will remain creatures, but our bodies will be glorified and made fit for the conditions of eternal life in the new creation.[14] As Paul puts it, we will put on immortality and incorruption.[15] While we cannot say much about the details—and we cannot answer all the "how" questions—it is very important to combat the confusion we noted earlier. It is far too common, even within the church, to believe that Christianity teaches that we live on for eternity as disembodied souls. It cannot be stressed often enough that the scriptural witness is that our eternal destiny is to receive a glorified resurrection body like Christ's glorified resurrection body (Phil. 3:20–21).

After the resurrection, all people will then face judgment. The Reformed tradition does not see the last judgment as *investigative*, as if God were only now weighing all the evidence and making up his mind at the last moment.

---

to God's separate plans and promises for Jews and Christians. See Hoekema, *The Bible and the Future*, esp. chap. 15, for a Reformed critique of dispensationalism. For a brief, popular account of the parousia and critique of "the rapture," see Wright, *Surprised by Hope*, 128–34.

14. There are important debates within disability theology concerning whether that which is experienced as a disability in this life will be "healed" in the resurrection body, or whether it will continue to characterize someone but will no longer be a hindrance to them in any way. The differences of opinion are often, but not always, between those who reflect on congenital conditions and those who reflect on acquired disabilities. This is one of those issues that we cannot resolve this side of the eschaton, but we can be sure that whatever takes place, it will lead to complete fulfillment and joy, and that nothing will hold anyone back from fullness of life with God, one another, and the whole of creation.

15. It is also important to note that when Paul speaks of our "spiritual body" (as *soma pneumatikon* is often translated) in 1 Cor. 15:42–47, he does not mean *nonphysical body*. The contrast in these verses is between our bodies with their creaturely limits and sinful tendencies and our bodies as they will be re-created and animated by the Holy Spirit.

The last judgment is *declarative*: It makes known the outcome of someone's life in the sovereign mercy and judgment of God.

For many, including many Christians, the idea of the last judgment is terrifying and even deeply objectionable. We live in a culture that is all too aware of the injustices that arise from human judgments and of the conflicting standards of right and wrong that make judgments within our own society, let alone for all human beings, seem deeply problematic. We also live in a culture that sometimes seems to find any concept of judgment to be *judgmental* and an infringement on others' rights. Under these circumstances, when all we can know are compromised and compromising human examples of (in)justice, we can find it hard to accept the idea of God as judge, or to fathom how the last judgment could possibly be fully and truly right or just. And yet we are also aware of deep-seated injustice and wrong in our world, and we have a deep longing for all of that to be put right.

This leads us to one of the predominant themes throughout Scripture when the prospect of the last judgment is raised: the longing for the time when God will fully and finally set all things right, when sin and evil will be fully exposed for what they are and utterly done away with. As N. T. Wright puts it, in a world of systematic injustice and oppression, "The thought that there might come a day when the wicked are put firmly in their place and the poor and weak are given their due is the best news there can be. Faced with a world full of exploitation and wickedness, a good God *must* be a God of judgment."[16] The promise that there will be a last judgment, then, is the promise that injustice will not prevail, and that sin and evil will not have the last word. And because, unlike sinful human beings and their flawed judgments, God knows all things and is unchanging in the fullness of his perfections as holy love, we can trust that the outcome will be holy, right, and good.

Perhaps most importantly, we can be assured that nothing about the last judgment (or any aspect of eschatology, for that matter) will be contrary to what we have seen of who God is in Jesus Christ. Sometimes you will hear even lifelong Christians express fear about the last judgment, saying something like, "I believe in Jesus, but when the judgment comes, well, *prepare to meet your Maker!*," as if suddenly we will all encounter a God who is very different from who God has shown himself to be in Jesus. Not so! This is one of the reasons the doctrines of the incarnation and the Trinity are so important. If you have come to know Jesus, you have already met your Maker. Moreover, Scripture indicates that Jesus Christ himself will be the judge, and the last judgment will make public, final, and universal what God has already done and shown

16. Wright, *Surprised by Hope*, 137.

in Christ. We can be assured that everything about the last judgment will be consistent with who God has shown himself to be in Jesus.

On the basis of Scripture, the Reformed tradition affirms that all human beings who have ever lived will be judged. You might have come across the idea that Christians will escape the last judgment, but Scripture is clear that they will not. To give one example among many, Paul tells the Corinthian Christians that "all of us must appear before the judgment seat of Christ, so that each may receive recompense for what has been done in the body, whether good or evil" (2 Cor. 5:10). For Christians, however, our sins are exposed as forgiven sins, and there is no need to fear. Christ has fully borne the penalty for our sins, and there is no condemnation for those who are in Christ Jesus (Rom. 8:1).

As 2 Corinthians 5:10 and many other places in the New Testament also make clear, judgment involves our *works*. The last judgment is the culmination of each person's life before God, based on the whole of who a person is, which is fully known by God in ways that none of us can know ourselves, let alone anyone else. In this way, the Reformed tradition on the last judgment reflects our understanding of the relationship between justification and sanctification. While we are not saved *by* works, neither are we saved *without* them, because what we do—and the whole of who we are—reflects the nature of our relationship to God in Christ. We therefore hold firmly to both poles of Scripture: Salvation is only by grace, through faith, and judgment is based in part on works. This does not at all mean that the final outcome of our salvation is ultimately based on what we do apart from faith. Salvation is based on what Jesus Christ has done, which we receive by faith. Our thoughts, words, and deeds reflect and express the relationship that we have with God. In this way, we do not need to fear anything arbitrary about the last judgment. The covenant Lord will be faithful to his character and to his will as revealed in Scripture, and God's judgment will be true to who each person truly is.

The historic Reformed tradition considers that the outcome of the last judgment will be either eternal life with God or eternal separation from the loving presence of God in hell. The doctrine of hell is difficult and has received a great deal of criticism in the last century; thus, it is all the more essential to revisit the basic biblical origins of the historic doctrine.

A historic Christian doctrine of hell emerges not only from numerous passages in the Gospels where Jesus warns about judgment (e.g., Matt. 25:30, 46) but also from many passages in the Pauline epistles and in Revelation. For example, 2 Thessalonians speaks of "the righteous judgment of God . . . inflicting vengeance on those who do not know God and on those who do not obey the gospel of our Lord Jesus"; they "will suffer the punishment of eternal destruction, separated from the presence of the Lord" (1:5, 8–9). Revelation 20 speaks of how "the book of life" is opened by Christ, with the works of all people recorded in the book. Then "anyone whose name was not found written in the book of life was thrown into the lake of fire" (Rev. 20:15). Based on such passages, the Reformed confessions concur with the pre-twentieth-century confessions of nearly every Christian tradition that hell is an eternal punishment of conscious separation from God's loving presence.

Stepping back for a wider biblical-theological perspective may give further insight here. As noted above, the Old Testament portrays God's original creation as a type of temple, a sanctuary for fellowship with his creation. With the fall, the world is contaminated by sin—yet the Lord lovingly provided a tabernacle, and then a temple, as places for communion. However, Israelites could not simply stroll into God's presence in the temple. They needed to cleanse themselves of signs of sin and death and offer sacrifices for atonement. God was lovingly present in the temple, but God's presence was also *dangerous*.

The loving-yet-dangerous presence of God is supremely concentrated in the incarnation of the Word: Jesus Christ. He himself is the temple, the perfect dwelling place of God, the one in whom heaven and earth have come together. Jesus demonstrates compassion toward outcasts, and in his parable of the wheat and the tares, he warns us against judging others as false believers (Matt. 13:24–30, 36–43). He says that he himself, as "the Son of Man," will perform this judgment at the end of the age—thus, we are called not to judgment but to repentance. Jesus is the judge, not us. But he will, in fact, judge. "When the Son of Man comes in his glory, and all the angels with him, then he will sit on the throne of his glory. All the nations will be gathered before him, and he will separate people one from another as a shepherd separates the sheep from the goats" (Matt. 25:31–32).

These passages should be taken not individually but collectively, as together pointing to God's larger work of making a dwelling place where he can be with his creation. "I will shake all the nations," the Lord says through the prophet Haggai. The nations will be shaken and judged so that the earth can once again be a temple for the glorious presence of the Lord (Hag. 2:6–9). Jesus embodies this and similar prophetic promises and will bring them to their consummation at the parousia, when creation itself will be judged and made fit to be a dwelling place for the holy Lord. Sin, the devil, and death—which presently appear to threaten creaturely communion with God—will be dealt with through God's love in the form of a warrior who will conquer the evil that afflicts his creation. The contamination of sin will be no more. Fleming Rutledge offers an environmental analogy: "If poisonous contamination has been released into the air and water, it must be permanently eliminated in order for God's new creatures to breathe and have eternal life."[17] The final consummation, then, follows the final judgment, as the cosmos itself will then have been cleansed to be a dwelling place of God with his creation.

This summation of the classical Christian teaching on hell, even with the biblical-theological supplement above, leaves many unanswered questions for modern Christians: How can we get our minds around a loving God sending sinners to hell? Are the "goats" who go into eternal punishment in passages like Matthew 25 annihilated, or do they consciously suffer? Is it possible that hell, prepared for the devil and his angels, will have only a small population, or even that it will eventually be empty?

In facing these questions, a Reformed doctrine of Scripture is particularly vital to remember in two particular senses. First, Scripture is not given to answer all our questions, or to make the justice of God's ways utterly clear to us; rather, it contains the will of God for us, and "everything one must believe to be saved is sufficiently taught in it."[18] We do not have a face-to-face knowledge of God. Even with Scripture, there is deep mystery. Second, Scripture, rather than our own urgent questions or even our own confessions and councils, has the final authority. "We must not consider human writings—no matter how holy their authors may have been—equal to the divine writings."[19] Thus, we cannot simply repeat the formulation of the Reformed confessions without returning to the biblical texts themselves, which have received a great deal of exegetical attention in the past century. Returning to these biblical texts, some Reformed theologians hold out a hope for the salvation of all, as noted in the chapter on election. This is not the position of the Reformed confessions, but these theologians' arguments should ultimately be evaluated on biblical grounds.

Eternal Life in the New Creation

Those who are saved will live in their glorified resurrection bodies in the fullness of the presence of the triune God for all eternity, in the transformed and glorified physical new creation. As we indicated earlier, God has prepared a glorious eschatological future for his good creation, as a fitting culmination to the way that Scripture has presented God's entire history with it. It is therefore not quite right to think of the separation of the final judgment as

17. Rutledge, *Crucifixion*, 322.
18. Belgic Confession, 7 (*Our Faith*, 29).
19. Belgic Confession, 7 (*Our Faith*, 30).

the final act of God's history with the world. The final act is *restoration* of God's righteous rule in *shalom* (peace)—the restoration of the communion God intended with us and with the whole of creation. Notably, of the Greek words for "new," in referring to the new heavens and the new earth, the New Testament only ever uses the word *kainos* (which suggests something *renewed* or *transformed*), rather than *neos* (which suggests something *brand new*).

Based on such insights, traditional Reformed thinkers such as Herman Bavinck do not end their discussions of eschatology with heaven and hell, but with the restoration and transformation of creation in the new creation. "All that is true, honorable, just, pure, pleasing, and commendable in the whole creation, in heaven and on earth, is gathered up in the future city of God—renewed, re-created, boosted to its highest glory."[20] The new heavens and the new earth will become the temple of God in the union of God's space (heaven) and the glorified creation, which will be saturated with the fullness of the presence of God.

The Reformed tradition, therefore, asserts that this world has a future, and that the new creation will be *this creation transformed*. Whether this will also involve the destruction of the present creation in some way—a death before its resurrection, so to speak—is a matter of debate, but the resurrection body of Jesus is our paradigm for both the continuity and the discontinuity between this creation and the new creation, as it is for our bodies now and our resurrection bodies to come. Just as it is *Jesus's* body—both the same and yet different—that is transformed and glorified, so it will be at the eschaton for our bodies and for the creation as a whole.

When it comes to our attempts to describe what eternal life in the new heavens and the new earth will be like for us, we must be very clear: We simply do not know the details, and anything we try to say will be almost entirely speculation. Given the prevalent and unscriptural confusion between the intermediate state and the final state, many contemporary theologians and biblical scholars have rightly emphasized that our final destiny involves our physicality, not just our "immaterial souls."[21] This is a crucial scriptural corrective. Once we move from this acknowledgment of physicality toward confident and detailed accounts of what exactly we will do and how we will do it, we have gone far beyond the scriptural witness. While we can be sure that the experience of eternal life with God in the new creation will far surpass anything our feeble imaginations can conceive, we also must take great

20. Bavinck, *Reformed Dogmatics*, 4:720.
21. Some important texts in this regard are Wright, *Surprised by Hope*; and Middleton, *New Heaven*.

care not to present our speculations as if they were actual depictions of what eternal life will be like.

We must also be careful not to lapse into a wholly creation- and human-centered approach to eternal life. If we are not careful, we can find ourselves focusing so much on the glorified physicality of the new creation, or projections of what we will do, or those whom we will meet or with whom we will be reunited, that God and our worship of God largely disappear from view. Any description of eternal life in the new creation that downplays its primarily God-ward focus cannot be a proper account of eternal life from a Reformed perspective. Scripturally speaking, and for the historic Reformed tradition, the glorious center of eternal life for the redeemed is what is called the *beatific vision*.[22] This is the indescribable fullness of our loving union and communion with God as we behold him face-to-face and are fully and finally transformed. It is our joyful adoration and worship of God with our whole being—glorified minds and resurrected bodies—as we behold God's glory in and through Christ above all, but also in everyone and everything else. As Samuel Parkison summarizes, the beatific vision will be the fulfillment of all creaturely desires because it is the destination toward which our desires have pointed all along, but it will also be a never-ending expansion of our capacity to apprehend and delight in the glory of God. The redeemed will be full to the brim, even as our capacity for satisfaction will grow forevermore.[23]

This does not mean that we have a purely individualistic understanding of eternal life, as if it were just about ourselves and our individual relationships with God. Nor does it rule out a range of possibilities for what we may do. We simply seek to maintain scriptural priorities for a properly God-oriented understanding of eternal life. Scripture makes clear that we were created for right relationship with God, and from that flows right relationships with one another and the rest of creation. We can be confident that eternal life with God will include the healing, glorification, and fulfillment of all these other sets of relationships. They will be experienced in their perfection as they flow out of our perfected relationship with God. In this way, two strands of thinking about the eschatological future that are often thought to be in tension are shown to be two sides of the one scriptural coin: our union and communion with God and the perfect *shalom* of the kingdom of God. These two strands belong together, both in the eschaton and also as we seek to live now in light of the life to come.

22. See, e.g., Allen, *Grounded in Heaven*. For an overview of the doctrine of the beatific vision and its relevance for our lives now, see Parkison, *To Gaze upon God*. For an outstanding account of Calvin's doctrine of the beatific vision, see Tyra, "*Neither the Spirit Without the Flesh.*"
23. Parkison, *To Gaze upon God*, 176–77.

From a Reformed perspective, then, eternal life with the Lord will be, first and foremost, God-centered; but it will also entail human-focused and creation-oriented elements. While we might not be able to fill in all the details or answer all the questions, we know that it will be indescribably glorious, that it will mean being drawn into infinite and ever-new depths of love and wonder, and that it will draw out of us ever more ecstatic love and adoration.

APPENDIX A

Why Is Reformed Theology Called "Reformed"?

Having spent years working in discipleship programs with middle schoolers, I (Todd) love their knack for asking the questions that may *seem* obvious but that adults in the room often have not really reflected on deeply. This is one of those questions, and it may prove difficult to answer for many who have been in congregations in the Reformed tradition for decades: *Why is Reformed theology called "Reformed," anyway?*

Put briefly, *Reformed* simply means *corrected* or *purified* (from what were perceived to be the errors of the Roman Catholic Church). The Reformed saw themselves as belonging to "the one, holy, catholic church" confessed in the Apostles' Creed, and they saw their calls for reform as in line with early Christian sources, though grounded finally on the Word of God in Scripture. While we will point to the history of the term *Reformed* below, the basic idea fits well with the notion of being catholic in a Reformed key, which we have developed in this book. In the words of William Perkins's 1598 book *Reformed Catholic*, "By a Reformed Catholic, I understand anyone that holds the same necessary heads of religion with the Roman Church; yet so as he pares off and rejects all errors in doctrine whereby the said religion is corrupted."[1] Thus, the label *Reformed* is shorthand for *Reformed Christian* or *Reformed catholic*—the historic Christian faith rectified of specific

1. W. Perkins, *Reformed Catholic*, 45.

159

errors in doctrine and practice in which the Roman Catholic Church had strayed from the more ancient Christian faith. Perkins sought to explain that the Reformed affirmed the core doctrines of the catholic faith, and that their disputes concerned later-developing accretions and novelties in Roman Catholic doctrine.[2]

The response to the question "What does the term *Reformed* mean?" is likely to strike some as anticlimactic. Today it means more than simply "Christians who seek to correct and renew the church's theology and practice" in response to late-medieval aberrations. It is a *tradition*, emerging historically from Huldrych Zwingli, John Calvin, Martin Bucer, and Heinrich Bullinger, extending in various forms and denominations through the centuries. *Reformed* is not a self-referential term; it does not mean "whatever a Reformed Christian thinks." It has specific origins in the sixteenth century and is defined by a particular theological confession. As we have noted elsewhere in the book, it is not a new church or even a new movement. The Reformers saw themselves as an extension of God's people in centuries past. But pragmatically, whether congregational or Presbyterian or Hungarian Reformed or nondenominational, belonging to the Reformed tradition refers to a particular *theological confession* with its roots in the sixteenth-century reform and renewal movement of catholic Christianity known as the Protestant Reformation.

In the classroom, some students are disappointed that *Reformed* doesn't capture the essence or excitement of the movement. However, the names of theological traditions often function more as labels than explanations of their deeper meanings.

Consider the Mennonites. Menno Simons, a leader in the Radical Reformation, did not intend to found a group known as Mennonites. As we saw in chapter 3, the Mennonites belong to a larger tradition of so-called Radical Reformers known as *Anabaptists*, which was originally a term of denigration by critics who saw their practice of baptizing confessing believers as a second baptism. While some in the Radical Reformation engaged in violent acts, Simons condemned these excesses and promoted nonviolence. Thus, *Mennonite* came to signify peace-loving Anabaptists, distinct from the factions that were willing to resort to violence.

Today, the term *Mennonite* connects believers to Menno Simons, but primarily it serves as a label indicating a specific group within Christianity. Historically, the Mennonite tradition actually disagreed with Simons on some points of doctrine, yet the term remains a label linking them to a historic set of communities, beliefs, and practices.

2. W. Perkins, *Reformed Catholic*, 52.

Similarly, *Reformed* should be understood as a label rather than an essence, marking a tradition without fully encapsulating its depth. Historically, *Reformed* emerged as a broad label for a set of Christians who objected to the office of the pope and certain late medieval teachings, and who professed the gospel in terms that the Roman Catholic Church condemned, particularly at the Council of Trent (1545–63).

How did these Christians refer to themselves within their own context? In the first three generations of the Reformation era, the groups that we now call Reformed and Lutheran had three terms for self-designation: *evangelical*,[3] *Protestant*,[4] and *Reformed*. The terms were used more or less synonymously for much of the sixteenth century and, in some regions, into the seventeenth century.[5] All of these considered themselves catholic Christians, as the term *catholic* is described in earlier chapters in this book. They saw themselves inhabiting a faith that endured through all ages of the church, including the medieval period, which embraced the trinitarian and christological doctrines confessed in the ecumenical councils of the fourth and fifth centuries. These Protestants saw themselves as catholic in confession and as belonging to the "holy catholic church" of the Apostles' Creed. But they were highly critical of the pope and of corruptions within the church; thus, they called for the reform of Roman Catholic doctrine and practice in light of Scripture.

The cultural and religious tumult of the Protestant Reformation was great, and readers unfamiliar with it would benefit from reading about the twists and turns of this extraordinary time.[6] But for the purposes of clarifying the term *Reformed*, along with *evangelical* and *Protestant*, the basic point is that the groups that described themselves this way had a view of catholicity

3. The term *evangelicals* referred to Christians who proclaimed the good news of God's promise in the gospel. This should be clearly distinguished from the meaning of the term *evangelical*, in both theological and political senses, in the early twenty-first century.

4. In the opening decades of the Reformation, Christians who were later known as Reformed and Lutheran both used the term *Reformed* as well as *Protestant* in self-designation. The term *Protestant* has had two main senses: protest and testimony. The term originated from the formal protest of Lutheran princes against the revocation of religious toleration demanded by the Second Diet of Speyer, held in 1529. Instead of allowing princes to choose the religion of each territory, it mandated that each region return to the Catholic religion and practice. But in addition to *protest*, the term *Protestant* also had a theological connotation: the Latin root, *protestari*, means *to bear witness* or *to testify*. Thus, early Protestants saw themselves as giving public testimony to the good news.

5. The finest short overview of the primary sources in using these terms is a dated-but-still-excellent account titled *The Spirit of the Reformed Tradition*, by M. Eugene Osterhaven, our predecessor at Western Theological Seminary.

6. A helpful introductory work on the Reformation for laypersons is Sunshine, *Reformation for Armchair Theologians*. For a more detailed historical work on the broader social, cultural, and religious movements of that historical era, see Lindberg, *European Reformations*.

that differed from that of the Roman Catholic Church. They advocated a Reformed, or corrected or purified, doctrine—one centered in the gospel of Jesus Christ (thus, *evangelical*), which bore witness to the faith, even when doing so involved protest against Roman Catholic abuses (the two senses of the term *Protestant*).

"We retain the Christian, sound, and catholic faith, whole and inviolable," Bullinger wrote in the Second Helvetic Confession. There is "one mediator" between God and human beings, "one shepherd of the whole flock, one head of this body"; there is "one church: which we, therefore, call catholic because it is universal," spread "abroad" through the world, and it "reaches unto all times." In contrast, "Roman clergy" presumptuously "vaunt that the Church of Rome alone is in a manner catholic," thus seeking to limit and contain the catholicity of the "whole flock" under Christ the shepherd.[7] With reasoning like this, the groups we now call Reformed and Lutheran sought to inhabit and defend their catholicity, their connection to the wholeness and oneness of the church in its history and life.

But as the excommunication of Luther and the persecution of early Protestants indicated, the Roman Catholic hierarchy rejected the substance of these early Protestant calls for reform. These rejections were solidified in the Council of Trent, the Roman Catholic council that took place between 1545 and 1563. Protestant accounts of justification by faith alone were rejected and condemned. Protestant calls, on the grounds of Scripture, to reform doctrines like purgatory and the powers of the pope were rejected as well, and the pope's authority was reinforced. However, Trent also endeavored to be responsive to some calls for reform by Roman Catholics and Protestants at the time, addressing concerns about corruption, the lack of theological and moral formation among clergy, and clarifying points of doctrine. As part of this response to the Protestant Reformation, which is sometimes called the Counter-Reformation or the Catholic Reformation, new orders developed, such as the Jesuits, founded in 1540 by Ignatius of Loyola, who sought to model a renewal of piety, education, and mission in the church. Nevertheless, within the papal and conciliar response to the Protestant Reformation, the magisterium (teaching office) of the Roman Catholic Church condemned key early Protestant teachings. This was significant, since the highest forms of tradition, in the Roman Catholic Church, have parity in authority with Holy Scripture.

So, the claims of catholicity from groups that we now call Lutheran and Reformed were rejected by the Roman Catholic Church. These Lutheran and

---

7. Second Helvetic Confession, 11, 17 (Dennison, *Reformed Confessions*, 2:831, 845).

Reformed groups differed from a number of other Protestant groups as well, given how they related to civil authorities. Lutheran and Reformed church leaders sought partnership with civil authorities (magistrates), both in giving pleas for clemency from persecution and in supporting the reform of the church. Other groups, those of the Radical Reformation, had a different approach: They separated themselves from civil authorities, emphasized a piety of returning to the New Testament and avoiding worldly contaminations, claimed that the baptism of believers was the only valid baptism, and tended to be much more skeptical about the value of the church's historic theology and practice.

Thus, *Reformed* is distinct from Roman Catholic or various groups in the Radical Reformation. But how did the term become distinct from *Lutheran* as well?

By the final decades of the sixteenth century, it was clear that the groups sharing the labels *Reformed*, *evangelical*, and *Protestant* would not remain fully united in their theological confession. But the acceptance of *Lutheran* as a self-designation among one strand of this larger tradition was slow, especially at first. Within the first decades of the Reformation, Martin Luther's close friend and fellow Reformer Philipp Melanchthon ruefully lamented that opponents called their proclamation of the gospel "Lutheran."[8] But after attempts in the opening generations to bridge the divides between Lutherans and non-Lutherans, the non-Lutherans who sought to inhabit the historic catholic tradition kept the label of *Reformed*, while those in the tradition of Luther and Melanchthon eventually accepted the term *Lutheran*. The term *Lutheran* became more common after the Book of Concord (1580) consolidated doctrinal standards, though the document itself doesn't use the term. Into the early seventeenth century, some Lutherans continued to refer to their churches as Reformed.[9] However, within two decades of the Book of Concord, *Lutheran* began shifting from an external label to a self-designation for churches identifying with Lutheran confessions, distinguishing themselves amid competing labels like *Philippist*, *Zwinglian*, and *Calvinist*.[10]

Does the term *Calvinist* for the Reformed tradition correspond to *Lutheran* for the tradition of Luther and Melanchthon? In short, no.

In both the Reformation and post-Reformation eras, well into the seventeenth century, the term *Calvinist* was used, at times, as an insult, not a term of self-designation. Calvin was one among several significant second-generation

8. "This blessed doctrine, the precious holy Gospel, they call Lutheran." Book of Concord, "Art. XV (VIII): Of Human Traditions."
9. Osterhaven, *Spirit of the Reformed Tradition*, 174.
10. Osterhaven, *Spirit of the Reformed Tradition*, 175.

theologians in the Reformed tradition. He did not seek to be the originator of the tradition. Unlike Luther, he was not the author of widely used catechisms or confessions.[11] Although, at points in history, the term *Calvinist* has been used as a label for the Reformed tradition as a whole, we feel that the practice is unhelpful and misleading. As Richard Muller succinctly puts it, "Calvin was not the sole arbiter of Reformed confessional identity in his own lifetime—and he ought not to be arbitrarily selected as the arbiter of what was Reformed in the generations following his death."[12] Using the term *Calvinist* tends to imply that Calvin's writings are the sources and criteria for the Reformed theological tradition.

Thus, for clarity in contemporary theological conversation, we agree with Michael Allen at Reformed Theological Seminary that "the term 'Calvinist' ought to be dropped entirely."[13] Yet, we also recognize that no term is perfect and that *Calvinist* is sometimes used pragmatically as a label, because that is the term that is being used by others. In addition, in certain cases, the term *Calvinism* cannot easily be avoided. For example, *neo-Calvinism* is a technical designation for a school of thought emerging in the Reformed tradition from Abraham Kuyper and Herman Bavinck.[14]

Thus, as we often need to do amid the contingencies and limitations of human discourse about God, we recommend doing what one can to avoid the reductionistic renderings of what *Reformed theology* means. Do the best you can with the language that is used in your context, listen to others with humility, and be willing to laugh at yourself. "Some droll sensibility is required to keep in due proportion the pompous pretensions of the study of divinity," Thomas Oden rightly reminds us, for "comedy glimpses refractions of God's own delight in creation."[15] We are all on the road of faith seeking understanding. Our terms and categories are laughably imperfect. Yet, as we stumble on this rocky path, the Spirit is still free to restore our delight in God and creation and to renew our hearts and minds as we commune more deeply with Christ, who is our life.

11. Osterhaven, *Spirit of the Reformed Tradition*, 171–73.
12. Muller, *After Calvin*, 8.
13. Allen, *Reformed Theology*, 3.
14. See Sutanto and Brock, *Neo-Calvinism*, for an excellent introduction to the neo-Calvinist theological tradition.
15. Oden, *Classic Christianity*, 3, 857.

APPENDIX B

A Misunderstood Motto: "Reformed and Always Reforming"

One of the most misunderstood and misused sayings describing the Reformed theological tradition is also widely used—the saying that we are "Reformed and always reforming." This phrase is potentially illuminating, but the insights are bundled together with deep inaccuracies, given how this maxim is used. Most often, the adage is framed as a motto for the Reformed tradition, wherein *Reformed* as a label is defined by the task of ongoing reformation. It occurs in various forms, but the shared assumption is that Reformed theology is fundamentally related to the principle of reforming, or to an ongoing process of being reformed and transformed by God.

The maxim has become remarkably widespread in the past half century, with a multilingual reach around the globe. The modern popularity of the motto likely derives, in part, from Karl Barth's use and adaptation of it in the mid-twentieth century.[1] But as a motto, it is rarely associated with Barth; it is framed as a principle of the Reformation. Among both conservative and progressive Presbyterians, "Reformed and always reforming" is common in denominational statements and discussions. In internal debates, it shows up as a "gotcha" argument for progressives against conservatives, as any revision

1. Bush, *Calvin and the Reformanda Sayings*, 289–90.

of doctrine or practice can be championed as "reforming," or progressing, the church. In more conservative discussions, the climax of the motto usually includes a final phrase, grounding the ongoing reformation "according to the Word of God." Thus, it is often used as a battle cry on various sides. It becomes a touchpoint for relating Scripture, tradition, and the theological task of the church in its current historical-cultural context.

Today, the widespread use of this phrase extends far beyond that of the Presbyterian tradition. Other Reformed groups, such as members of the French Reformed and Dutch Reformed confessional traditions, have made significant use of this maxim as a principle. It is used also in Baptist and nondenominational discussions, functioning as a shorthand to speak about a distinctively Protestant way to inhabit tradition. Whether in book titles, blog posts, or conference talks, the maxim has become almost ubiquitous.

Usually when this maxim is referenced, even in scholarly literature, no specific source is given. Often the references are parenthetical, such as, "As the Reformers would say, we are 'Reformed and always reforming.'" Even historians sometimes assume that the maxim encapsulates a concept that was operative in the sixteenth-century Protestant Reformation.[2] One historian criticizes the French Reformed Confession of 1612 because "it brought to an end the previous commitment to the concept of *semper reformanda* (always reforming)."[3]

But here's the trouble: After decades of historical research, scholars have not found this maxim, or an advocacy of the idea that to be *Reformed* is to be characterized by an "ongoing reformation," in the work of any sixteenth-century Reformers. Indeed, there is good reason to think that such a concept would have been rejected.[4] The first form of it occurred in 1674, and as we will see later, even the underlying concept in that instance varies sharply from the maxim's uses today. While many scholars and laypeople today apply a variation of the "Reformed and always reforming" maxim to the Reformation, it first appeared 150 years after the beginning of the Reformation—and not as a slogan or motto or Reformed confession.

Positively, we think it is important to recognize that the "Reformed and always reforming" motif can still have value in some circumstances. The reason for finding value here is somewhat pragmatic: Since it has become a widely used motif to describe the Reformed, it can still be illuminating as a brief

2. This assumption can lead historians and theologians to evaluate sixteenth- and early seventeenth-century Protestants by the norm of "Reformed and always reforming," even though they held no such norm.
3. Armstrong, *Semper Reformanda*, 136.
4. See Bush, *Calvin and the Reformanda Sayings*, 285–300, esp. 291–98.

heuristic (or lesson) when used with care.[5] We do not think that it should be considered a core principle of the Reformation. It has no formal authority from a confessional standpoint. The danger of misusing the maxim is quite serious. It risks distorting the very principles of the Reformed theological method that it seeks to illuminate. Yet, used circumspectly, it can serve as an entry point to a more substantial Reformed account of Scripture and tradition.

Detective Work: Digging into the Origins of the Maxim

Despite variations in wording, most who invoke the maxim rely on a play between the terms *Reformed* and *reforming*, with the latter clarifying the meaning of the former. But is this assumption justified?

Whether the maxim is referenced in English, French, or other contemporary languages, those invoking it often quote the Latin (which adds to the apparent authority of the phrase): *ecclesia reformata, semper reformanda* ("the church reformed, always to be reformed"). Sometimes the additional Latin phrase *secundum verbi Dei* ("according to the Word of God") is added. Whether referenced in parts or the whole of this sentence fragment, it is translated and used in a variety of quite divergent ways. If one takes the whole set of phrases together, it can be rendered "Reformed and always being Reformed according to the Word of God." This emphasizes the principle of *being Reformed* (by God) through the Word of God in Scripture. While advocates of this form of the maxim sometimes say that it is incomplete if not quoted in full, that is not quite correct. There is no codified form of the maxim in Reformed confessions or other Reformed documents, and, historically, it is not clear that the longest form was the earliest. The argument for embracing or rejecting this long form needs to be made on more pragmatic grounds.[6]

Most often in today's English-speaking discussions, a shorter form of the maxim is used: "Reformed and always being Reformed" or "Reformed and always reforming." Both accent the crucial role of an ongoing reformation in understanding what it means to be Reformed.

Some rhetorical uses of this short version are simply affirming a "both/and" about Reformed identity: that the Reformed affirm both Reformed doctrine and the task of being reformed and reshaped in our life, worship, and witness

5. On the necessary role, yet profound limitations, of heuristics in theological discussions in the church, see "Heuristics for Reformed Theology, Keywords, and Group Identity," in chap. 1.

6. Stated differently, determining the original usage of the maxim is not crucial in the decision about whether to include the phrase *secundum verbi Dei* if we use the maxim as shorthand for how Reformed Christians inhabit their theological tradition. The various wordings of this motto historically suggest no single, original source.

through Scripture. With this, the use of the passive tense in English, "being Reformed," gives a more accurate translation of the Latin's term *reformanda*, but more importantly for our own purposes, the passive framing properly accents divine agency, such that "we are the recipients of the activity of the Holy Spirit which reforms the church in accordance with the Word of God."[7]

But often the shorter maxim is used as a way to imply that "newer is better," as well as to imply that the purpose and end of what it means to be Reformed is to be reforming. Used in this sense, to be Reformed is to be always reforming the Reformed theology and practice that Reformed Christians profess. Addressing the use of the maxim in a mainline Presbyterian context, Anna Case-Winters notes that it is often used to imply that "newer is always better" and that "the church can reform itself."[8] Indeed, when Reformed Christians debate one another on an area of dispute, a common rhetorical question is, How can one claim the title *Reformed* if reforming isn't central to one's Christian identity? Jürgen Moltmann turns this into its own maxim: "Reformed theology is *reforming theology*."[9] While Moltmann's intent is to urge the Reformed to stay attentive to context and Scripture's voice, the notion that Reformed theology must always be reforming can easily become a bundle of self-contradictions. Consider this situation: Presbyterian confessions teach infant baptism. But to be *truly Reforming*, a Presbyterian could argue that one needs to reject it. Thus, by this person's claim, those who agree with the Westminster Standards on infant baptism are not Reformed enough. Likewise, I (Todd) recall a theologian commended for being Reformed, especially in the sense of "always Reforming," whose published theology rejected basic components of the Apostles' and Nicene creeds in relation to the saving person and work of Christ. Admittedly, these examples may seem extreme, and they are. But they point to the logical outworking of a notion that expresses itself in much more subtle ways as well: that to be Reformed theologically is to stand at odds with Reformed theology itself, under the banner of "reforming theology," in the words of Moltmann. For many observers, this version of "always reforming" seems less like a call to faithful renewal than a license for perpetual dissent.

Each of these renderings has different layers and assumptions built into it. And precisely because the phrase (in various forms) is used so widely, it is important to clarify some misunderstandings about how it is used. First, we need to disentangle two different questions that are usually conflated when

---

7. Nebelsick, "Ecclesia Reformata Semper Reformanda," 62.
8. Case-Winters, "Ecclesia Reformata, Semper Reformanda."
9. Moltmann, "Theologia Reformata et Semper Reformanda," 121.

this set of phrases is used. The first is *descriptive*: Is the phrase "always being Reformed" at the root of the label, describing what it means to be called Reformed? The second question is *evaluative*: Is this an illuminating and helpful principle for the way in which Reformed Christians inhabit the theological tradition, particularly in relation to innovation and change (in "reforming") and also in relation to Scripture ("according to the Word of God")?

On the first question, the answer is relatively simple and will come as a surprise to most Reformed Christians who use the motto. The phrase *semper reformanda* ("always to be reformed") dates back to the late seventeenth century in the Netherlands, with the first known printed use coming from Jodocus van Lodenstein in 1674.[10] Within this context, it was used by writers in the Dutch "further Reformation" (*Nadere Reformatie*) to indicate the importance of not only being Reformed theologically but also offering one's own practical life to "always reforming" by the Spirit's power through God's Word in Scripture. A movement with some parallels to the Puritans in England, the *Nadere Reformatie* sought to explore and embrace the importance of personal piety and deep discipleship in all areas and spheres of life. It was theologically astute and embraced the theology of the Reformed confessions. But it did so in a way that emphasized the deeply formational direction of the Christian life, advocating for growth in Christ in practical and communal ways.

Thus, *semper reformanda*, as a play on words, was intended to encourage the ongoing reform of our lives to the lordship of Christ. It did not advocate a need to reform, or change, one's doctrine. Nor was it an overall motto on how to be Reformed. It was not offering an authoritative principle for how the Reformed ought to relate to tradition, innovation, or Scripture. The play on words, in Latin, is meant to point to a piety that shows we have not "arrived" in the Christian life, but we live as sinners who are always in need of ongoing reform, repentance, and renewal by the Spirit. Indeed, as noted above in chapter 6, the gift and calling of sanctification is ongoing for every Christian and every Christian community. Justification and sanctification are distinct yet inseparable, in union with Christ by the Spirit. The piety of the *Nadere Reformatie* embraces and extends this point, giving a portrait of the Christian life as an ongoing process of pilgrimage.

What did *Reformed* mean, then, in the context of the *Nadere Reformatie*? Quite simply, it meant embracing reformed theology as expressed by the confessions. Thus, the representatives of this movement were theologically Reformed and yet always being reformed in life and action by God's Word. In some sense, this is not surprising. No references to *Reformed* are found

10. See Bush, *Calvin and the Reformanda Sayings*, 286–89.

in catechisms or confessions as pertaining to the act of reforming. Although today the *semper reformanda* formulation is frequently used as a core motto or principle for the Reformed tradition, or a core principle of what it means to be Reformed, this practice is both misleading and historically implausible. The emergence of the title *Reformed* had absolutely nothing to do with the notion of "always reforming," or even "always being reformed according to the Word of God." Reformed Christians had been called Reformed for approximately 150 years before the *semper reformanda* formulation was even used; and when it was used, this saying was pedagogical and pragmatic (a play on words), not an attempt to define what *Reformed* means.

Given this history of misunderstanding the *semper reformanda* sayings, what are some guidelines to keep in mind when the phrase comes up in conversation today?

1. *The maxim can be a useful shorthand for how the Reformed tradition inhabits the historic Christian tradition.* It is not accurate to apply it to the Reformation era, or to treat it as a confessional statement. And don't expect this short sentence to do a lot of conceptual work or teaching; it is only a heuristic. We all need key words and phrases to remind us of larger ideas, especially in theology. But the *semper reformanda* maxim alone is not grounds for presenting a full theology of the church, or tradition, or the use of the Bible. It is a shorthand for a larger set of theological claims and questions. As Case-Winters notes, in recent decades it has become a "misused motto" that is "appropriated in times of disagreement and pressed into the service of our own agendas."[11] Rather than using it as a weapon against opponents, this shorthand can remind us of the humbling reality that we embrace a Reformed faith as a witness to God's work in Christ through the Spirit, and in our lives, worship, and ministry, we are all in need of ongoing formation and re-formation into the fullness of Christ as we continue to receive God's life-giving Word by the Spirit.

2. *When used, the motif is most helpful in its full form—namely, when the passive form ("being Reformed") is used and "according to the Word of God" is included:* "Reformed and always being Reformed according to the Word of God." Although our grounds for this recommendation are pragmatic rather than historical, emphasizing the passive sense of *reformanda* clarifies how the triune God alone is the reformer. This, in combination with including the phrase "according to the Word of

11. Case-Winters, "Ecclesia Reformata, Semper Reformanda."

God," clarifies the normative character of Scripture in this process. If the maxim is used to say "Newer is always better," then any innovation (e.g., a rejection of claims within the Reformed confessions) becomes a way to be *more Reformed* than actually sharing in a Reformed confession. Moved in this direction, there is literally no limit to what could be called Reformed. *Reformed* could be used to embrace white supremacy, a capricious mutability of God, or anything else that differs from the Reformed confession. A short form of the maxim—"Reformed and always reforming"—may imply that the job of the church is to reform itself by catching up with the times, accommodating to new cultural trends. But the long form is a bit more resistant to both of these understandings: The *ground* of what it means to be Reformed is the Word of God, not chasing trends or innovations. The passive tense of the church "being reformed" recognizes God as the agent of reform, rather than us in our own attempts to fix the church, as if it belonged to us rather than Christ.

3. *When used carefully, it can remind us of the ongoing calling to hear Scripture deeply in various cultural contexts.* In a Reformed vision, we are pilgrims on the road of theological understanding. God addresses us through Scripture, and we have not exhausted the depths of Scripture or finished the task of hearing in obedience.

Although not addressing the *semper reformanda* motto directly, Herman Bavinck insightfully identifies a characteristic of the Reformed tradition that aligns well with a thoughtful application of this phrase: "Those who profess the Reformed religion can and must, as long as they remain true to their origins, never give the impression that for them orthodoxy per se is the highest truth. However high the church's confession may be estimated, it is a *norma normata* ('a normed norm'), subservient to Holy Scripture and thus always remains subject to revision and expansion."[12]

Rather than conformity to the church's confession (like the Reformed confessions), Bavinck describes the dynamic life of the church as finding nourishment and new life through the hearing of God in Scripture. With his use of the Latin phrase *norma normata*, Scripture is the norm, or standard, that rules all other norms. The church's confessions are also a norm, but their authority is secondary in service to the Word of God in Scripture; they are always subject to Scripture as the supreme and final norm.

Bavinck's framing is characteristic of a Reformed approach to theological traditions more generally. Traditions have value as shared, provisional norms,

---

12. Bavinck, "Modernism and Orthodoxy," 155.

but the final norm is Scripture. This speech about different levels of norms may sound like a set of abstractions, or formal relations between different sources. But these relations flow from a larger and deeper drama: We are sinners who have been incorporated into Christ and addressed by the risen Christ through his Word, by the power and illumination of the Spirit. In this new family of adoptive fellowship, the Spirit enables us to be nourished in our growth into the Father's household, as children of God through the beloved Son. Our testimony in word and in life to this—the triune God's deliverance and new life—is always partial, limited by our finitude and tainted by sin. Yet, this imperfect testimony, emerging from the historic household of God, can also help the church deepen her reception of the Spirit's Word through Scripture. The sustenance and renewal of the church's life depends not on upholding its confession above all else but on receiving the continuing nourishment of God's Word, through the Spirit. The church's confession is an instrument to serve that end.

Stated differently, for the Reformed, the church's theological confession as a norm is distorted if it functions as the final measure for rightness or orthodoxy, at the expense of the ongoing path of continuing to hear God's address through Scripture. Certainly, Bavinck was not suggesting that the theological markers of the Reformed confessions are roadblocks to being authentically Reformed. But they are not ends in themselves. Being Reformed is not a doctrinal contest to see who can win the game of being most doctrinally strict, or who can be reforming in a way that is most innovative. Rather, the church's whole life is as a creature of God's Word. The church is called to live and grow as children of God adopted in Christ by the Spirit. This God-given identity and calling expresses itself through deepening worship, service, and self-offering to God and his purposes.

Bibliography

Allen, Michael. *Ephesians*. Brazos, 2020.

———. *Grounded in Heaven: Recentering Christian Hope and Life on God*. Eerdmans, 2018.

———. *Reformed Theology*. T&T Clark, 2010.

Armstrong, Brian G. *Semper Reformanda: The Case of the French Reformed Church (1559–1620)*. Edited by W. Fred Graham. Truman State University Press, 1994.

Athanasian Creed. Christian Classics Ethereal Library. https://www.ccel.org/creeds /athanasian.creed.html.

Bacote, Vincent E. Foreword to *Ownership: The Evangelical Legacy of Slavery in Edwards, Wesley, and Whitefield*, by Sean McGever. IVP, 2024.

———. "Kuyper and Race." In *Calvinism for a Secular Age: A Twenty-First-Century Reading of Abraham Kuyper's Stone Lectures*, edited by Jessica R. Joustra and Robert J. Joustra. IVP Academic, 2022.

Barmen Declaration. In *Book of Confessions: Study Edition*. Geneva Press, 1999.

Barna Group. "Is There a 'Reformed' Movement in American Churches?" November 15, 2010. https://www.barna.com/research/is-there-a-reformed-movement-in -american-churches/.

Barth, Karl. *Church Dogmatics*. Edited by T. F. Torrance and G. W. Bromiley. 13 vols. T&T Clark, 1936–77.

Bauckham, Richard. *Bible and Mission: Christian Witness in a Postmodern World*. Baker Academic, 2004.

Bavinck, Herman. "Modernism and Orthodoxy." In *On Theology: Herman Bavinck's Academic Orations*, edited by Bruce R. Pass. Brill, 2020.

———. *Reformed Dogmatics*. 4 vols. Edited by John Bolt. Translated by John Vriend. Baker Academic, 2003–8.

———. *Reformed Dogmatics: Abridged in One Volume*. Edited by John Bolt. Baker Academic, 2011.

Bechtel, Carol M. *Touching the Altar: The Old Testament for Christian Worship*. Eerdmans, 2008.

Bender, Kimlyn. "5 Lessons Christians Can Learn from the Barmen Declaration." *Christianity Today*, October 9, 2024. https://www.christianitytoday.com/2024/10/barth-bonhoeffer-barmen-declaration-evangelical-confession-5-lessons/.

Benedetto, Robert, and Donald K. McKim. *Historical Dictionary of the Reformed Churches*. 2nd ed. Scarecrow, 2009.

———. *Historical Dictionary of the Reformed Churches*. 3rd ed. Rowman & Littlefield, 2023.

Bierma, Lyle D. *Font of Pardon and New Life: John Calvin and the Efficacy of Baptism*. Oxford University Press, 2021.

Billings, J. Todd. "Calvin on 'Distracting Emotions' and 'Sinful Complaints' in Lament Psalms: Receiving Laments as Christian Scripture." In *The Old Testament, Calvin, and the Reformed Tradition*, edited by Yudha Thianto. Brill, 2024. https://doi.org/10.1163/9789004688025_005.

———. *Calvin, Participation, and the Gift: The Activity of Believers in Union with Christ*. Oxford University Press, 2007.

———. "The Problem with TULIP, or More Than TULIPs in This Field." *Reformed Journal*. March 1, 2011. https://reformedjournal.com/the-problem-with-tulip-or-more-than-tulips-in-this-field/.

———. *Rejoicing in Lament: Wrestling with Incurable Cancer and Life in Christ*. Brazos, 2015.

———. *Remembrance, Communion, and Hope: Rediscovering the Gospel at the Lord's Table*. Eerdmans, 2018.

———. *Union with Christ: Reframing Theology and Ministry for the Church*. Baker Academic, 2011.

Book of Concord. "Art. XV (VIII): Of Human Traditions in the Church." December 10, 2019. https://thebookofconcord.org/apology-of-the-augsburg-confession/article-xv/.

Book of Order 2023–2025. Presbyterian Church (U.S.A.), 2023.

Bradley, James E., and Richard A. Muller. *Church History: An Introduction to Research, Reference Works, and Methods*. Eerdmans, 1995.

Brink, Emily. "A Reformed Approach to Psalmody: The Legacy of the Genevan Psalter." *The Hymn: A Journal of Congregational Song* 56, no. 1 (Winter 2005): 16–25.

Bromiley, Geoffrey W. *Children of Promise: The Case for Baptizing Infants*. Eerdmans, 1979.

Brownson, James V. *The Promise of Baptism: An Introduction to Baptism in Scripture and the Reformed Tradition*. Eerdmans, 2006.

Bush, Michael. *Calvin and the Reformanda Sayings*. Edited by Herman J. Selderhuis. Calvinus Sacrarum Literarum Interpres: Papers of the International Congress on Calvin Research. Vandenhoeck & Ruprecht, 2008.

Calvin, John. *Commentary on the Book of Psalms*. Edited by James Anderson. 5 vols. Calvin Translation Society, 1845–49. Available online through Christian Classics Ethereal Library: https://ccel.org/ccel/calvin/commentaries.i.html.

———. *Institutes of the Christian Religion*. Edited by John T. McNeill. Translated by Ford Lewis Battles. Westminster, 1960.

———. *John Calvin's Sermons on the Ten Commandments*. Edited by Benjamin W. Farley. Wipf & Stock, 2019.

Camus, Albert. *The Rebel: An Essay on Man in Revolt*. Vintage, 1997.

Case-Winters, Anna. "Ecclesia Reformata, Semper Reformanda: Our Misused Motto." *Presbyterians Today*, May 2004. PC(USA). https://pcusa.org/ecclesia-reformata -semper-reformanda.

Chatonnet, Francoise Briquel, and Muriel Debie. *The Syriac World: In Search of a Forgotten Christianity*. Translated by Jeffrey Haines. Yale University Press, 2023.

Chrysostom, St. John. *On Wealth and Poverty*. 2nd ed. St. Vladimir's Seminary Press, 2020.

Church Order and Its Supplements. Christian Reformed Church in North America, 2024.

Cochrane, Arthur C., ed. *Reformed Confessions of the Sixteenth Century*. Westminster John Knox, 2003.

Cooper, John W. *Body, Soul, and Life Everlasting: Biblical Anthropology and the Monism-Dualism Debate*. Eerdmans, 2000.

"A Declaration on the 'Russian World' (Russkii mir) Teaching." Public Orthodoxy, March 13, 2022. https://publicorthodoxy.org/2022/03/13/a-declaration-on-the -russian-world-russkii-mir-teaching/.

de Gruchy, John W. *Liberating Reformed Theology: A South African Contribution to an Ecumenical Debate*. Eerdmans, 1991.

Dennison, James T., Jr., ed. *Reformed Confessions of the 16th and 17th Centuries in English Translation*. 4 vols. Reformation Heritage Books, 2008–21.

DeYoung, Kevin, and Greg Gilbert. *What Is the Mission of the Church? Making Sense of Social Justice, Shalom, and the Great Commission*. Crossway, 2011.

Dostoevsky, Fyodor. *The Brothers Karamazov*. Translated by Richard Pevear and Larissa Volokhonsky. North Point, 1990.

Eglinton, James. "Varia Americana and Race: Kuyper as Antagonist and Protagonist." *Journal of Reformed Theology* 11, nos. 1–2 (January 21, 2017): 65–80.

Emerson, Michael O., and Christian Smith. *Divided by Faith: Evangelical Religion and the Problem of Race in America*. Oxford University Press, 2001.

Fesko, J. V. *The Theology of the Westminster Standards: Historical Context and Theological Insights*. Crossway, 2014.

Fox, Maggie. "Fewer Americans Believe in God—Yet They Still Believe in Afterlife." NBC News. March 22, 2016. https://www.nbcnews.com/better/wellness/fewer-americans-believe-god-yet-they-still-believe-afterlife-n542966.

Garces-Foley, Kathleen. *Crossing the Ethnic Divide: The Multiethnic Church on a Mission.* Oxford University Press, 2007.

Global Ministries. "Reformed Church in Hungary." Accessed June 30, 2024. https://www.globalministries.org/partner/reformed_church_in_hungary_1/.

Gockel, Matthias. *Barth and Schleiermacher on the Doctrine of Election.* Oxford University Press, 2006.

González, Justo L. *Mañana: Christian Theology from a Hispanic Perspective.* Abingdon, 1990.

———. *The Story of Christianity.* 2 vols. HarperOne, 2010.

Green, Michael. *Baptism: Its Purpose, Practice, and Power.* Paternoster, 1987.

Guder, Darrell L., and George R. Hunsberger, eds. *Missional Church: A Vision for the Sending of the Church in North America.* Eerdmans, 1998.

Haas, Guenther H. *The Concept of Equity in Calvin's Ethics.* Wilfrid Laurier University Press, 1997.

Hart, David Bentley. *The Doors of the Sea: Where Was God in the Tsunami?* Eerdmans, 2011.

Hayes, Josh. "Interview with Michael Horton: For Calvinism." *Credo*, December 14, 2011. https://credomag.com/2011/12/interview-with-michael-horton-for-calvinism/.

Hesselink, I. John. *On Being Reformed: Distinctive Characteristics and Common Misunderstandings.* Reformed Church Press, 1988.

Hoang, Bethany Hanke, and Kristen Deede Johnson. *The Justice Calling: Where Passion Meets Perseverance.* Brazos, 2017.

Hoekema, Anthony A. *The Bible and the Future.* Eerdmans, 1994.

Holy See. "Catechism of the Catholic Church." https://www.vatican.va/content/catechism/en/part_two/section_two/chapter_two/article_4/x_indulgences.html.

Horton, Michael. *The Christian Faith: A Systematic Theology for Pilgrims on the Way.* Zondervan Academic, 2011.

———. *Covenant and Eschatology: The Divine Drama.* Westminster John Knox, 2002.

———. *For Calvinism.* Zondervan Academic, 2011.

Jacobs, Alan. *How to Think: A Survival Guide for a World at Odds.* Crown Currency, 2017.

Johnson, Kristen Deede. "The Way of Jesus in a Divided Nation." The Center for Pastor Theologians, November 6, 2020. https://www.pastortheologians.com/articles/2020/11/6/the-way-of-jesus-in-a-divided-nation.

Junius, Franciscus. *A Treatise on True Theology with the Life of Franciscus Junius.* Translated by David C. Noe. Reformation Heritage Books, 2020.

Kaemingk, Matthew, and Cory B. Wilson. *Work and Worship: Reconnecting Our Labor and Liturgy.* Baker Academic, 2020.

Kahneman, Daniel. *Thinking, Fast and Slow.* Farrar, Straus & Giroux, 2013.

Kaminsky, Joel S. *Yet I Loved Jacob: Reclaiming the Biblical Concept of Election.* Wipf & Stock, 2016.

Kantzer Komline, Han-luen. *Augustine on the Will: A Theological Account.* Oxford University Press, 2019.

Kapic, Kelly M., and Wesley Vander Lugt. *Pocket Dictionary of the Reformed Tradition.* IVP Academic, 2013.

Keller, Timothy. *Generous Justice: How God's Grace Makes Us Just.* Penguin Books, 2012.

———. *Walking with God Through Pain and Suffering.* Penguin Books, 2015.

Kinnaman, David, and Gabe Lyons. *Good Faith: Being a Christian When Society Thinks You're Irrelevant and Extreme.* Baker Books, 2017.

Kleist, James A., trans. and ed. *The Didache, The Epistle of Barnabas, The Epistles and The Martyrdom of St. Polycarp, The Fragments of Papias, The Epistle to Diognetus.* Ancient Christian Writers, vol. 6. Newman, 1948.

Leith, John Haddon. *An Introduction to the Reformed Tradition: A Way of Being the Christian Community.* Rev. ed. Westminster John Knox, 1981.

Levenson, Jon D. *The Death and Resurrection of the Beloved Son: The Transformation of Child Sacrifice in Judaism and Christianity.* Yale University Press, 1995.

———. *Resurrection and the Restoration of Israel: The Ultimate Victory of the God of Life.* Yale University Press, 2008.

Levering, Matthew. *Predestination: Biblical and Theological Paths.* Oxford University Press, 2011.

Lindberg, Carter. *The European Reformations.* Blackwell, 2009.

Luther, Martin. *The Bondage of the Will.* Baker, 1957.

———. "Concerning the Ministry." In *Church and Ministry II.* Vol. 40 of *Luther's Works*, edited by C. Bergendoff and H. T. Lehmann. Fortress, 1999.

———. Smalcald Articles. In *The Book of Concord: The Confessions of the Evangelical Lutheran Church*, edited by Robert Kolb and Timothy J. Wengert. Fortress, 2000.

McCracken, Brett. "The Rise of Reformed Charismatics: A Global Movement Brings Together Doctrine and Spiritual Gifts." *Christianity Today*, January/February 2018.

McDonald, Suzanne. "Calvin's Theology of Election: Modern Reception and Contemporary Possibilities." In *Calvin's Theology and Its Reception: Disputes, Developments, and New Possibilities*, edited by J. Todd Billings and I. John Hesselink. Westminster John Knox, 2012.

———. "The Canons of Dordt for the Church Today: Polemics, Pastoring, and Pulling Up TULIPs." *Calvin Theological Journal* 54, no. 2 (2019): 407–20.

———. *Re-Imaging Election: Divine Election as Representing God to Others and Others to God.* Eerdmans, 2003.

McGever, Sean. *Ownership: The Evangelical Legacy of Slavery in Edwards, Wesley, and Whitefield.* IVP, 2024.

McKim, Donald K. *Reformed Theology from A to Z.* Rowman & Littlefield, 2023.

McMaken, W. Travis. *The Sign of the Gospel: Toward an Evangelical Doctrine of Infant Baptism After Karl Barth.* Augsburg Fortress, 2013.

Middleton, J. Richard. *A New Heaven and a New Earth: Reclaiming Biblical Eschatology.* Baker Academic, 2014.

Moltmann, Jürgen. "Theologia Reformata et Semper Reformanda." In *Toward the Future of Reformed Theology: Tasks, Topics, Traditions*, edited by David Willis and Michael Welker. Eerdmans, 1998.

Muller, Richard. *After Calvin: Studies in the Development of a Theological Tradition.* Oxford University Press, 2003.

———. *Calvin and the Reformed Tradition: On the Work of Christ and the Order of Salvation.* Baker Academic, 2012.

———. *Divine Will and Human Choice.* Baker Academic, 2017.

———. "How Many Points?" *Calvin Theological Journal* 28, no. 2 (1993): 427–33.

Nebelsick, Harold P. "Ecclesia Reformata Semper Reformanda." *Reformed Liturgy and Music* 18, no. 2 (Spring 1984): 62.

Noll, Mark A. *The Civil War as a Theological Crisis.* University of North Carolina Press, 2006.

Oden, Thomas C. *Classic Christianity: A Systematic Theology.* HarperCollins, 2009.

———. *The Living God.* Vol. 1 of *Systemic Theology.* HarperOne, 1992.

Ortlund, Gavin. *What It Means to Be Protestant: The Case for an Always-Reforming Church.* Zondervan, 2024.

Osterhaven, M. Eugene. *The Spirit of the Reformed Tradition.* Eerdmans, 1971.

Our Faith: Ecumenical Creeds, Reformed Confessions, and Other Resources, by Faith Alive Christian Resources, Christian Reformed Church in North America, and Reformed Church in America. Faith Alive Christian Resources, 2013.

Padilla, C. René. *Mission Between the Times: Essays on the Kingdom.* 2nd ed. Langham Global Library, 2010.

———. *What Is Integral Mission?* Translated by Rebecca Breekveldt. Regnum Books International, 2021.

Parkison, Samuel. *To Gaze upon God: The Beatific Vision in Doctrine, Tradition, and Practice.* IVP Academic, 2024.

Pascal, Blaise. *Pensées.* Translated by A. J. Krailsheimer. Penguin Classics, 1995.

Pelikan, Jaroslav. *The Vindication of Tradition.* Yale University Press, 1984.

Pemberton, Glenn. *Hurting with God: Learning to Lament with the Psalms*. Abilene Christian University Press, 2012.

Perkins, Harrison. *Reformed Covenant Theology: A Systematic Introduction*. Lexham Academic, 2024.

Perkins, William. *Reformed Catholic*. Edited by Shawn D. Wright. Reformation Heritage Books, 2018.

Pew Research Center. "Spirit and Power—A 10-Country Survey of Pentecostals." October 5, 2006. https://www.pewresearch.org/religion/2006/10/05/spirit-and-power/.

Piper, John. "Is It Ever Right to Be Angry at God?" *Desiring God*, October 16, 2002. https://www.desiringgod.org/articles/is-it-ever-right-to-be-angry-at-god.

———. "It Is Never Right to Be Angry with God." *Desiring God*, November 13, 2000. https://www.desiringgod.org/articles/it-is-never-right-to-be-angry-with-god.

———. *Lessons from a Hospital Bed*. Crossway, 2016.

———. *Providence*. Crossway, 2021.

Pitikoe, Dr. Molefi Seth. "Ecumenical Address from the Rev. Dr. Pitikoe." Reformed Church in America, Acts and Proceedings of the 196th Regular Session of the General Synod. Reformed Church Press, 1982.

Pope Leo X. "Exsurge Domine." June 15, 1520. https://www.papalencyclicals.net/leo10/l10exdom.htm.

Pope Paul VI. "Unitatis Redintegratio." November 21, 1964. https://www.vatican.va/archive/hist_councils/ii_vatican_council/documents/vat-ii_decree_19641121_unitatis-redintegratio_en.html.

Pope Pius XI. "Mortalium Animos." January 6, 1928. https://www.vatican.va/content/pius-xi/en/encyclicals/documents/hf_p-xi_enc_19280106_mortalium-animos.html.

Rankin, Russ. "SBC Pastors Polled on Calvinism and Its Effect." *Baptist Press*, June 20, 2012. https://www.baptistpress.com/resource-library/news/sbc-pastors-polled-on-calvinism-and-its-effect/.

Rhee, Helen. *Loving the Poor, Saving the Rich: Wealth, Poverty, and Early Christian Formation*. Baker Academic, 2012.

Richter, Sandra L. *The Epic of Eden: A Christian Entry into the Old Testament*. IVP Academic, 2008.

Robinson, David, and Jeff Liou. "Our Racist Inheritance: A Conversation Kuyperians Need to Have." *Comment Magazine*, May 14, 2015. https://comment.org/our-racist-inheritance-a-conversation-kuyperians-need-to-have/.

Rutledge, Fleming. *The Crucifixion: Understanding the Death of Jesus Christ*. Eerdmans, 2017.

Said, Edward W. *Orientalism*. Pantheon Books, 1978.

Saillant, John. *Black Puritan, Black Republican: The Life and Thought of Lemuel Haynes, 1753–1833*. Oxford University Press, 2002.

Schleiermacher, Friedrich. *Christian Faith*. Edited by Terrence N. Tice and Catherine L. Kelsey. 2 vols. Westminster John Knox, 2016.

———. *On the Doctrine of Election, with Special Reference to the Aphorisms of Dr. Bretschneider*. Translated by Iain G. Nicol and Allen G. Jorgenson. Westminster John Knox, 2012.

Schreiner, Thomas. "Why I Am a Cessationist." *The Gospel Coalition*, January 22, 2014. https://www.thegospelcoalition.org/article/cessationist/.

Selderhuis, Herman J., ed. *Psalms 73–150*. Vol. 8 of *Old Testament*. Reformation Commentary on Scripture. IVP Academic, 2018.

Sittser, Gerald. *Resilient Faith*. Brazos, 2019.

Small, Joseph D. *Flawed Church, Faithful God: A Reformed Ecclesiology for the Real World*. Eerdmans, 2018.

———. "Reformed." In *The Oxford Handbook of Ecumenical Studies*, edited by Geoffrey Wainwright and Paul McPartlan. Oxford University Press, 2021.

Smit, Dirk J. "Reformed Faith, Justice and the Struggle Against Apartheid." In *Essays in Public Theology: Collected Essays 1*, edited by Ernst Conradie. Sun, 2007.

———. "South Africa." In *Essays in Public Theology: Collected Essays 1*, edited by Ernst Conradie. Sun, 2007.

Smith, Christian, and Melina Lundquist Denton. *Soul Searching: The Religious and Spiritual Lives of American Teenagers*. Oxford University Press, 2009.

Smith, James K. A. "Teaching a Calvinist to Dance: In Pentecostal Worship, My Reformed Theology Finds Its Groove." *Christianity Today*, May 2008.

Sproul, R. C. "Is It a Sin to Be Angry with God?" Ligonier Ministries, 2015. https://www.ligonier.org/learn/qas/is-it-a-sin-to-be-angry-with-god.

———. "The Locus of Astonishment." Ligonier Ministries, March 16, 2014. https://learn.ligonier.org/sermons/locus-astonishment.

———. *What Is Reformed Theology? Understanding the Basics*. Baker Books, 2016.

Steenwyk, Carrie, and John D. Witvliet. *At Your Baptism*. Eerdmans, 2011.

Stewart, Kenneth J. *Ten Myths About Calvinism: Recovering the Breadth of the Reformed Tradition*. IVP Academic, 2011.

Sunshine, Glenn S. *The Reformation for Armchair Theologians*. Westminster John Knox, 2005.

Sutanto, N. Gray. "Bavinck Warned That Without Christianity, Racism and Nationalism Thrive." *Christianity Today*, June 17, 2024. https://www.christianitytoday.com/2024/06/herman-bavinck-kuyper-nazi-racism-christian-nationalism/.

Sutanto, N. Gray, and Cory C. Brock. *Neo-Calvinism: A Theological Introduction*. Lexham Academic, 2023.

Terpstra, Nicholas. *Religious Refugees in the Early Modern World: An Alternative History of the Reformation*. Cambridge University Press, 2015.

Thompson, John L. "Do You Really Want to Be Saved Sola Gratia?" *Modern Reformation*, June 29, 2007. https://www.modernreformation.org/resources/articles/do-you-really-want-to-be-saved-sola-gratia.

———. *Reading the Bible with the Dead: What You Can Learn from the History of Exegesis That You Can't Learn from Exegesis Alone*. Eerdmans, 2007.

Tisby, Jemar. *The Color of Compromise: The Truth About the American Church's Complicity in Racism*. Zondervan, 2019.

Tyra, Steven W. *"Neither the Spirit Without the Flesh": John Calvin's Doctrine of the Beatific Vision*. T&T Clark, 2024.

Van Biema, David. "The New Calvinism." *Time*, March 12, 2009. https://content.time.com/time/specials/packages/article/0,28804,1884779_1884782_1884760,00.html.

van Driel, Edwin Chr., ed. *T&T Clark Handbook of Election*. Bloomsbury, 2023.

Vischer, Lukas, ed. *Christian Worship in Reformed Churches Past and Present*. Eerdmans, 2003.

———, ed. *Reformed Witness Today: A Collection of Confessions and Statements of Faith Issued by Reformed Churches*. Evangelische Arbeitsstelle Oekumene Schweiz, 1982.

World Council of Churches. "Member Churches." https://www.oikoumene.org/member-churches.

"The World Reformed Fellowship Statement of Faith." World Reformed Fellowship. Accessed October 29, 2024. https://wrf.global/about/wrf-theological-statements/statement-of-faith.

Wright, N. T. *Surprised by Hope: Rethinking Heaven, the Resurrection, and the Mission of the Church*. HarperOne, 2008.

Scripture Index

Subject Index

Abraham
  and God's covenant, 59–61, 64, 75
  as hero of the faith, 49–50
adoption, xxi, 20, 23, 63, 70, 97, 123, 125, 135, 172
Against Calvinism (Olson), 16
Allen, Michael, 33, 164
anabaptism, 57, 59, 64, 67, 160
apartheid, 42, 75, 118, 132–34
Apostles' Creed, xviii, 30, 95, 140–41, 159, 161, 168
archetypal knowledge of God, 23
Arminianism, 16–17
  and Calvinism, 73, 75, 80
  and the Canons of Dort, 82–86
Arminian Remonstrance, 80–86
Assyrian Church of the East, 34
Athanasian Creed, 96
atonement, 154
  limited, 68, 83–84
Augsburg Confession, 31
Augustine, 76–77, 79

Bacote, Vince, 44–48
baptism
  believers, 163
  as dying and rising with Christ, 51
  as foretaste of eschatological fulfillment, 144
  oneness of, 29, 32–33
  as ordinance, 68
  saving work of Christ in, 55, 62–66, 69
  second, 160

as sign and seal, 55, 61, 63, 136
  and sin, 62, 65–66
  as social rite, 57
  and union with Christ, 136
baptism, infant
  and adoption, 70
  continuities of with circumcision, 59–65
  and covenantal theology, 59–63, 68
  and faith, 54–55, 57, 60–71
  in French Reformed liturgy, 66
  historical Reformed justifications for, 58–59, 168
  importance of community, 63
  objections to, 53–54
  pastoral issues, 69–71
  and prevenient grace, 66–67
  Reformed distinction from Roman Catholic approach to, 57–58
  and the saving work of Christ, 55, 62–66, 69
  and Scripture, 54–57, 59–66
  and *sola scriptura*, 55–57
  varied Reformed approaches to, 67–69
Barmen Declaration (1934), 40–41, 118
Barth, Karl, 2, 41, 165
  on election, 87–88
  on infant baptism, 54n2
Basil of Caesarea, 117
Bavinck, Herman
  on the catholicity of the church, 5, 42, 46
  on eschatology, 156
  as neo-Calvinist, 164
  on providence, 112, 114

185

"With a rare combination of precision and warmth, Todd Billings, Suzanne McDonald, and Alberto La Rosa Rojas invite us to approach Reformed faith and practice as a dynamic, diverse tradition that continues to gather the church—as creature of the Word—around the Word of God in Christ as nourishment for weary pilgrims. Longtime devotees and the newly curious alike will find much in these pages that clarifies and commends Reformed theology's deep roots and expansive vision of God and God's commitment to us."

—**Kenneth J. Woo**, Pittsburgh Theological Seminary

"This wonderful book is surely destined to take its place among the classics of Reformed theology. It goes deep and wide in covering the strengths (and weaknesses) of the Reformed tradition while also placing it in the larger context of the universal body of Christ. And all of this points us to the depth and breadth of God's amazing grace!"

—**Richard Mouw**, Fuller Seminary

"Navigating the Reformed church landscape is far from simple. As someone counted among the tradition through the Presbyterian branch, I am grateful to the authors for their generosity of time and approach in answering questions that range from the simple to the complex. This book offers an insightful, thought-provoking, and gracious response to the question of what it means, and does not mean, to be Reformed."

—**Jennifer Powell McNutt**, Wheaton College

"As a Latino pastor and theologian in the Presbyterian Church, I am often asked, 'Why are you Presbyterian?' This wonderful volume offers several excellent responses to the naysayers and critics. It also reminds those of us in the Reformed tradition why we stay. The Reformed tradition cannot be reduced to any one confession or creed but rather encompasses an ecumenical and global family of churches united by certain theological themes ranging from faith in the benevolent sovereignty of God to the presence of the Holy Spirit in the church's compassionate ministries, all grounded in the Word of God as revealed in Christ. In other words, there are many branches in the Reformed genealogical tree, and they reach far and wide because, as Reformed believers, we are committed to the Nicene Creed's vision of one, holy, catholic, and apostolic church."

—**Rubén Rosario Rodríguez**, Saint Louis University

"We have needed this book for years, and at long last we have it—a generous, thoughtful, accessible introduction to the Reformed tradition. In this exceptionally well-written book by three 'converts,' we see the beauty of Reformed theology without overlooking its shadow side. *Generously Reformed* invites all Christians—not just those with Reformed inclinations—to consider how they inhabit their faith in relation to the wider beliefs and traditions of Christianity writ large. For that reason, this book is a must-read for Christians today. As those in ministry grapple with how to encourage deep roots in this complex time, as those in theological education wonder how to help their students become more grounded in their faith, as all of us seek to be rooted in Christ and bear fruit in this world, this book will be a good and trustworthy guide."

—**Kristen Deede Johnson**, Wycliffe College, University of Toronto

"We have needed this book for some time. Resisting the overly narrow (and often distorting) approach that reduces Reformed theology to TULIP, *Generously Reformed* moves in different directions. While remaining brief and accessible, this book reminds us of the historic and global nature of the Reformed tradition, underscoring its breadth even as it explains its unifying confessional roots. I am grateful not only for the content of this volume but also, and just as importantly, for its generous tone."

—**Kelly M. Kapic**, Covenant College

"If you associate Reformed theology mainly with tulips, this book will deepen and broaden your impression. The topics are expertly selected and handled by three veteran Reformed scholars. Highly recommended!"

—**Michael Horton**, Westminster Seminary California